LENIN AND GANDHI

LENIN
(from a portrait by Andreev)

LENIN AND GANDHI

By

RENÉ FÜLÖP-MILLER

Translated from the German by
F. S. FLINT and D. F. TAIT

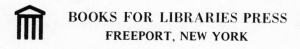

BOOKS FOR LIBRARIES PRESS
FREEPORT, NEW YORK

First Published 1927
Reprinted 1972

Library of Congress Cataloging in Publication Data

Fülöp-Miller, René, 1891–1963.
    Lenin and Gandhi.

    Reprint of the 1927 ed.
    Bibliography: p.
    1. Lenin, Vladimir Il'ich, 1870–1924. 2. Gandhi
Mohandas Karamchand, 1869–1948. I. Title.
DK254.L46F813 1972   335   72-7057
ISBN 0-8369-6932-4

CONTENTS

INTRODUCTION

THE aim of this book is to describe the life and work of the two men whose personalities, in the author's opinion, most forcibly embody the spirit of the present age. The ideas preached by Lenin and Gandhi, their words and actions, will perhaps afford future generations clearer evidence than anything else of the motives of our time, of what spheres it accomplished permanent work in, and of how far it fell short of our hopes. Later ages will measure the significance of our epoch by the standard of the work of Lenin and Gandhi, and the inadequacy of these two men will show the tragic deficiencies of our age, which set itself the task of attaining the unattainable, the concrete realization of age-old Utopias.

Both of them, Lenin as well as Gandhi, in different ways undertook the heroic and at the same time adventurous experiment of putting into practice the long cherished dreams of humanity. They were both rooted deeply in their own nations, and their reforms and their methods were entirely the result of the destinies of their countries, of the limitations of Russian and Indian conditions, and that at a moment when both nations had arrived at a turning point in their national development. But the political enterprise of both the Russian and the Hindu goes far beyond the narrow boundaries of the national and the temporary. Russia and India were merely to be the subjects of a great and universally valid experiment whose success was to give an example to the world and to spread the new doctrines of the two reformers over the whole earth. Lenin and Gandhi were upheld by the emotion of an ecstatic faith, the faith that their country was called to redeem humanity.

Therefore the words of these two men have the

fascination, and at the same time the disturbing and repelling arrogance, of a Gospel. Like two prophets they stand at the opening of the twentieth century. If we listen to them, their age will be the beginning of a new epoch in the history of the world. They desire to lead humanity to salvation in different ways and they point in opposite directions, each with the same gesture of most profound conviction. Lenin regarded the unlimited—though only temporary—use of violence as the means for bringing about an ideal world order, whereas Gandhi is trying to reach the goal by an absolute rejection of all violence. Lenin tried to free humanity by complete mechanization, Gandhi, by repudiating machinery in principle. The one regarded machinery as the salvation from all evil, the other as a delusion of the devil.

But in spite of these apparent antagonisms, the deep kinship and the common spiritual origin of the two may be seen at every turn, often more clearly in the differences between them than in the obvious resemblances in their lives. Lenin and Gandhi both sprang from the race of the great rebels, and what unites them in all their resemblances as well as in all their differences is that both were convulsed by one and the same great experience, that both belong to an age which was stirred to its deepest foundations, in which need and misery began to arouse not only an inactive or friendly and charitable pity, but that genuine sympathy which leads to consciousness of personal responsibility for every evil, and, therefore, necessarily to rebellion against the existing political and social order. It was their profound feeling of responsibility for the sufferings of all the disinherited that lent compelling force to the words of these two great leaders, gave weight to their actions, and was the cause of their overwhelming influence on the masses.

Lenin associated personally with the oppressed and shared their life, their sorrows, and their imprisonments. He formed his doctrine on the injustice they suffered

and drew his power from the hatred that seethed in
their souls. Lenin the dictator was the outcome of the
appeal of a dispossessed nation. From the moment he
entered the Kremlin in the name of the masses and
seized power in Russia, through him the hitherto dumb
world of the disinherited began to reign. Their indictment became the new political ideal, their hunger for
power created the new brutal machinery of state, their
dumb instincts decided the ethics of the new social
order, the continued existence of which seems very
problematical.

The same historical phenomenon also occurred in
India, with the difference natural to another cultural
zone and another national character. Gandhi also
shared the life of the oppressed, their humiliations and
imprisonments. With every success of Gandhi, the
countless millions of oppressed Indians also gained a
victory, and in his rise they too rose to power. When
the people of India appointed Gandhi dictator, the
enslaved Hindu appeared as the accuser of the foreign
authorities and the despised pariah as the accuser of the
proud Brahman. The cry and accusation of the humble
in Russia and India assumed for the first time a concrete
and personified power, which confronted the still existing old order on equal terms. In the faces of Lenin and
Gandhi, the physiognomy of the impersonal millionfold
mass, which no one had ever looked at before, took on
the form and austere features of two great personalities,
features which will be stamped on history for all time.

The Russian and the Indian gospels, in spite of their
differences, are both animated by the same spirit of
indictment of European culture. This indictment is
brought by two men, to whom the moral right and,
therefore, the sincerity, behind their harshness cannot
be denied. We cannot disregard their words.

Europe cannot, however, accept the accusations of
Lenin and Gandhi as both a judgment and an indictment,
for like all accusations, these too show only a part of the

truth. Asia, whose spirit rises against Europe in the words of the Hindu, and also in those of the Russian, may be superior to us in many respects, but only Europe has been able to struggle to the recognition of one truth, the truth that the accuser may never be at the same time the judge.

Thus Europe will listen to both accusers, but will be able consciously to oppose to this damning verdict the defence of a rich and manifold culture based on the moral freedom of personality. For the West has hitherto known how to transform all great ideas coming from the East into a new and organic enrichment of its own nature.

In his attempt to present a reliable, objective, and true picture of Lenin's character and career, the author found a most inadequate literature at his disposal. For most of the books on Lenin misrepresent the figure of the Russian dictator either from uncritical admiration or party hate. The author was, however, able to supplement the sources quoted at the end of the book mainly by impressions and experiences gathered in Soviet Russia, by documents and conversations with people who had been connected with Lenin from his earliest youth, followed his career as fellow workers, or been his opponents in political warfare.

In painting the picture of Gandhi, the author chiefly used the Indian editions of the writings, speeches, and letters of Gandhi, the files of *Young India* and *Current Thought*, and the writings and pamphlets of Gandhi's Indian opponents. Moreover the careful German selection of Gandhi's works by Emil Roniger, a model of editing, supplied many valuable hints.

It is unnecessary to say that the well-known monograph by Romain Rolland was also consulted, and also the other works on Gandhi, especially Hans Prager's profound study of the Indian apostolate. In investigating the connections between Gandhi's teaching and Buddhism, the abridged and longer collections of

Buddha's speeches in the classical translation of Karl
Eugen Neumann was used.

Herr Percy Eckstein also gave the author valuable
assistance with his book, for which he is especially
thanked here. Mention must also be made of the kindness of Messrs. Romain Rolland, Bernard Shaw, Upton
Sinclair, Dilip Kumar Roy, Professor C. F. Andrews,
Sir N. Chandavarkar, and Professor T. L. Vaswani, who
gave the author their views on non-violence by letter.

RENÉ FÜLÖP-MILLER.

VIENNA, *March* 1927.

LENIN

Lenin to Gor'kiĭ :

" I know nothing more beautiful than the ' Appassionata,' I could hear it every day. It is marvellous, unearthly music. Every time I hear these notes, I think with pride and perhaps childlike naïveté, that it is wonderful what man can accomplish. But I cannot listen to music often, it affects my nerves. I want to say amiable stupidities and stroke the heads of the people who can create such beauty in a filthy hell. But to-day is not the time to stroke people's heads; to-day hands descend to split skulls open, split them open ruthlessly, although opposition to all violence is our ultimate ideal—it is a hellishly hard task. . . . "

LENIN

I

IN the year 1889 there appeared at a meeting of the
Committee for the Relief of Famine in Samara a
young student who had been " sent down." In the
midst of an anxious and zealous discussion by the members of the committee of the measures to be taken to
fight the catastrophe, which was assuming more and
more alarming proportions, the unknown student rose
and declared, to the general consternation, that it would
be a crime to try to help the starving population, for all
measures of relief would mean support for the Tsarist
dominion. Any increase in the famine should, on the
other hand, be welcomed, for it caused difficulties for
the authorities and contributed to the overthrow of the
existing regime. That was the real evil and only its
destruction could once and for all put an end to future
famines.

This utterance of the nineteen-year-old Lenin, which
sounded so extraordinary to those who heard it, already
contains all that is most characteristic in his later
doctrine: in the next three decades, with the same
disregard of the effect of his opinions, obsessed by this
one idea, he applied all his mental and physical energies
to bringing about the overthrow of the existing world
order.

As one of the countless political conspirators of that
period, in Petersburg as well as in exile in Siberia, shut
up in his poor little attic room in Germany, France,
Italy, or Switzerland, in libraries, and in little smoky
coffee houses, he worked unremittingly on his great
campaign for the overthrow of the mighty Russian

Empire. Years and decades were spent in nightlong debates on quite trifling details of the party programme and on the revolutionary tactics to be adopted at the moment. In these thirty years, he alienated his former partisans increasingly, and cast them off one after the other, until in the end only three or four remained with him.

From the complete isolation of the life of an uprooted emigrant, he was suddenly, as it were overnight, in an apparently mysterious manner, called to be the all-powerful ruler of a hundred and fifty million men. In the struggle with Imperialist war aims, he had evolved quite a new social idea, and now threatened Europe with a titanic upheaval, negotiated on equal terms with the most powerful statesmen of his time, and succeeded in forcing them to recognize the new political organization which he had created.

This " little theorist of revolution," whom even many of his partisans made fun of, who had spent the last few decades in apparently fruitless discussions in the coffee houses of Geneva, Paris, and London, all at once took his place before the world as a truly great statesman, who gradually compelled the political and personal recognition even of his enemies. Bertrand Russell, one of the most distinguished and profound thinkers of our age, and a man who can certainly not be suspected of a bias in Lenin's favour, saw the dictator Lenin at work and wrote of him that one day our century would be described as the century of Lenin. A mighty historical process did, it is true, precede the Bolshevik upheaval, and yet, between that which, before the coming of Lenin, had been fermenting in the masses so powerfully that it needed only translation into word and deed to become a living reality, and that which then took shape through the word and deed of Lenin, lies an ever-mysterious something, the marvel of the individual word and the individual deed, the secret of the great personality.

No other historical example, perhaps, so strikingly

confirms the indispensability and wonderful uniqueness of personal greatness as the mighty historical achievement of Lenin, the man who created the empire of the impersonal mass. For never was there such inseparable connection between the word and him who spoke it, the doctrine and its teacher, the deed and the man, and the movement of the mass and the example of its leader. Nothing can be detached from this personality, everything abides sure and certain in it as in a mighty cosmos.

Bolshevism is entirely the achievement of Lenin, understandable only through him and possible only through him. In the comparison which Trotskiĭ drew between Marx and Lenin this remark is especially significant : " The whole of Marx is in the *Communist Manifesto*, in the preface to his critique in *Kapital*," says Trotskiĭ. " Even if he had never been destined to become the founder of the First International, he would remain for all time as he stands before us to-day. But Lenin, on the other hand, is wholly expressed in revolutionary action. His theoretical work is merely a preparation for action. Had he not published a single book he would still live in history, as he has already entered it, as the leader of the proletarian Revolution, and the creator of the Third International."

This inseparable union between the work and its master can be seen unmistakably, not only in every one of Lenin's utterances and actions, but also in all the events of Bolshevism.

When Lenin spoke, the audience heard words which had often been uttered before, or at least thought of, turns of speech which were sometimes entirely unoriginal and well worn, and which would perhaps have been utterly commonplace if it had not been he who used them; but they all received significance from his enigmatic personality; each of his simple words had an invisible power, each of his gestures was fashioned to a great historical event, whose image was to be impressed on the hearer for ever.

This magic is even felt in Lenin's writings. If we read them without thinking of the personality of the author, we must describe them for the most part as written in a mediocre and not particularly logical way, and sometimes even as one-sided and flat. But the figure of the writer, which is felt behind the written word, holds the reader in thrall, compels him to let sober judgment go, and demands attention, for what is said has beyond all doubt the authority of a great personality. The fact that sentences which in themselves express no particularly profound thought exercise so strong and impressive an effect, speaks more convincingly than anything else for that mysterious power which dwells in personality alone.

One of Lenin's bitterest enemies, the Russian Socialist M. A. Landau-Aldanov, tells how the dictator once, in the midst of the most important State business, received an unknown workman who came to bring him some rather trifling message. " I saw," writes Aldanov, " this workman at the moment when he returned from his audience with Lenin. He was powerfully moved, not the same man. Usually a quiet and reasonable being, he spoke all at once like a man in ecstasy. ' That is a man,' he repeated over and over, ' that is a man for whom I would give my life! . . . With him a new life begins for me! . . . Ah, if we had had a Tsar like him! ' ' But what did he say to you then? ' I asked when he was a little quieter. I received only a vague reply. ' Everything belongs to you,' Lenin had said, ' everything. Take everything. The world belongs to the proletariat. But believe no one but us. The workers have no other friends. We alone are the friends of the workers.' The workman had already heard a hundred times these absurd demagogical sentences, this promise of an earthly paradise instead of a long life of want. Was it the infection of deep faith that had so excited him? Was it the magnetic influence of an outstanding personality? "

Countless numbers hated Lenin and regarded him as
Antichrist. Countless others worshipped him as the
liberator of Russia. But they all, disciples as well as
enemies, felt him in the same way, as a great elemental
phenomenon such as occurs only once in centuries.
In the love and hatred of the Russian peasants his figure
immediately rose to a mystical greatness; the Russian
poetess, Seïfulina, tells how, even in Lenin's lifetime,
legends had formed about him in the stuffy peasants'
cabins of the farthest parts of Russia, as about a being
from a higher, superhuman world. In these descriptions
of Seïfulina's, that fascination which the figure of Lenin
exercised over the Russian peasants appears with a lively
power: " I used to hear Old Believers and sectarians
shrieking by heart, in furious devotion, a sort of ecstasy,
whole pages of the Bible; they attributed to Il'ich Lenin
the number of the beast, the number of Antichrist. . . .
But another of the sectarians, a saddler by trade, spoke
in the country town in support of Lenin, with great
gestures, also quoting Holy Scripture. Lenin, in his
view, acted according to the Bible when he took from
the wealthy their rich acres. ' Woe unto them who add
house to house, field to field, so that no place remains
for the rest, as though they were alone on this earth.'
For this particular sectarian, Lenin was the bearer of
the righteous wrath of God, who was to fulfil the
prophecies of Isaiah. In a settlement of Orthodox
believers there was a thin, red-headed man who fanatic-
ally and, in his own words, scripturally, professed his
faith in Lenin. He joined the party, slung on a rifle,
brandished it threateningly at every meeting, and
bellowed out scriptural texts to prove the justice of
Lenin's political acts. . . . The stories which were
current about Il'ich Lenin testified alike to admiration,
and hate, and repugnance; but all were equally passionate, none was indifferent: land-hungry settlers, labourers, all this poor population wove a garland of legends
about the figure of Lenin."

The whole success of Lenin, the explanation of how it was possible for him, with a few hundred thousand adherents, to assume dominion over a hundred and fifty millions, is plainly due entirely to the influence of his personality, which communicated itself to all who came into touch with him, and then penetrated into the cabins of the peasants in the remotest villages. It is true that the Bolshevist system of dominion is maintained by armed power, by the terror inspired by the secret police, by espionage, and persecution; but what keeps this whole apparatus of power in motion is nothing but the force that proceeds from the great name of Lenin, the spell of his authority.

Never yet, therefore, has the name of its originator been given to a creation with such complete justification as in this case. The word " Leninism " often signifies Bolshevism in Russia to-day, and in this, the name of the leader given to the whole movement, the true essence of the whole system is completely expressed. For Bolshevism is, in content and doctrine, the achievement of Lenin, and it was the mysteriously strong personal influence that he exercised that afterwards grew and waxed to an historic influence, to the mighty upheaval, which is Bolshevism.

After Lenin himself had denied the existence and value of personality, his stalwarts felt obliged to explain the uniqueness of Lenin as a mere product of historical and economic development, and they tried hard, especially the Soviet professor of history, M. Pokrovskiï, to explain Lenin as a " special appliance," or, like a Bolshevist poet, attempted to describe him as a " greater screw " within the collective machine. However, they were not able to argue away the unique element in the existence and appearance of Lenin. When Zinov'ev set himself to relate the history of the Communist Party, even he had . to recognize the magnificent personal achievement of the leader. Speaking of the October Revolution and the part played by the Party in these

events, Zinov'ev says that " nine-tenths of it was the
work of Lenin, if in revolutionary times one may speak
of a single personality at all.   But if any man was able
to convince the doubters, to compel the waverers to a
decision, and to precipitate the fight, that man was
Lenin."

And immediately after Dora Kaflan's attempt on the
life of Lenin, Trotskiĭ declared: " When we think that
Lenin may die, our whole life seems useless and we
cease to want to live."   A greater and more unqualified
recognition of personality, a deeper homage to its unique
nature, has seldom been paid.   For do not these words
imply an avowal that the famous, historically conditioned evolution to which Bolshevist theory ascribes
the " revolutionary achievement," was in reality nine-
tenths the work of a single great individuality?   And for
Trotskiĭ simply to obliterate everything else, the whole
of the rest of the world, in order to fill himself completely with the image of the great leader, does that not
signify that the impression of his personality was of the
most profoundly overwhelming character?

However one-sidedly Soviet historians may urge their
claim to Lenin as a proof of their materialist dogma, they
can by no means explain how his personality differed
from all others, what made it " special " and " greater "
than that of the other two hundred thousand communists,
greater even than that of his whole generation.   But the
strength of the impression which the personal greatness
of Lenin really made, even on those Bolshevists who
were determined to see in him an " appliance " or a
" screw," is shown by the fanatical cult of Lenin which
followed his death.   In Bolshevist Russia, in the empire
of the impersonal mass man, the man who created the
doctrine of the unimportance of the individual, has been
glorified as scarcely any ruler before him.   The funeral
procession of the " appliance, Lenin " was a ceremony
such as Russia had never before seen: from the farthest
districts of the realm came hosts of peasants merely to

file once past the bier of the great dead, and to be able
to gaze for a few moments on the face of Lenin. Very
soon after his death, the mausoleum on the " Red
Square " before the Kremlin, the last resting-place of
his embalmed body, venerated like the relics of a saint,
became a place of pilgrimage. Hosts of men streamed
unceasingly past the glass catafalque in which the dead
man lay on his bier, clad in his military coat, the " Order
of the Red Flag " on his breast and his right fist clenched.

And just as in former times the hearts of the saints
were enclosed in golden caskets and preserved as wonder-
working relics, the most valuable part of Lenin, his
brain, was also enclosed in a casket and preserved as a
sacred relic.

But does not all this imply an avowal that no idea
and no movement can be effective of itself without the
strong driving force of a great personality? Even the
Bolshevik Revolution, through which the " coming
world of the impersonal mass " was to arise, needed to
an overwhelming degree the achievement of the great
man, needed for its system the name of an individual,
just as it had need of sacred relics and a legend for the
establishment of the communist world-church. But it
actually seemed as if Bolshevism more than any other
idea required a personality, Lenin, for it could not be
separated from him; it was nothing but the powerful
historical effect of a mighty individuality which was
used to thinking into and dealing with the brains of the
mass.

II

Of course, in Lenin we are dealing with an entirely
new type of historical greatness, and to understand his
historical importance we must make a fundamental
change in all our former views about truly eminent men.

For, just as the Bolshevik world created by him is without precedent, just as everyone who wants to understand it must get rid of all his ordinary conceptions, so any understanding of the significance of Lenin also demands a complete revision of all current notions about historical greatness.

Even in the external image of this modern hero, in Lenin's whole figure and attitude, the conventional gesture of the great man is lacking. His exterior was completely that of any everyday man of the mass, and clashed with all the pictures of a hero which the imagination is used to make. On the thousands of Soviet flags, propaganda pictures, emblems and badges, Lenin is now portrayed as an orator, standing on the globe, or set amid the rays of the rising sun; but the man himself, beneath whose feet the terrestrial sphere rests as a footstool, whose face emerges from the brightness of the sunlight, is in no way distinguished from thousands and tens of thousands of his fellow citizens. He stands before us, his head covered with an ordinary cloth cap, his right hand in his trousers pocket, and we search his countenance in vain for any trace which might betray the important man. Lenin had the face of an average Russian, and all his friends and disciples who had opportunity to observe him at close quarters, and all the painters and sculptors who fixed his features, are unanimous in stating that his face was entirely lacking in anything remarkable; only the little black eyes made a certain impression. The things that might strike a stranger as characteristic, the high, somewhat conical shape of the skull, the Asiatic cheekbones, and the Mongolian eyebrows, are all quite ordinary in Russia; Lenin's physiognomy has the features which one may meet at every turn in Moscow among the many Russians from the Eastern provinces. Lunacharskiĭ, Lenin's friend, disciple, and biographer, himself confesses that the dictator had the commonplace face of a merchant of peasant stock from, say, Iaroslav.

But not only was there nothing remarkable in Lenin's appearance, even the first impression made by his whole manner was in no way remarkable. And yet he was a popular orator, who carried his audiences on to the most violent upheaval in history, although his speech was entirely lacking in the fiery impulse which is, as a rule, absolutely necessary to capture the masses and bend them to your will. His voice was almost always dimmed with huskiness, it generally sounded flat and colourless, and his turns of speech lacked all appeal, all oratorical adornment. The style of this man, whose words put a whole continent out of joint, both in writing and speech, was entirely insignificant. Trotskiĭ, the second great leader of Russia, was master of the practice of the persuasive orator; his speech had rhythm, dramatic power, and artistic structure; Lenin's oratory had none of these talents at its command.

When Trotskiĭ compared Lenin to Marx, he had to mention this deficiency in the speeches of his leader: " The style of Marx is rich and splendid," he writes, " a skilful blend of strength and suppleness, wrath and irony, harshness and elegance. Marx united in his style the literary and aesthetic achievements of all preceding political literature; Lenin's literary and oratorical style, on the other hand, is simple, utilitarian, almost ascetic." Another interesting analysis of Lenin's peculiarly jejune style is found in the Left periodical Lev; it is an investigation of that mode of speech which, in spite of its insignificance, resulted in one of the most important upheavals in the history of mankind. It is there pointed out that Lenin's style consisted exactly in that avoidance of the revolutionary phrase, in the substitution of simple expressions from daily life for the traditional grandiose language.

" The word was not to him a profession or a career, but the right act; agitation itself is the subject of the majority of his articles and speeches. He had always on the one side opponents or enemies, and on the

other the mass who had to be influenced and convinced."

While Lenin himself set not the slightest value on
style, he nevertheless reacted very decidedly to the
language and stylistic peculiarities of others. The
parties were to him not only symbols of a definite
philosophy of life, but also characteristic systems of
oratorical expression. He passionately condemned all
" fine rhetoric," and regarded it as a sign of intellectual
weakness and moral emptiness. The fight against the
revolutionary phrase runs through all his works and
appeals; he rejected everything which smacked of
meaningless rhetoric and literature. Any high-flown
sentences in his comrades called forth his angry rejection,
a " grand gesture " roused the sharpest criticism and
biting scorn; anything " poetic " or " sublime " incited
him to furious outbursts of contempt.

Only language taken from simple talk had value for
him, and he himself used to introduce into his style
popular, easily understood words and phrases which
often had even a touch of the coarseness of the speech
of the people. But he also loved Latin proverbs, of
which he appreciated the force, terseness, and concentration. Apart from these excursions into the manner
of speech of the educated world, however, he spoke as
simply as possible, and endeavoured as far as possible
to maintain the modulation of easy conversation.

The instructions which he gave in a letter to the
management of a communist paper on the proper
journalist style are characteristic of Lenin's views on this
subject: " Why do you not write ten or twenty lines
instead of your two or four hundred—and these as
simple, easily understandable, and clear as possible—on
events which have penetrated into the flesh and blood
of the masses." Lenin was also always endeavouring
to give fresh content to expression, and to free threadbare
turns of speech and designations from the commonplace
and stereotyped, often merely by giving special import-

ance to conjunctions and adverbs. He was the enemy
of all introductory flourishes, and nearly always plunged
into the middle of his subject.

In his polemics, as *Lev* maintains, he relied chiefly on
emphasis, and when he attacked his enemies, he built
up a whole system of angrily ironic interjections by
which he exposed his foe to general scorn and turned
the whole dispute into a kind of satiric dialogue.

In Lenin's written style, the inverted commas with
which his articles swarm are highly characteristic. He
loved to use his opponent's words, set them in a con-
temptible light, rob them of their force, as it were, strip
off their shell. By preference he made an increasingly
reiterated use of one and the same formula, which
seemed suited to direct the attention of the public to
an important point. He never appealed to emotion
and imagination, but always to will and resolution;
his sentences struggled with the hearer, forced him to a
decision, left him no choice.

His images and comparisons were always entirely
sober and simple; on the whole, he used them only to
make the concrete and visible even clearer; he liked to use
proverbs and easy images, especially from the Gospels and
Krylov's fables; but he never quoted present-day writers.

Not only was Lenin's terse and homely language
entirely lacking in all pathos, and his writings free from
captivating phrases; even the content of his utterances
was always directed entirely to the practical and necessary. He, who had prophesied the victory of Bolshevism
twenty years before, never made great promises. His
friends can point out now how, even in his book on the
future state of society free from class distinctions, no
trace of " exuberance " is to be found, although the
theme demanded and would have excused a certain
passionate exaltation. In all Lenin's utterances, sober
and clearly-felt practical considerations alone prevail;
all his writings are dry discussions of practical politics
or utilitarian instructions.

The result was that with Lenin, who had striven for the Utopian kingdom of the future, Utopia was always adjusted exclusively to the nearest momentary interests of the masses; although he had evolved the most violent programme for the overthrow of the whole world and all its century-old conditions, yet in practice he concerned himself only with the next steps which seemed to him necessary to attain his end.

In Lenin's mind every doctrine or theory, even if it were an idea which embraced the whole of humanity, always assumed the form of a directly necessary, practical demand. Therefore, even in his oratory as an agitator and his propagandist writings, he always dealt only with the tasks which must be immediately carried out.

" Lenin," wrote Trotskiĭ on one occasion, " always sings the same tune, the necessity for fundamentally altering the social differences between men, and above all the best means of attaining this end." The Bolshevist critic, Voronskiĭ, also is of opinion that Lenin always spoke only on one and the same theme: " He deals with the same statement from the most varied and least expected angles, often ten times over. He speaks like a man who has always the same idea, the idea of ideas, about which the splinters of all other thoughts revolve, like the planets round the sun. The innermost core is never lost, never gives place to another thought. To live thus must in the end be very burdensome."

Thus Lenin's whole purpose was as far as possible to express the scientific content of his theory in such a way that it would be comprehensible even to the Russian peasants, uneducated and unused to political speculation, and rouse them to action. Every one of his words was always aimed at its object and at direct action, and for this reason was so loaded with will-power that it was immediately of its own force translated into action. Gor'kiĭ remarks that Lenin's logic was as sharp as an axe. His words were not only a call to battle, but also at the same time practical instructions for the conduct of the fight. His motto was: Revolutions must not remain on paper; they must be carried out in action. He often declared that the proper execution of even the most unimportant measure was more important for the existence of Soviet Russia than all theory, more important than ten Soviet resolutions.

III

The unvarnished simplicity, this peasant rationalism, directed always towards the practical, which was manifest in Lenin's political activity, was deeply rooted in his whole nature; Lenin, the man, was as simple in his personal life as Lenin, the politician, and strove in the same way for practical ends. In his private life, too, his actions and behaviour were in no way prominent; simple, without flourish, free from all superfluity, his whole mode of life was unpretentious, even ascetic.

But this asceticism, which has brought him so much posthumous fame, had no affectation about it, it was not the result of a moral principle, but rather the expression of a nature whose needs were few, the expression of a simple and resolute man, whose whole mind and will were bent on the practical and the carrying-out of principles once and for all recognized as right. Everything else not directly connected with his aims had no interest whatever for him. " It is difficult to draw his portrait," Gor'kiĭ says about Lenin; " he was forthright and simple like all he said. His heroism lacked almost all external glitter. It was the modest ascetic zeal, not seldom seen in Russia, of a revolutionary who believed in the possibility of justice on earth, the heroism of a man who, for the sake of his heavy task, renounced all worldly joys."

Since he was a fanatical believer in the rightness of his ideas, he was troubled by no doubts, no attacks of despondency, or spiritual conflicts; he was exclusively occupied with realizing his projects at any cost. Therefore, even the superhuman labour, the enormous task, which he performed in order to work out and prepare his ideas and translate them into reality, was not an overstrain which could be said to have in any way twisted and distorted his compact nature, but rather the natural expansion of the immense powers possessed by this inimitable and unique being.

Lenin's whole activity had the charm of harmonious freshness and ease. Lunacharskiĭ states that Lenin was by no means a friend of toil, and was but rarely seen with a book, or at a desk. He wrote infinitely fast in large writing and threw his articles on to paper without the least exertion, at any odd time, whenever opportunity offered. He read only in a piecemeal fashion, and never kept long to one book, but he had a sure eye for the significant, and especially for passages which he could use in fighting speeches. It was not so much ideas akin to his own as ideas opposed to his that set him on fire, for the fighter was always alive in him, and his mind was mainly kindled in criticism. Not only did Lenin write occasional pamphlets with this calmness, speed, and objectivity, but also all those decrees which plunged half a continent into upheaval; for his measures as dictator were to him nothing but the natural expression of what he had recognized to be right, and, for this reason, had resolved to realize. None of the violent and terrible conflicts in which Lenin was involved in his lifetime could disturb his calm or upset even for a moment his inner equilibrium.

His friends tell us that he knew, to a degree found in perhaps few other men, the secret of complete relaxation, of the " breathing space," and could procure for himself hours of absolute peace and gaiety, even in the midst of the most stirring events and the most strenuous work.

This may explain his playing for hours with children and kittens after a tiring day's work.

From the unanimous descriptions of all his friends, we see that Lenin was anything but a gloomy, reserved man. Nay, we are always hearing of his childish gaiety, his care-free, jolly laugh, which seems to have been particularly characteristic. " Lenin is genuine right through, filled up to the brim with the sap of life," Voronskiĭ wrote of him. " He tries in vain to control his laughter, which, when he puts his hand over his mouth, bursts out at the side."

Lunacharskiĭ also testifies to Lenin's cheerfulness in private life : " In the unhappiest moments of his exist- ence, he was serene and always prone to gay laughter; even his anger, terrible though it could be in its effects, had something extraordinarily lovable, almost jovial, about it."

This even temperament made it possible for Lenin to preserve his calm and his prudent glance even in the most difficult and catastrophic moments of the political struggle. He was never nervous, impatient, or excited, but always uniformly attentive, interested, and objective. He was always ready to listen attentively to the most trifling communications of the soldiers, workers, or peasants who came from the most remote villages to lay their grievances before him. He was entirely merged in the mass of his partisans, Klara Zetkin reports; he became homogeneous with them, and never by gesture or attitude tried to obtrude his personality. Klara Zetkin also speaks of his comradely way with young people, and of the fatherly note he knew how to strike in his intercourse with the younger Party members.

IV

There is no doubt that a large part of his success with
the Russian masses may be traced to the unpretentious-
ness of his character; he laid all who came to him under
a spell, and he was obeyed as one obeys a trusted and
experienced adviser, who is distinguished from those
about him merely by greater shrewdness. Even the
poorest peasant faced Lenin with a feeling that he was
meeting a friend on an equal footing.

Lenin had much of the peasant in him; his simple,
reliable character, his prudent eye for practical advantage,
are all characteristic features of the Russian peasant.
" This undoubtedly great proletarian leader," wrote
Trotskiï once, " not only has the appearance of a
peasant, but his rugged bearing as well. When he
shuts his left eye in deciphering a radio-telegram or an
important document, he is the very image of a shrewd
peasant who is not to be got round by empty words.
His shrewdness is exactly a peasant's shrewdness, but
raised to the highest power and equipped with the keenest
scientific methods of thought."

Lenin had in common with the peasants not only their
shrewdness, but also their tendency to violence; he was
intimately one with all the primitive forces of the people,
and it was through this that he was able to bring about
such a colossal upheaval. This basic trait of his personality explains his political success also, for he saw
in politics exactly the field of activity in which his nature
could best prove itself.

All his acts, speeches, and writings always breathed
this simple feeling for the practical, and also that inflexible energy which was so pre-eminently characteristic of him.

" If we take the little slips of paper," says Voronskiï,
" which Lenin sends out all over the place, we find in
them simple instructions on, say, what attitude should

C

be taken to England, or what advice must be given to
the German workers, cheek by jowl with a request that
some peasant woman or other should be allowed to take
four poods of corn from one station to another, because
she has three children to keep."

But it was just in such little everyday things, in
practical activity like this, that Lenin's real strength lay.
When he died, and his disciples, as is customary after
the death of all important men, were collecting proofs
of the greatness of their master and seeking for " unforgettable words," it was found that Lenin's utterances were mere dry orders, brief instructions, or official
arrangements.

One of these notes, which is regarded by Leninists as
" immortal," is an order which he issued in the year
1921, in the most critical period of " militant communism." The district immediately round Moscow was
then threatened by the enemy, and it was generally
believed that the days of Soviet dominion were numbered. In this most perilous of all moments, Lenin
thought the introduction of electric light into the villages
was an all important task and issued an ordinance:
" The peasants in the localities of Gor'kiĭ and Ziianova
are immediately to be supplied with electric light!"

Another instruction of that period deals with the
improvement of the radio-telephone, and the rest of the
utterances of the great revolutionary have a similar
ring: " Investigate immediately why the Collegium of
the Central Naphtha Syndicate has assigned to the
workers ten and not thirty arshin per head." " Thor-
ough study of the scientific organization of labour
necessary." " Care must be taken to make the com-
position of the bills laid before the Ministerial Council
clearer and plainer." " Investigate how wind-motors
could be utilized for lighting the villages with electricity."
This is how Lenin's great utterances look; in these
sentences lies the secret of the mysterious way in which
Utopias can be created by means of purely practical

transactions. A special commission was recently set up
at the Lenin Institute in Moscow to investigate how
changes of world-wide importance have in the course of
time resulted from Lenin's individual and practical
measures.

All the descriptions of his friends and fellow workers
discover for us again and again the man whose whole
attention was always given to the meticulous carrying
out of everyday tasks. Even the legend which is now
beginning to form around the figure of Lenin in Russia
celebrates the " prudent hero of Utilitarianism "; it
paints the mighty ruler of Russia who, in the midst of
the most difficult affairs of world politics, bothered
himself about whether the women workers in some
factory or other had actually received the new aprons
assigned to them. The legend extols Lenin as the ruler
of an immense empire, who, after sending a letter to some
office under his authority, telephoned immediately
himself to ask whether the document had arrived.

It was this capacity for being able to think of everything at once, never to let any course of action, once
begun, out of his sight again, to put the world out of
joint and at the same time worry over the most trifling
needs of workwomen, it was this capacity that gained
Lenin so many adherents. It is on account of this that,
after his death, all his apparently uninteresting practical
instructions were treated by the Bolsheviks as sacred
words, as unforgettable utterances. Thus Lenin's note
about the electrification of the villages by means of
wind-motors is quoted in Russia like a text from the
Gospels. It is remembered at great festivals, and from
it strength is drawn for fresh struggles.

Finally, Lenin's influence on the multitude is also to
be explained by the fact that he succeeded Kerenskiï, a
professed rhetorician, who loved a well-sounding phrase
above all else. He appeared exactly at the moment
when Russia was tired of high-flown words and longed
for terse dryness, for action and deeds. The Russian

mind was at that moment involved in one of its most
serious crises, and Lenin was then the right man, who
proclaimed deeds and practical action as the one
salvation, and himself set the example. Had Lenin
appeared in a Western European State, his practical
principles and civilizing schemes would perhaps have
roused little attention; but in Russia, utterly behind the
times in modern civilization, this gospel of utilitarianism
must have seemed in truth a new religion.

V

Lenin subjected the whole domain of intellectual and
spiritual life to this utilitarian method of treatment,
philosophy, literature, art, and even morality. His
judgment of philosophy, in particular, is permeated by
utilitarian and party political notions.

Like the princes of the Church in old days, Lenin is
one of those thinkers who rightly recognize the important
political background of philosophy. In his view,
adherence to one philosophy or another was far more
than the mere private business of a limited number of
philosophically trained men; he saw the different
philosophies rather as " ideological weapons " in the
class war, idealistic philosophical tendencies representing a class remote from the direct process of production,
materialistic views, on the other hand, representing the
working class, the producer of goods.

Therefore, in the interest of the Communist State, the
most ruthless warfare had to be waged against idealist
philosophy, a warfare which should crown the victory
Bolshevism had already won in the political and economic
fields. If the epoch of " militant communism," the
terrorizing and persecution of all political opponents,
signified the external fortification of Soviet rule, and the

subsequent " new economic policy " an economic
consolidation and a new organization of production, the
" ideological front " now formed against idealistic
philosophy corresponded to the third and final phase of
Lenin's struggle for dominion in Russia.

It is not necessary to emphasize here that Lenin
always dealt with all forms of religiousness in the most
drastic fashion; he regarded the piety of the people as
the worst obstacle in the way of the carrying out of his
new ideas. Again and again in his writing and in his
speeches he pointed out that the Communist proletariat
and its leaders must work with might and main to overthrow God, " the arch-enemy of the Communist social
order."

For this purpose, he organized a regular atheistic
propaganda. " It would be the worst possible mistake,"
he wrote on one occasion, " for Marxists to imagine
that the great millions of the people can be liberated
from their intellectual darkness and ignorance merely by
the direct road of Marxist enlightenment. They must
rather supply the masses with the most varied atheistical
propaganda, present them with scientifically proved
facts, approach them now in one way, now in another,
awaken their interest and try to arouse them by every
possible means from every possible angle.

" The journalism of the atheists of the eighteenth
century, which openly attacked parsondom in a ready,
lively, clever, and witty fashion, was a thousand times
more fitted to rouse men from their religious slumber
than the boring, dry, and clumsy popular expositions
of Marxism such as predominate in our literature and
often even distort Marxism. The chief thing is and
will continue to be, to awaken the interest of the wholly
undeveloped masses to a conscious criticism of religion."

This fight against idealism seemed necessary to him
mainly because this philosophy was based on the idea
of a teleological unity, in accordance with which, both
in nature and in human life, everything advances

towards ends infinitely distant in a process of continual perfectibility.

In such a theory of design, Lenin saw a " concealed religiousness," for the concept of the end, in his view, presupposes the concept of a supreme being who has determined an end. Lenin rejected with the greatest rigour this " immanent teleology," which speaks of a striving towards an end, indwelling in nature and society, and gradually revealed, and, therefore, shifts the end, the design, to the process of evolution. Lenin believed that he recognized a " disguised God-concept " in this theory, even though it was " washed with all the waters of thought."

In a manuscript fragment found among Lenin's papers after his death and edited by Deborin, he states:

" Philosophic idealism is not quite an absolute lie, for it springs from the same soil as materialism. None the less, philosophic idealism becomes a lie, a barren bloom, if it turns to clericalism, for it makes of one of the gradations in the infinitely complicated system of knowledge, an absolute, and a fragment of reality, the whole.

" Philosophical idealism, considered from the standpoint of dialectical materialism, represents a one-sided and exaggerated expansion of one of the features, one of the sides, one of the boundaries of the knowledge of the absolute, which is torn apart from matter, from nature, and deified.

" The idealists, by taking a fragment of the totality of phenomena, and depriving it of its relation with matter, at the same time inflate the part to a whole, and allow it to assume absolute dimensions. Dialectical materialism, on the other hand, is always conscious that such a fragment, torn from its general relation and divorced from matter, lacks all reality and is a barren blossom. We therefore see in subjectivism, in subjective delusion, in that narrow-minded and one-sided attitude which takes a part of an integer for the whole integer, blows it up into a complete system, and makes it pass for the absolute, the gnoseological roots of idealism."

To Lenin not only the religions, but also all the doctrines and methods of non-materialistic philosophy seemed a great intellectual menace to the proletarian regime; idealism, in particular, he regarded as a focus of counter-revolution, the ruthless destruction of which seemed to him to be the most important and urgent task of the Revolution.

In order to protect the rising generation, the young Communists, from the "intellectual poison of the old outlook on the world," Lenin staked everything on a complete transformation of the universities. For him all idealistic doctrine was as false and as dangerous as religion itself; its propagators must, therefore, be rendered harmless. Even in the science of jurisprudence Lenin discerned a remnant of the idealist system, for jurisprudence presupposes individual rights, and is, therefore, opposed to the collectivist principles of Bolshevism. But even the exact sciences could only be tolerated under strict communist control, for fear that one or other result might creep into their experimental researches which might permit of arguments for the existence and sway of a spiritual world.

But how extraordinary this " spiritual dictatorship of materialism " really is can only be understood by a somewhat closer study of the past history of Bolshevik ideology. This same party, which now pitilessly and ruthlessly fights any form of idealism, not so very long ago championed idealistic principles against the materialism of the Mensheviks. Lenin, who for long had taken practically no interest in philosophical problems, suddenly imposed dictatorially on his party a quite different view of life. He was asked for his verdict in the ideological controversy between Bolsheviks and Mensheviks, proceeded to London, there pursued philosophical studies ostensibly for two years but, according to other accounts, for only six weeks, and then gave his vote for the materialistic philosophy hitherto championed by his Menshevik opponent, Plekhanov. The " empirio-criticism " of his fellow Bolshevik, Bogdanov, seemed to him unsuited to practical class war, and this was enough to sway his verdict against it.

When Lenin read philosophical wᴏrks, he skimmed through them rather than studied them. Madame Lepeshinskiĭ, who once made a steamer journey with Lenin, describes how he used to hold some heavy work in his hand and turn the leaves continually. At last she asked Lenin whether he merely glanced at the pages or really read them. He replied with a laugh and some surprise: " Of course I read them and very carefully, for the book is worth it. . . . " The socialist, Landau-Aldanov, justly remarks on Lenin's philosophical studies:

" It is clear that Lenin was interested in philosophy only as one is interested in an enemy. He had studied a pile of philosophical books, or rather had glanced through them, but he was inspired by the same motives as made German officers study the Russian language."

In fact, it was only the practical polemical side of philosophical discussion that attracted Lenin's interest, and this also explains the unusual note always struck by his own work in this field: he is continually breaking off his argument to hurl furious insults at his opponents and a hail of malicious and caustic wit.

After Lenin had spoken his mighty word in favour of materialism in the dispute between Mensheviks and Bolsheviks, all his imitators immediately began to make the most violent attacks on Bogdanov's doctrines, which had hitherto been regarded as the only true ones, and eventually they drove him out of the Bolshevist party. But a considerable time had still to elapse before this inner change of front in Bolshevism found a chance of making itself externally felt. Up to the outbreak of the world war, the Party had led only a semblance of life, and later even, at the time of the February Revolution, it had to devote its whole attention to purely political matters. It was not till November 1917, when the Bolshevist Party attained to power, that it was at last possible to make a clear definitive statement of the ideological side of Bolshevism; then the problem was decided in Lenin's sense, in favour of dialectical material-ism. The treatise which Lenin had published earlier on the idealo-materialist dispute was reissued, and with all due form elevated to the position of the Bolshevik State religion.

Starting from a well-known dictum of Karl Marx, Lenin made practice the touchstone of all theoretical knowledge. " Life, practice," he once declared, " is the basic angle from which the theory of knowledge must be treated. It leads inevitably to materialism, by driving out the endless tomfooleries of philosophical scholastic-ism at the very threshold. . . . What is confirmed by Marxist practice, both in the purely theoretical and also in the social sphere, is the only objective truth."

For this reason, Lenin made it his particular endeavour " not only to know the world but to reform it," to turn theory into practice. His theoretical recognition of the necessity for freeing the proletariat must not merely, according to this doctrine, maintain a dispassionate attitude to reality; it must before everything itself lead to a change of this reality; at the same time, the regard for practice should also re-fructify the theory and carry it to a further stage of development. In his view the function of the theorists was to work out " a detailed Marxist version of Russian history and reality," at the same time to popularize this theory, make it compre-hensible to the working class, and create a form of organization for the spreading of Communism. " Marx-ist theory undertakes the task of revealing the antagon-ism and the methods of exploitation in the bourgeois social order, of tracing its evolution, and in this way making it easier for the proletariat to abolish it."

The secret of Lenin's successes lies not least in his

capacity for making theory influence practice and practice influence theory alternately. He did not put off for a moment the realization of theoretically acquired knowledge, but he also had no scruples about subjecting theory to revision, if practical results made this course desirable. " The practical empiricist," writes Deborin, Lenin's philosophic commentator, " deals, so to speak, with each case as it crops up. He does not see phenomena as a whole, their inner relation, and their obedience to laws. The revolutionary thinker, on the other hand, does not rest content with the casual fact, he is not satisfied with the surface of phenomena, but endeavours to base his activity on the real essence of phenomena, on their laws. The laws of society are its inner motives and levers, and the ceaseless changes and developments in reality are accomplished in accordance with these inner laws. Humanity has been blind and wandered in darkness for so long that these laws have become mysteries; but its sight will be restored as soon as it recognizes them. . . . Without a right and objectively true theory, there is no rationally conscious historic and social activity. Such a theory is an indispensable condition for any conscious influencing of the historical process."

This indispensable theory Lenin found in dialectic, of which he said on one occasion that it shows " how opposites can be and actually are identical, under what conditions they are transformed into each other and become identical, and why human reason must regard these opposites not as dead and fixed, but as vital, conditioned, movable, and in process of transformation into one another."

Lenin distinguishes two conceptions of evolution: one sees in it nothing but a waxing and waning, a recurrence; the other view, on the contrary, which he thinks is the only true one, sees the basis of evolution " in the unity of opposites and in the division of this unity."

A posthumous fragment of Lenin dealing with dialectic contains, in addition to interesting notes on Heraclitus, Aristotle, Philo, and Hegel, a sort of tabular comparison of the sciences in their relation to this dialectical " struggle of opposites." In this table Lenin tries to discover in mathematics, mechanics, physics, and chemistry dialectical opposites inextricably bound up with each other, and to prove from this that all the sciences, the natural sciences no less than those of social life, are fundamentally dialectical and proceed from dialectical opposites.

But if dialectical materialism is to be valid as a scientific method, it must also find confirmation in the exact natural sciences. Engels had already declared that nature was the touchstone for dialectic, and that the materialist must be grateful to the natural sciences, which every day afforded new material for testing his theory. Lenin adopted this view and tried to find the necessary confirmation of his philosophical theories in modern physics.

But as exact science, so far from producing results which confirmed materialism, seemed on the contrary to be pressing on to idealistic conclusions, Lenin increasingly felt the necessity of subjecting all the achievements of exact research to a " Marxist revision " from the standpoint of dialectical materialism. Therefore, he called for a rigorous, purely materialistic control over the entire activities of all scientific research, and the suppression of all idealistic conclusions, which he regarded as false, in order to prevent any theistic ideas from springing up afresh within the natural sciences.

VI

Lenin's materialistic philosophy involved his regarding art also not as an independent spiritual phenomenon, but merely as one dependent on the economic conditions of the moment. Thus his personal attitude to art was that of a practical politician: he valued it according to its usefulness as propaganda.

" Down with literati not belonging to the Party! " he wrote as early as the year 1905. " Down with the supermen literati! Literature must form a part of the universal proletarian cause, a screw or a cog in the great democratic mechanism set in motion by the whole class-conscious working-class."

He made the same demand for party political utility on the visual arts: he could only allow that they were justified if it were possible to make them useful for purposes of political propaganda: he raised the cry of " making art political " throughout the whole revolutionary period.

Lunacharskiĭ relates how Lenin sent for him in 1918, and explained to him that art must be used as a means of propaganda. Hereupon he evolved two schemes for the People's Commissar : buildings and walls must be supplied with great revolutionary inscriptions; and in addition it was necessary to erect memorials to the great revolutionaries. Both schemes were realized immediately. In particular, the houses of the small towns in Russia resembled for a time gigantic poster hoardings, while at the same time in Moscow and Leningrad numerous monuments to revolutionary heroes were set up.

It is true that Lenin later seemed not to have been particularly well satisfied with the carrying out of his scheme; on one occasion he visited an exhibition of plans for a new memorial, examined all the work with a critical eye, and did not approve of a single plan. He

stood for a long time in amazement before a monument
of strongly futurist style, and finally declared, on being
asked for his opinion, that he did not understand anything about it, they must ask Lunacharskiĭ. On the
latter's stating that he did not consider any of the plans
exhibited worth carrying out, Lenin was delighted and
cried: " I was so afraid that you would erect one of
these futurist scarecrows! "

Lenin did not care much for futurism. Once he
visited an artists' home, and had long conversations with
the futurist painters and sculptors there, in which he
took a highly ironic tone and seemed to make fun of the
whole movement. It is true that at the end he declared
placatingly that he really understood nothing about it.

The men engaged on the renaissance of Russian art,
the Bolshevik poets, painters,, sculptors, and architects,
who were endeavouring in their creative work to put a
spiritual crown on Lenin's great social work, complained
despairingly of the Master's utter blindness and deaf-
ness: he was unable to comprehend the supreme and
ultimate achievements of his own system as manifested
in modern art.

The reason for Lenin's inability to understand art
should to some extent be ascribed to the fact that he had
had little time in his life to devote to the things of art.
During the first revolution, in 1905, he once had the
opportunity to glance through some monographs on
artists at the house of a party comrade. Next morning
he declared: " What a marvellous and vast domain the
history of art is! Last night I could not get asleep till
morning, and I looked through one book after the other;
it distressed me to think that I have no time to devote
to art, and that it is unlikely I shall ever have any leisure
for it." And as he loathed all dilettanteism he refused,
as a rule, to speak on artistic subjects; nevertheless his
taste was pretty decided, and knew strong sympathies
and antipathies.

Russian literature of the revolutionary period was

entirely and peculiarly alien to him, although he sometimes praised the work of Il'ia Ehrenburg and individual
poems of Maiakovskiĭ and Dem'ian Bednyĭ. But whenever he read literary works, it was mostly those of the
old school.

Nadezhda Krupskaia, Lenin's widow, has given us
some interesting information about her husband's
literary interests. During his stay in Siberia, according
to her account, there always lay on his bedside table, in
addition to Hegel's works, books by Pushkin, Lermontov,
and Nekrasov, which he read frequently. Of all these
authors, he was particularly fond of Pushkin, whereas
he had little use for Dostoevskiĭ's works. He regarded
Dostoevskiĭ as a reactionary, and thought that the great
enthusiasm for his work was a disguised form of counter-
revolution. Tolstoĭ, especially his social and ethical
doctrines, he had studied closely, only to reject them
violently in the end: the spread of Tolstoĭ's ideas
seemed to him a real misfortune for Russia. As early
as the year 1908 he published in his periodical, *Proletar*,
an article on Tolstoĭ which bluntly expressed his views
of the novelist-apostle: " To set the name of this great
artist," he wrote on that occasion, " alongside the
Revolution, which he clearly did not understand and
which he consciously avoided, may at the first glance
seem strange and unnatural. . . . But our Revolution is
an extremely complicated phenomenon; among the
multitude of those who directly carry it out and participate in it, there are many elements which do not understand events and evade the real historic tasks. When
we have to do with a truly great artist, he cannot help
but reflect in his work at least one of the important
aspects of the Revolution. . . .

" The inconsistencies in Tolstoĭ's views should not be
judged from the point of view of the modern labour
movement and socialism, but from that of the protest
against the advance of capitalism as it inevitably appeared
in the patriarchal Russian village. As a prophet who

has discovered new receipts for the salvation of humanity Tolstoï is ridiculous; the foreign and Russian Tolstoïans are quite pitiful creatures, because they try to elevate into a dogma the weakest side of his teaching. Tolstoï is great in so far as he succeeded in expressing the ideas and moods of the peasantry at the time of the bourgeois revolution in Russia; he is original because, although his views are as a whole harmful, he does reveal the peculiar character of our Revolution as a bourgeois-peasant rebellion. . . .

" Tolstoï reproduced the accumulated hate, the matured striving after better things, the desire to be free of the past, but he also reflected the crudities of all visionariness, the lack of political training and revolutionary flabbiness. Historical and economic conditions explain both the necessity of the revolutionary struggle and the lack of preparation for this struggle; the Tolstoïan doctrine ' of non-resistance to evil ' was in any event one of the chief causes of our defeat in the first revolutionary campaign. . . .

" The inconsistencies in the works, the opinions, the teaching, and the school of Tolstoï are glaring. On the one hand, we have an author of genius, who has produced incomparable pictures of Russian life, even classical works in the literature of the world; on the other hand we have the landowner and the fool in Christ. On the one hand, he makes a most zealous, direct, and sincere protest against the falsehood and dishonesty of the existing social order; on the other, he produced the Tolstoïans, worn out, hysterical, pitiable rags of Russian intellectuals, who openly beat their breasts and cry: ' I am a sinner, a miserable sinner, but I am devoting myself to my moral perfection. I no longer eat meat, and I feed on rice cutlets! ' On the one side, unsparing criticism of capitalist exploitation, unmasking of the Government and its violence, of the comedy of justice and the contrasts between the growth of the plutocracy and the increase of poverty among the working classes;

on the other, imbecile preaching about not resisting evil
with force. Here, the most sober realism, the tearing off
of all masks, there, the preaching of the most infamous
thing in all the world, religion—the attempt to replace
the official priests by priests by moral conviction, and
thus to cultivate a refined and hateful form of parsondom. . . ."

Lenin, however, had all his life the greatest admiration
for Tolstoĭ, the artist. A volume of Tolstoĭ was often
to be found on his desk in the Kremlin.

" To-day I wanted to re-read the hunting scene in
War and Peace," he once said to Gor'kiĭ, " but I
remembered that I had still to write to a comrade.
I have almost no time for reading, but to-night I will
bury myself resolutely in Tolstoĭ." He smiled, shut
his eyes, stretched himself in a chair and went on:
" Tolstoĭ, what a mass! my friend, what a wealth of
material! Tolstoĭ, my dear fellow, there's a true artist!
The really splendid thing in him is his peasant voice,
his peasant thought! He is a real peasant as no other
man has ever been. Until this nobleman appeared, the
true peasant was unknown in literature." Then he fixed
his Asiatic eyes on Gor'kiĭ and asked: " What has
Europe to compare with Tolstoĭ? Nothing." He smiled
and rubbed his hands contentedly.

Lenin's library, Nadezhda Krupskaia tells us, also
included Goethe's *Faust* and a volume of Heine's poems
in German; but he set particular store on Chernishevskiĭ's novel, *What is to be done?* At the time of his
stay in Paris, he read Victor Hugo and Verhaeren with
pleasure; during the war he studied with interest
Barbusse's *Le Feu*. During his illness, his wife read
aloud to him books by Shchedrin, Jack London, and
Maxim Gor'kiĭ, but he took no interest then in modern
Russian literature.

Lunacharskiĭ gives a similar report of Lenin's dislike
of contemporary Russian literature: " Vladimir Il'ich
did not altogether deny the significance of the prole-

tarian poets' groups; but generally he paid no attention
to the work of the new literary associations formed
during the Revolution. He had no time to devote to
them." However, he found leisure enough to read
Maiakovskiĭ's *Hundred and Fifty Million*, and to express
plainly his disapproval of this work, which he called
affected and superficial.

Lenin was mostly repelled by the modern theatre,
and seldom stayed till the end of a play. His last visit
to the Moscow Artists' Theatre was to see a dramatiza-
tion of Dickens' well-known story, *The Cricket on the
Hearth*, the sentimentality of which he thought intolerable; Gor'kiĭ's *Night Refuge* was also a great disappointment to him. On the other hand, he liked the perform-
ances at the same theatre of Hauptmann's *Fuhrmann
Henschel* and Chekhov's *Uncle Vania*. During his
wandering period, a performance of Tolstoĭ's *Living
Corpse* at the Berne Municipal Theatre made a profound
impression on him.

But Lenin's attitude to art and to the modern
Bolshevik tendencies may be most plainly seen from a
conversation he had with Klara Zetkin, the well-known
German Communist, his wife, and his sister.

" Why worship the new," he cried, " merely because
it is new? That is nonsense, sheer nonsense. But there
is besides much conventional hypocrisy and respect for
artistic fashions at work here, even if it is unconscious.
We are good revolutionaries, but we feel obliged to prove
that we stand on the summit of contemporary culture.
I have the courage to recognize myself to be a barbarian;
I cannot extol the products of expressionism, futurism,
cubism, and the other 'isms' as the supreme revelations
of artistic genius. I do not understand them, and they
give me no pleasure."

When Klara Zetkin thereupon confessed that she also
lacked the organ for seeing why an enthusiastic soul
should necessarily be represented as a triangle, and why
revolutionary zeal should transform the human body

into a shapeless sack on two wooden legs, Lenin laughed
heartily. " Ah, yes, my dear Klara, it's because we are
both old people. We must be content sometimes still
to feel young and progressive in the Revolution; we
cannot keep pace with the new art, we just hobble along
in its wake."

" However," he went on, " our opinion of art is of
no importance, nor is what art can give to a few hundred
or even a few thousand people important either. Art
belongs to the people, it must have its deepest roots in
the great producing masses, it must be understood and
loved by them. Art must unite and elevate the mass in
their emotion, thought, and will, it must awaken and
develop the artist in them. Are we to hand a sweet,
delicately flavoured biscuit to a minority, while the
masses of the workers and peasants lack even black
bread? Of course, I mean that not only literally but
figuratively as well. We must always keep the workers
and peasants before our eyes and learn to reckon with
them even in matters of art and culture.

" In order that art can come to the people and the
people to art, we must first raise the general level of
education and culture. How do things look in our
country? People are enthusiastic about the enormous
amount of cultural work that has been done since
Bolshevism seized power. And we can say, without
boasting, that we have really done a great deal in this
domain: we have not only ' cut off heads,' we have also
enlightened heads, many heads! But they are many
only in comparison with the past, when measured
against the sins of the former ruling class. We are faced
with the gigantic awakened need of the workers and
peasants for education and culture, not only in Petrograd
and Moscow, in the industrial centres, but also away
there in the villages. And we are a poor nation, beggarly
poor! Whether we like it or not, most old people must
remain victims, disinherited, when it comes to culture.
It is true that we are carrying on an energetic campaign

against illiteracy and are sending trains for national education and circulating exhibitions all over the country. But I repeat, what is all this compared with the many millions who lack the most elementary knowledge, the most primitive culture? In Moscow to-day ten thousand and to-morrow another ten thousand may listen intoxicated to a fine theatrical performance, but out there the need of the millions for the art of spelling and arithmetic cries aloud, the people cry for the culture which can teach them that the earth is round!"

"Do not complain so bitterly about illiteracy," interposed Klara Zetkin. "It to some extent made the Revolution easier for you. Your propaganda fell on virgin soil; it is easier to sow and to reap when you have not first to uproot a whole primaeval forest."

"That is quite true," answered Lenin, "but only to a limited extent, for a certain period of our struggle. I grant that illiteracy was useful when it was a question of demolishing the old political machinery; but are we destroying merely for the sake of destruction? We are destroying in order to build up something better. . . ."

There was some speculation on which of the conspicuous manifestations of artistic life could be explained by the situation existing at the moment, and Lenin replied: "I am quite aware that many people are honestly convinced that all the difficulties of the moment could be overcome with the old receipt *panem et circenses*. *Panem*, yes: *circenses*,—for all I care! But it should not be forgotten that circuses are not truly great art, but more or less fine entertainment. It should not be forgotten that our workers and peasants are not the rabble proletariat of Rome. They are not maintained by the State; they maintain the State by their labour. Our workers and peasants deserve something better than circuses: they have a right to genuine, great art. Therefore I say our main aim must be national education and national instruction in the widest sense."

Lenin was convinced that it was impossible to establish the Communist social order in a country without national education, and that the chief task of Russian Communism was to " liquidate " illiteracy, so that the rising generation should no longer know even the connotation of the word. He regarded the fight against illiteracy as the duty of every Bolshevist, a duty as urgent as armed opposition to the counter-revolution, for, as he remarked in one of his speeches, he thought it absurd to pursue political enlightenment, so long as the country was swarming with illiterates: " A man who can neither read nor write, is outside politics; he must first learn the A B C, without which there can be no such thing as politics, but merely rumours, gossip, fairy tales, and prejudices." For this reason he considered that all strivings after a new Bolshevik art were for the present doomed to failure. Once when asked for his opinion in the course of a literary argument, he declared again that the convulsive efforts to produce a new art and poetry were vain and useless, it was infinitely more important to devote attention to elementary national education, since reading and writing are necessary conditions for a true proletarian culture.

But although Lenin sought in literature and art mainly social and political utility, and refused to allow any validity to abstract aesthetic values, he could not entirely escape from the spell of music, the most mysterious and direct of all arts. He, who always aimed at sober utilitarianism, who so steadfastly shut himself off from all the seductions of art, could not quite save his soul from the assaults of music. He stopped his ears with wax to preserve his level-headedness, but the song of the sirens sometimes penetrated to his heart, and stained his immaculately utilitarian mind with lewd magic.

" Vladimir Il'ich loved music," says Lunacharskiĭ, " but it affected him too strongly. I used to arrange good concerts at my house at one time; Shaliapin often sang, and Meĭchik, Romanovskiĭ, the Stradivarius Quartet, and other artists used to play. More than once

I asked Lenin to come to one of these evenings, but he was always otherwise employed. Once he said to me frankly: ' It is certainly very delightful to hear music, but it affects me too strongly, so that I feel oppressed. I stand music badly.' "

And that other remark Lenin made to Gor'kiĭ after hearing Beethoven's *Appassionata*, that music seduced him into uttering amiable stupidities and stroking people's heads, while it was his duty to split skulls open ruthlessly, shows in an appalling way the inner conflict which went on in the soul of this " apostle of level-headedness." Those Bolsheviks who spoke after him had no longer any trace of the profound disunion which made the tragic greatness of Lenin. They belonged to a time which was completely steeped in flat, unspiritual utilitarianism. They had no longer any artistic feeling; they were dull and level-headed to the innermost core of their nature, utterly degenerated into the " cold madness " of rationalism.

VII

All Lenin's conceptions of ethics and morality, of good and evil were also completely subordinated to the momentary political interests of Bolshevism. He ventured with a bold gesture to relegate the ideal of moral freedom to the position of a worthless phrase: " Freedom is a bourgeois prejudice."

In these words, Lenin reduced to its crudest form the idea that humanity can participate in the revolutionary regeneration only through a dictatorship aided by a reliable army and a horde of spies, prison warders, and torturers. He substituted the " Katorga "[1] of to-day for

[1] A word meaning " hard labour," [which sums up for the Russian mind exile in Siberia with all its attendant miseries and tortures. (Translator's note.)

the " Katorga " of yesterday, the Bolshevik " Cheka "
for the Tsarist " Okhrana "—for the liberation of the
former oppressed and disinherited seemed to him
synonymous with fresh oppression and fresh disinherit-
ance. The kingdom of Communism was to be ushered
in with violence, gaols, and gallows, with the abolition
of freedom of speech and of the Press, with all kinds of
material and spiritual terrorism.

In this connection, a remark made by Lenin in 1907,
at the time of the London Congress and reported by the
Polish revolutionary Krajevski, is very interesting.
During a meal, there was a discussion on whether
Bolsheviks and Mensheviks could ever act in harmony.
One of those present was of opinion that it would
perhaps be possible, in spite of all differences of opinion,
to bridge the gulf between the two parties and restore
Socialist unity. Lenin was silent for a minute or two
and then said with his characteristic smile: " Why
should we imitate the example of Western Europe?
I recognize only one form of conciliation with regard to
political opponents, *écraser*—smash them! " Krajevski
remarks that these words, spoken without any emotion,
were stamped on his mind for the rest of his life.

When the Council of People's Commissars, soon after
the Revolution, in Lenin's absence, again abolished the
death penalty in the Army which Kerenskiĭ had introduced, Lenin, on hearing of it, was beside himself with
excitement over this decision. " Madness! " he repeated
again and again. " How can you carry out a revolution
without executions? Do you really believe that you can
make an end of your enemies without the death penalty?
What measures are left then? Prison? Who worries
about imprisonment during a civil war, when both
parties hope to win? "

Even when Kamenev explained to him that it was only
a question of abolishing the death penalty for deserters,
Lenin merely went on repeating: " It's a mistake, an
unpardonable weakness, a pacifist illusion! " He urged

with all his force that the decree must be immediately repealed. Finally, it was agreed not to withdraw the order, but simply to take no notice of it and go quietly on with the executions.

In the early days of the Bolshevik regime, when the opposition press was agitating violently against the Soviet Government, Lenin used to ask at every opportunity: " Are we never going to put an end to the carryings on of this crew? Devil take it, what kind of a dictatorship is this? "

A remark which he once made during a debate on the drafting of an appeal to the people is characteristic of Lenin's point of view with regard to unrestricted terrorism. It was a question of including in the appeal a clause to the effect that anyone who helped the enemy would be executed on the spot; Steinberg, the social revolutionary, then a member of the Government, protested against this threat on the plea that it would spoil the " emotional effect of the appeal." " On the contrary," declared Lenin, " that is the very revolutionary emotional effect. Do you really think then that we can emerge victoriously from the Revolution without rabid terrorism? "

Trotskiĭ tells us that, at this period, Lenin at every opportunity emphasized in the strongest possible way the inevitability of terrorism: " Our so-called revolutionaries imagine then," he cried, " that we can make a revolution in the most friendly and kindly fashion? Where did they learn this? What do they really understand by a dictatorship? Theirs is a dictatorship of sleepy-heads! " Such remarks could be heard dozens of times every day, and they were always directed against some person present who was suspected of " pacifism." When people spoke of revolution and dictatorship in his presence, Lenin never let an opportunity slip without interposing with " Where's the dictatorship there? Show it to me. All that is pap, not dictatorship! If we are unable to shoot a White Guard guilty of sabotage, our Revolution has not made much advance. Look at what the bourgeois rabble is writing in the newspapers! Where is the dictatorship hiding then? Nothing but pap and babble!" These speeches, as Trotskiĭ remarks, express his real temper, although he had at the same time a definite aim. In pursuance of his method, he hammered into the consciousness of those about him the necessity of exceptionally harsh measures.

Gor'kiĭ relates in his memoirs how once, during a walk, Lenin pointed to a crowd of children at play and said: " The life of these children will be happier than ours: they will no longer have personal experience of much that we have lived through. Their fate will be less cruel. I do not envy them, however, for our generation has succeeded in work of enormous historic significance. Circumstances have compelled us to be cruel, but later ages will justify us; then everything will be understood, everything. . . ."

Gor'kiĭ also attempted to remonstrate with Lenin on the subject of terrorism. Lenin answered with irritated amazement: " What would you have? Is humanity possible in such a furious struggle? Can we allow ourselves to be soft-hearted and magnanimous, when Europe is blockading us and the hoped-for assistance from the European proletariat has failed, and counter-revolution is rising against us on every side? No, excuse me, we are not imbeciles! We know what we want, and no one can stop us from doing what we think right! " On Gor'kiĭ's pointing out that useless cruelty would deter many people from participating in the revolutionary movement, Lenin said with dissatisfaction:

" Between ourselves, there are many workers who are disloyal and treacherous to us; this is due partly to cowardice, partly to confusion and fear that their beloved theory will be injured by coming into conflict with practice. We are not afraid of that; for us theory is not a sacred thing, but merely a working tool."

When some condemned prisoner attempted to appeal

for mercy to his wife, Lenin sent the following brief communication to the newspapers: " People are appealing to my wife for pardon for prisoners sentenced to death. I beg that no such letters shall be sent to my wife, as they are useless."

By the proclamation of the maxim that " freedom is a bourgeois prejudice," Lenin accomplished a revolution which, perhaps more than all political and economic events, divided Bolshevism for ever from the revolutionary movements of earlier times. The ideal of moral and civil freedom, previously held to be the supreme and ultimate aim of all popular movements, was from now onwards to dwindle into a lie, since the dictatorship, formerly regarded as abhorrent, now became the sole moral necessity. The distinction between good and evil must not in future be made by feeling, but weighed solely by the understanding; henceforward everything politically useful was good, and everything which could injure the cause championed by the Bolsheviks was to be condemned. The moral judgment of human action thus lost its absolute character, and morality became a " dialectically " relative value, whose principles were conditioned solely by the class interests of the moment. Since Lenin was fighting for the rise of the working class, everything that could advance this class seemed a moral necessity: he declared that the extermination of the bourgeoisie was justified, and at the same time he tried to prosecute any injustice, however slight, done to a worker, as a serious crime.

" We repudiate," he said in a speech to young people, " all morality which proceeds from supernatural ideas or ideas which are outside class conceptions. In our opinion, morality is entirely subordinate to the interests of the class war; everything is moral which is necessary for the annihilation of the old exploiting social order and for the uniting of the proletariat. Our morality thus consists solely in close discipline and in conscious war against the exploiters. We do not believe in external principles of morality, and we will expose this deception. Communist morality is identical with the fight for the strengthening of the dictatorship of the proletariat."

E. Preobrazhenskiĭ, a pupil and follower of Lenin, later collected all the " moral and class norms " preached by Lenin and important for the Bolshevist system: it is somewhat significant that the work is dedicated to Dzerzhinskiĭ, the chief of the " Cheka." This dedication, however, becomes immediately understandable when we read in Preobrazhenskiĭ that the concept of morality, when " translated from the misty language of morals into that of ordinary life," means what is advantageous, useful, and expedient for a definite group of people; everything, on the other hand, is immoral which seems injurious and inexpedient to this group. There has never been a system of ethics whose claims were not based on the needs of definite social classes. What is necessary for a given society, class, or group is always regarded by it as moral, everything harmful to it as immoral.

Once Lenin had come to regard the functional connection between class interests and morality as a proved truth, he consciously and openly professed his conviction that there was no such thing as absolute morality, and that the immediate practical value to the proletariat of individual actions must be regarded as the sole ethical and moral standard. The logical consequence of this was that no means, neither crime, lies, nor deceit, could in itself be reprehensible, if it was used for a useful purpose.

" Whereas in a society in which there are no classes," writes Preobrazhenskiĭ, " lying is a disadvantage in itself, because it compels the members of the society to use their energy in discovering the truth, the case is quite different in a society based on class. In the struggle of an exploited class against their enemies, lying and deceit are often very important weapons; all the subterranean work of revolutionary organizations actually depends on over-reaching the power of the State. The workers' State, surrounded as it is on all sides by hostile capitalist countries, finds lying very necessary and useful in its foreign policy. Therefore, the attitude of the working class and the Communist Party to the open recognition of the right to lie is quite different from that of the Western European Socialists, those God-fearing *petits bourgeois*, who are systematically deceived and treated as fools by the representatives of capital. . . . The lie is a consequence of the oppression of one man by another, the result of the class and group war."

From the beginning, Lenin stood for the use of force in the class war. The armed rising in 1905 is attributed to a large extent to his influence, and even after it failed he continued to consider aggressive armed methods to be the only ones for freeing the proletariat. In the years which followed the first Revolution, he formed the well-known " five and three groups " to serve as an embryo organization for the armed mass war.

When Plekhanov wrote in 1905, after the collapse of the rising, that recourse to arms was bound to fail, Lenin replied to him in his *Proletar*: " Nothing can be more shortsighted than Plekhanov's view that we should not have embarked on the abortive strike and that we should not have had recourse to arms. On the contrary, we should have gone to work in a much more resolute, energetic, and aggressive fashion, and made it clear to the masses that it was impossible to succeed by peaceful means alone. At last, we must openly proclaim that political strikes are not sufficiently effective; it is necessary to agitate among the masses for an armed rising and make no concealment of the fact that the next revolution will resemble a desperate, bloody, and destructive war. . . .

" Grouping in accordance with political programmes is not enough: anyone who is opposed to armed rebellion and refuses to prepare for it must be ruthlessly

banished from the ranks of the revolutionaries to the
camp of the enemy, among the traitors or cowards.
For the day is at hand when the force of events will
compel us to distinguish friends from foes by this sign.
We must not confine ourselves to waiting passively for
the moment when the army will come over to us; we
must cry aloud the necessity of a bold attack arms in
hand. . . .

" The attack on the enemy must be as energetic as
possible; the watchword of the masses should be
' attack,' not ' defence.' . . ."

It will thus be seen that Lenin, the champion of force
and civil war, even of war in general, could have little use
for pacifism in any of its varieties. For him the word
pacifism had a definitely despicable sound; if he used it,
it was always in an ironical sense. It is true that during
the world war he co-operated for a time with the international pacifist associations which assembled in Switzerland, but this was only for tactical reasons. He supported the ending of the world war, but, as he himself
declared, this was not for the sake of civic peace, but
with the purpose of bringing about an even greater war,
the " war between classes."

The manifesto which he addressed to the Swiss
workers on the day of his departure for Russia is very
interesting: " We are not essentially pacifists," he
states in it, " we are opponents of the imperialist war,
but we have always declared that it would be absurd
for the proletariat to bind itself not to wage those
revolutionary wars, which are possible and which may
be necessary in the future in the interests of socialism."

VIII

The path followed by Lenin and his ultimate success have no parallel. It is only if we look back on his whole career that we can judge their really unprecedented character. Vladimir Il'ich Ul'ianov Lenin was born on 10th April 1870 at Simbirsk on the Volga. He was the son of noble parents; his father held the office of State Councillor and curator of the national schools. While he was still at the grammar school, at the age of seventeen, the young Vladimir was drawn into revolutionary circles for the first time through the influence of his brother Alexander, and became acquainted with inflammatory books. Even at that age he spent every evening studying political writings in the company of his elder brother. Immediately after breakfast he would retire to a corner of the garden laden with books, periodicals, and works of reference, and study there. His sister tells us that the zeal and earnestness of the young Vladimir Il'ich made a deep impression on her, so that his occasional praise seemed to her high distinction.

" All day long," she writes, " Vladimir Il'ich sat at his books, from which he was separated only to go for a walk or to talk or argue in the little circle of his comrades, who, like himself, were imbued with revolutionary ideas. This tenacity and power of work he never lost during the whole of his life. Later, too, both in exile in Siberia and in his sojourns abroad, he used every leisure moment, every leisure hour, to study in libraries. We still possess many periodicals and extracts which show what an enormous quantity of literature dealing with all branches of knowledge Vladimir Il'ich studied in the course of his life."

His brother Alexander was his mentor in all these studies. Alexander had become acquainted with Marx's *Kapital*, and recommended Vladimir Il'ich to study it; the brothers often discussed this book for hours, although Alexander Il'ich, a supporter of terrorist revolutionary ideas, never himself became an adherent of Marxism.

In 1887 the revolutionary association to which Lenin's brother belonged decided to make an attempt on the life of the Tsar Alexander III. The attempt was to be carried out in Petersburg, on the Neyskiĭ Prospekt, by means of infernal machines. The first of March, the anniversary of the successful attempt on Alexander II, was chosen for the attack. The young revolutionaries had decided to carry their bombs concealed in thick books which were to be thrown after the Tsar's carriage.

Hardly was this decision made when the whole group of revolutionaries was arrested. It was later learned that there had been a police spy among them, who played the part of *agent provocateur* and handed over the young conspirators to the authorities. Alexander Ul'ianov and four of his comrades were executed immediately after.

Vladimir was still at the grammar school at the time; his brother's death made a deep impression on him. " In the spring of 1887," his sister relates, " we received the news of the execution of our eldest brother. I shall never forget the expression on Vladimir Il'ich's face as he said: ' No, we cannot succeed in this way, it is not the right way.' From that time he began to prepare the way which seemed to him the right one for freeing Russia from the yoke of the Tsars."

Lenin, in later years, told his wife how all the acquaintances of the family avoided them after Alexander Ul'ianov's imprisonment, even the old teacher who had been used to come often in the evenings to play chess gave up his visits. Lenin's mother travelled from Simbirsk to Petersburg with great difficulty to visit her son in prison; Vladimir Il'ich tried in vain to find a travelling companion for her, but no one wanted to accompany the mother of a prisoner. This universal cowardice made a deep impression on Lenin, and even then inspired him with hate for bourgeois society.

' Lenin often spoke to me about his brother, whom he loved dearly," writes Krupskaia. " The two youths had the same views on many subjects, understood each other very well, and kept somewhat apart from their other relations. The fate of Alexander Ul'ianov had a great influence on Lenin, and largely contributed to making him a bitter enemy of Tsarist rule."

At the end of his time at the grammar school, Lenin studied law at the University of Kazan. He had meanwhile become a convinced Marxist, and at Kazan joined revolutionary students' associations. For this reason he was soon sent down from the University and banished to Kukushino in the Samara Government.

His first public appearance dates from that time. In the year 1889 a severe famine broke out in Samara, and a Relief Committee of Intellectuals was formed. At one of its preliminary meetings Lenin appeared, listened to the various speeches for a while, and then rose and briefly expressed his own views. He regarded all relief as foolish and harmful, for the misery of the people was due entirely to the political regime. It may be imagined that these views were received with the greatest indignation, and that Lenin had to leave the committee immediately. Soon afterwards he moved to Petersburg and there passed the State law examinations.

After he had practised the profession of barrister for a brief space, really only for a few days, he decided for the future to devote all his energies to revolutionary agitation. He became a professional revolutionary, like many another Russian fighter in the cause of freedom both before and after him. " A legal career," says Zinov'ev, in his reminiscences of Lenin, " could not attract him. Vladimir Il'ich often told me humorous stories of his few days of barristerhood."

In the years from 1890 to 1893 he travelled about Russia, always in search of comrades of like views, who would be ready to take up the revolutionary struggle on a Marxian basis. Most revolutionaries rejected these

ideas and regarded them as foolish dreaming. Again and
again Lenin was assailed from all sides with objections
that there was no working class in Russia, let alone a
class-conscious proletariat, since the overwhelming
majority of the population were peasants; therefore, the
Marxian doctrines could not be applied to Russia.
Lenin paid no attention to these objections, but persisted in his convictions and worked steadily to unite
the workers in a class-conscious organization.

It was in these years that his real political activity
began; it already showed the characteristics which were
later to make the greatness of Lenin, and cause his
extraordinary success, his sense of the practical, of
political and economic detail, his untiring energy and
his capacity for taking into account the seemingly most
trifling circumstances. His wife, N. K. Krupskaia,
thinks that Lenin did not approach Karl Marx as a
theorist or a bookworm, but rather as a man seeking
answers to urgent and troubling questions. " It was in
the 'nineties, at a time when he was still unable to speak
in national assemblies. Lenin went to Petersburg, to
the workers, and talked to them of all he had discovered
in Marx. But he did not only talk, he could also listen
attentively to all that the workers had to say to him.
Vladimir Il'ich recognized then that the working class
must be the vanguard for the whole of the oppressed
masses, and that its historic task was to free the whole
of the populace from slavery. This idea illuminated
all his further activities and determined every step he
took."

Lenin was able to make his way into the great industrial undertakings and workshops; he visited the
workers, talked with them, instructed them, and was in
his turn instructed by them. He contrived to make
skilful propagandist use of their complaints about their
supervisors, about wages and fines, and in this way
succeeded in rousing discontent among Russian workers
and adding fuel to the flame.

Lenin's first literary work was also devoted to simple everyday problems of proletarian life. " This great revolutionary," says Zinov'ev, " who set his stamp on a whole epoch, began his literary activity in a very modest sphere. In conjunction with Babushkin, Sheldunov, and other workers united in the social democratic organization which had sprung up, he began to compose illicit broadsheets, and to run off copies on a hectograph, appeals which dealt with the economic problems of working-class life. The broadsheets written by Lenin at that time spoke of the position of the proletariat, the treatment of the workers—especially the women workers —by the engineers, of the drinking water in the factories, of the length of the working day and of fines, that is, of obvious things which no longer seem of much import-ance to us after the lapse of thirty years."

Thus Lenin succeeded in founding a real labour organization in Petersburg, which received the name of the " Association for the Emancipation of the Working Class." His broadsheets led to the breaking out of " mutinies "—the name then given to strikes—in a few Petersburg factories. " Here," says Zinov'ev, " in these trifling events of economic everyday life, we must see the beginning of the great battles, which were enacted in the following decades and which led to the Revolutions of 1905 and 1917."

Krupskaia gives an arresting account in her memoirs of this first Petersburg period:

" Vladimir Il'ich Lenin came to Petersburg in the autumn of 1893; I did not get to know him till later. I heard from some comrades that a disciple of Marx had arrived from the Volga district, and later someone brought me a pamphlet, *On Markets*, which set forth the views both of the engineer, Hermann Krassin, our Petersburg Marxist leader, and of Lenin, the Marxist from the Volga. I desired to make the further acquaint-ance of the stranger, and to hear his views.

" The first time I saw Vladimir Lenin was during

E

Carnival. Since the gathering had officially the character
of a festivity, the *bliny* (pancakes) customary in Russia in
' butter week ' were served. At this meeting, besides
Lenin and Krassin, Peter Struve and some other comrades were present. During the festivities Lenin did
not say much; he looked at the guests and his sharp
eye had a painful effect on those present.

" In the autumn of 1894 Vladimir Lenin read his
work, *Friends of the People*, to our circle; the book got
hold of us, for it showed us as clear as daylight how we
must set about the fight for the people. The brochure
was hectographed and circulated anonymously among
the people, and made Lenin's name popular.

" In the winter of 1894-95 I got to know Vladimir
Il'ich better. He was then engaged in propaganda work
in the workers' quarters of Petersburg, while I was a
teacher in a Sunday school in one of these quarters, and
so had a fairly exact knowledge of labour life. A large
number of workers belonged to the circle in which
Lenin was carrying on his propagandist activities. The
Smolenskaia School had six hundred pupils: the
workers had blind confidence in us women teachers.
Since there was a secret spy in nearly every class, we did
not dare to mention the dangerous word ' strike.' I was
then living in the suburb of Staro-Nevskaia, in a house
with a thoroughfare through it. Vladimir Lenin visited
me every Sunday after his work in the secret circle was
over, and endless talk began between us. I was in love
with my school at that time, and was capable of forgetting about meal times when the talk was of schools
and scholars. Vladimir Lenin was interested in the
smallest details of the lives of the workers; he was
trying by the help of these details to comprehend the
spirit of the proletariat, in order to make it easier to find
the way to revolutionary propaganda among the industrial
proletariat. The majority of the Russian intelligentsia
at that time were but ill-acquainted with the workers.
They mixed with the people and addressed them in

learned lectures; Vladimir Lenin was the first to contrive to unite theory and practice in his propaganda. He first read passages from Marx's *Kapital* to the workers, and then explained the content of the book, but he went on to ask his audience about their own work and their lives, and showed them the connection between their personal lot and the structure of society, and explained to them how the existing order could be changed. This kind of agitation made a great impression on the workers; it was not till later, when in exile in France I went through the great Paris postal strike, that I fully recognized how right this method was.

"Vladimir Il'ich, however, never forgot the other forms of agitation. In 1895 appeared his pamphlet on fines, in which he showed how the workers could be won over to the socialist movement. Our frequent visits in working-class circles had attracted the attention of the police, and we began to be watched. Of all the members of our group Vladimir Lenin was most skilled in all the conspirators' tricks. he knew all the houses with thoroughfares through them, was extraordinarily clever at leading police spies by the nose, and taught us to write letters in books with chemical ink and to put dots under individual letters; he also thought of secret names for everyone of us. The spies began to watch us more closely, and Lenin declared that they must fix on a successor who should be informed of everything. As I was the most reliable person politically, I was chosen as Lenin's deputy.

"On the Saturday before Easter, five or six of us went to Tsarskoe-Selo to spend Easter with a member of the group, a certain Silvin. During the railway journey we did not look at each other and behaved as if we were strangers. On this excursion Vladimir Lenin explained to us how we were to write in cipher and how to establish connections with the people. He was master of the great art of picking out from the mass those that were suitable for revolutionary work. Thus he once organized a discussion with a group of women teachers in the Sunday school; almost all of them later became good social democrats. Among these was Lydia Knipovich, who at once recognized Lenin as the great revolutionary: she undertook to establish contact with a secret printing press, to conceal the printed manuscripts among her acquaintances, and to organize the distribution of the propagandist literature among the workers. She was later imprisoned through the treachery of a compositor; on this occasion twelve boxes of illicit pamphlets were found in the houses of her friends. Lydia Knipovich died in the Crimea during its occupation by the White Army. On her death-bed she talked in delirium of the future of Communism; she died with Lenin's name on her lips.

" In the summer of 1895 Vladimir Lenin went abroad, and spent almost all his time in Berlin attending labour meetings; he then went on to Switzerland, where he met Plekhanov, Axelrod, and Vera Sasulich. He returned full of new impressions and brought a box with a false bottom under which illicit literature was concealed.

" The spies began at once to watch Lenin; he and his box were followed. One of my cousins was then working in the Registration Office, and she told me that when she was on night duty a spy came to the office and made inquiries about Lenin's address. He said to her: ' We have established the fact that this Vladimir Lenin is a dangerous revolutionary; his brother was hanged : he himself has now come back from abroad and won't give us the slip any longer.'

" My cousin was aware that I knew Lenin and she begged me to inform him of the danger, which I did immediately. We decided to go to work cautiously. The work was apportioned and distributed according to districts. We were now engaged in circulating the first propagandist sheets; the first broadsheet composed by Lenin, written by hand in printed letters, was destined for the workers in the Zemenikovskiĭ factory; later the sheets were circulated in other factories as well. They met with such great response among the workers that we decided, since we had a printing press at our disposal, to publish a secret newspaper; every line of every issue had to pass through Lenin's hand.

" A meeting had been fixed for the eighth of December in my rooms for a further revision of the issue which was ready. We had arranged with Lenin that I should apply in doubtful points to a friend of his, a railway official called Chbotarev, at whose house Lenin took his mid-day meal. When Lenin did not turn up at the meeting, I went to see Chbotarev and learned that Lenin had not come that day. We knew that he had been arrested, and that same evening we learned that many other members of our group had suffered the same fate. I handed over the copy of the secret labour newspaper to a friend of mine, afterwards the wife of Peter Struve, to keep, and we decided not to print it, as we wished to avoid further arrests. This Petersburg period of Lenin's work was very important, for it was then that he established close relations with the working classes, got near the masses, and succeeded in directing them.· It was in these years that Lenin gradually developed into a proletarian leader.

" Contact between our group and Vladimir Lenin was rapidly re-established after his imprisonment. At that time, it was permitted to take as many books as you liked to prisoners awaiting preliminary examination. These books were only casually examined, and no one noticed that dots had been placed under certain letters or that many pages had been written on in milk. Lenin's anxiety about the arrest of his comrades was very characteristic of him: in every letter which he smuggled out of the prison, he advised us not to compromise So-and-so by visits, or asked us to tell a prisoner to look for a letter in a certain book in the prison library. Or again he would beg us to procure warm shoes for another comrade.

" Lenin's letters breathed great confidence. All who received these communications forgot that Lenin was in prison, and began to work as if he were supervising them. I remember the impression a letter of this kind made on me, after I had been arrested in August 1896. We received these communications written in milk on the days on which it was permitted to bring books to prisoners. You looked for a certain mark on the books smuggled in, and when you saw it, you knew that a letter was concealed in it. We took tea at six o'clock, and afterwards the prisoners went to church. Before going to church we tore the letter into long strips, made our tea, and when the wardress had left our cell, we dipped the strips into the hot liquid, whereupon the writing became immediately visible. It was not possible in prison to hold the letters over a flame, so Lenin had devised this method of developing the invisible writing in hot water.

" Whether in prison or at liberty, Lenin was the centre of our movement. In addition, he was working very hard on the preliminary studies for his book, *The Development of Capitalism*. In order not to be surprised while he was writing his secret letters in milk, he made little 'ink pots' out of bread, which he filled with milk and hid in his mouth the moment the warder opened the door. ' To-day I swallowed six ink-pots,' he once wrote in a postscript in a book.

" As Lenin found it difficult to endure restraint, and disliked to be confined to the limits of a fixed regime, he was not enamoured of life in prison; he wanted to see his friends, as he was unaccustomed to loneliness. In one of his letters, he proposed that a friend and I should be on a certain spot on the pavement at a certain hour, where he could see us if the prisoners were taken along the corridor for a walk. My friend could not come, nor could I until several days later; I remained for a few minutes on the spot indicated, but I could not see Lenin.

" During the whole time Lenin was in prison, the

labour movement developed strongly; it was not till after Martov's arrest that a slight decline set in.

"When Lenin was released I was still in prison, and was not set free until after the political prisoner, Vetrova, had burnt herself alive in prison. I was quite aware that spies dogged my every step.

"In the winter of 1897-98 I often visited Peter Struve on Lenin's behalf. Lenin was later exiled to the village of Shushensk in the Minusinsk government in Siberia, and I was also sent to the Ufa government for three years. When I declared that I was Lenin's betrothed and wished to follow him into exile at Shushensk, the authorities granted my request and I rejoined Lenin."

IX

Lenin's years of exile in Siberia also emerge with the vividness of a picture from Krupskaia's description:

"My mother accompanied me to Minusinsk, whither I journeyed on my own account. We met on the 1st of May 1898 at Krasnoiarsk, and were to proceed from there along the Enisseï by boat, but it appeared that the boats were no longer running. In Krasnoiarsk I made the acquaintance of Tuchev, a relation of mine, and his wife, who, as experienced people, enabled me to meet a group of socialists in exile at Krasnoiarsk; Silvin was one of these revolutionaries. The soldiers brought the prisoners to be photographed and likenesses of them were taken; they then withdrew and ate sausage sandwiches we had given them, so that we were able to speak to the political prisoners in peace.

"Towards evening we arrived in the village of Shushensk, where Vladimir Lenin was living. Lenin was out shooting. We got down from our sleighs and were taken at once to his abode. In the Minusinsk

district in Siberia, the peasants are extraordinarily clean;
the floors of their houses are covered with bright carpets
made by themselves and the walls are painted white.
" Lenin's room was not large, but it was very clean.
He lived in one wing and the other part of the house
was assigned to Mama and me. The owners of the
house and their neighbours at once visited us, took a
good look at us and asked questions. At last Lenin
came back from his shooting and was amazed to see a
light burning in his room. The master of the house
told him in joke that an exile, a Petersburg workman,
had burst into his room drunk and scattered all the
books in his library. Lenin came into the room and
was much astonished to see me. Then we talked the
whole night.
" Lenin had made a good recovery and looked
splendid. He had formed a friendship with only two
of the exiles in Shushensk, a Polish social democrat from
Lodz called Prominski, and a Petersburg workman, a
Finn, Engebert by name. Both were good comrades.
Prominski was a quiet but very energetic man who
would have been glad to go back to Poland, but could
not manage it. He then looked for a home in the neighbourhood of Krasnoiarsk, and earned his living as a
railway worker; later he became a communist. He fell
in the war, while Engebert died of typhus in 1923.
Lenin also visited a certain Shuravlev, whom he liked
very much. Shuravlev suffered from tuberculosis. He
was thirty years old, and had been a clerk, and was,
according to his lights, an agitator and a revolutionary.
He devoted all his energies to the fight against the
injustice of the rich, but soon died of tuberculosis.
" Another acquaintance of Lenin's was a poor devil
of a peasant called Sosipatich. By his help Lenin
learned to know the Siberian village; his method was
peculiar. Every Sunday he held a kind of legal consultation, and gained great popularity among the
inhabitants as a lawyer, especially after he had helped a

worker who had been dismissed from his job to obtain redress.

" The report of this successful case spread rapidly among the peasants. They came to Lenin with their complaints in increasing numbers; he listened to them attentively and gave them advice. Once a peasant came from a distance of twenty versts to ask him how he should deal with his father-in-law for not having invited him to a wedding; soon afterwards the father-in-law also turned up and Lenin spent almost an hour in making peace between the two peasants.

" He became very well acquainted with the Siberian village, and soon he knew it as intimately as he knew the Volga villages. He used often to say: ' My mother would be pleased to see me occupied with agriculture. I tried it for a time, but gave it up when I recognized that our relations with the peasants were fundamentally wrong.'

" As an exile Lenin had really no right to be engaging in legal affairs, but the authorities in the Minusinsk district were liberal, and did not trouble about what the deported prisoners did. The mayor, a rich peasant, was much more interested in selling veal to the political prisoners than in watching for their attempts at escape.

" Living was very cheap in Shushensk. Lenin received the Government allowance of eight roubles a month, and for that got a clean room, food, drink, and laundry; and it was said that he paid too much. Dinner and supper were simple meals; once a week a sheep was killed for him, and he had to eat mutton day in day out. When the sheep was eaten, meat was again prepared for a week, and there were cutlets for eight days. There was plenty of milk available for Lenin and his dog.

" As the peasants often got drunk at Lenin's hosts' and the family life was unpleasant in many respects, we soon moved to another abode and rented for four roubles half a house with a garden and court; there we had a regular family household. In the summer it was generally difficult to get servants, so that Mama and I had to struggle with the malicious ways of the stove; to start with I often enough upset the soup pot, but I soon became accustomed to cooking.

" My particular pride at that time was the kitchen garden, where I had planted cucumbers, melons, roots, and other vegetables. A communist " cell " is now established in this house; the garden has run wild, the fence is rotting, and the house will soon fall to pieces.

" In October we engaged a servant girl, a young person not quite thirteen, who soon, however, assumed the management of the whole household. I instructed her in reading and writing and soon she was adorning the walls of the house with mottoes like ' Never spill tea.' Later she made such progress that she was able to keep a regular diary. At this time, we also made friends with a child, a boy of six, with a pale, transparent face, whose father, an exile from Lettonia, was given to drunkenness. My mother was very fond of him and Lenin also liked to talk with him. Later when we left Minusinsk, the child missed us so much that he became quite ill. We afterwards increased our home circle by the addition of a cat.

" In the mornings I used to work with Lenin: we translated the works of Webb, which Struve had sent to us. After dinner we translated the *Development of Capitalism*, if we did not do other work. Once we got hold of Kautsky's monograph against Bernstein; we stopped our ordinary work immediately and translated the book into Russian in a fortnight.

" When Lenin had finished his work, he took a walk or went shooting; he was very fond of shooting. He had had a pair of leather breeches made for him, and so was able to face any bog, however deep. When spring arrived Prominski came to us with a smiling face and announced that the ducks were here; then we talked for hours of where and when one of those birds had been seen. When the winter ice melted there was much life in the woods and swamps, turkey cocks and wild boars were to be met with there. At this time Lenin liked to go to the forest, but he left his hunting dog behind so as not to scare the game.

" Lenin also devoted much time to hunting hares. In autumn he generally resolved not to shoot these animals if he met them, but he soon forgot his good resolutions and pulled his gun from his shoulder whenever a hare came his way. In late harvest, when the Enisseï began to bring down floating ice, the little islands in the middle of the river were full of hares, who ran about helplessly, because they could not find their way back to the mainland. Our hunters got fine bags and brought in the slaughtered animals by boat.

" Lenin used sometimes to praise the joys of hunting at a later time, when he lived in Moscow, but not with the same passion as in Siberia. Once we took part in a fox hunt, which interested Lenin very much. A fox ran right up to him, Lenin took aim, the animal stopped for an instant and looked at him, then it turned and fled into the forest. ' Why did you not shoot? ' asked his companions. ' The fox was too beautiful,' was his answer.

" In late autumn, before the first snow fell, we often walked on the banks of the ice-covered river to look at the fish which could be seen quite clearly under the crystal clear coating of ice. In winter, we enjoyed skating, a pastime Lenin was very fond of. During the long winter evenings, he read either philosophical works by Hegel and Kant or the writings of the French materialists. When he was tired with study, he refreshed himself with the poems of Nekrasov and Pushkin.

" When Lenin first appeared in Petersburg, his friends told me to my amazement that he had never read a novel. In Siberia I discovered that these statements were not correct: he had not only read the works of Turgenev, Tolstoï, and Chernishevskiï, but knew and loved all the Russian classics. In his photograph album,

in addition to the likenesses of his comrades in exile, are
to be found those of Emile Zola, Herzen, and Chernishevskiĭ; on one of the photographs of Chernishevskiĭ is a
note in Lenin's own hand: ' Died in 1889.'

" The post came twice a week. Our correspondence
was copious; we received books and letters from Russia.
Not only did Lenin's mother write regularly from
Petersburg, Nina Struve also sent accounts of her son.
Sometimes letters came from other exiles: Martov
wrote from Turukhansk, but most frequently we got
news from the comrades who were staying in neighbouring villages. We corresponded on all sorts of subjects,
recent news from Russia, our plans for the future, new
books, and philosophical problems. For some time
Lenin was very much interested in chess and used to
play games by letter with a comrade. At that time he
was so absorbed in chess problems that he would often
call out in his sleep: ' If you move there with your
knight I shall come here with my king!'

" Lenin's father had also been very keen on this game.
Lenin himself told me that to begin with his brother and
he were always beaten by their father, but Alexander
Ul'ianov bought a book on chess, and after that their
relative strength soon changed. ' One evening,' according to Lenin's account, ' we saw our father coming
out of our room with the chess book in his hand. He
went back to his study, read the book, and was soon our
superior again.'

" Lenin gave up chess after his return from Siberia.
He said: ' I must stop chess; it claims too much of my
thoughts and prevents me from concentrating on any
work.'

" It had been his custom from his youth to give up
any occupation whenever it began to disturb his work.
' While I was still at school,' he told me, ' I was passionately fond of skiing, but as it tired me and made me very
sleepy, I felt obliged to give up this sport in the interests
of my work.' His attitude to his Latin studies was

similar; this occupation was too great a hindrance to his
important work to allow him to go on with it permanently.

" Lenin worked at Latin in order to learn the con-
structions in the speeches of the Roman orators; it often
struck me in later days how much his own speeches
sometimes resembled Roman models.

" Although he carried on a lively correspondence with
his exiled comrades, he very seldom visited them. I can
remember only one visit to Kurnatovskiĭ, an interesting
and well educated comrade, and a journey to Tes; the
back history of this excursion was peculiar. One day
some comrades in that locality wrote to us that the police
superintendent there was not favourable to them and
forbade them to leave the locality, but that in Tes there
was a mountain of geological interest, and Lenin should
apply for a permit to investigate this mountain.

" The trick succeeded and we were allowed to go to
Tes, where we had a chance of seeing our exiled comrades. At the New Year, we went to Minusinsk, where
some deported socialists were staying. Differences of
opinion arose on this occasion between these men and
us, and the social democrats declared that they had no
real confidence in us and did not regard us as sincere
socialists. Lenin, therefore, proposed a separation,
which was carried out, and henceforth both parties
worked on their own and neither troubled about the
other.

" Meanwhile, news from Russia had become scanty:
the attempt to publish some of Lenin's work through
the medium of our Petersburg comrades came to
nothing; the circulation of our ideas by means of
popular pamphlets also proved impossible in the end,
and also the frequent arrests were a great hindrance to
our work. It was at this time that Lenin developed his
plan for the organization which was later realized in the
publication of *Iskra*; he decided to found a paper,
have it printed abroad, and secretly circulated in Russia.

" He slept less and less, thought day and night about his plan, and became visibly thinner. He discussed it at length with me, corresponded with Martov, and planned to make a journey abroad with him and Potresov. The nearer the end of his exile approached, the more nervous did Lenin become, and the more strongly was he drawn to active political work.

" Suddenly a search was made of our house. They had somewhere or other found the receipt for a registered letter addressed to Lenin, and the gendarmes took the opportunity of carrying out a search. They found the letter, but its contents proved to be quite harmless. As we had done in Petersburg, we kept our legal correspondence strictly separate from our illicit in Siberia also. All the letters dealing with the revolutionary movement were in the lower part of the cupboard. Lenin supplied the gendarmes with a chair so that they would begin their investigation with the upper shelves of the library, on which there was nothing but statistical works. They soon became so tired that they were content with my statement that there were only educational books on the lower shelves. So the search passed without any bad results, but the matter had hung in the balance; it would have easily been possible for the authorities to use the discovery of compromising writings to prolong our period of exile.

" In the March of 1900 our time in Siberia came to an end, and we returned to European Russia. Basha, our maid, who had grown into a pretty girl in the course of the two years, wept bitterly at our departure, and our little friend, the six year old boy, took our pictures, pencils, and paper as mementoes. Our house-mates and neighbours kept arriving all the time to say good-bye, and even Lenin's dog looked questioningly at us.

" We went to Minusinsk, where Starkov and Olga Silvina were to join us; all the exiled comrades had assembled there to wave us farewell. The atmosphere was as it always is when an exile is returning to Russia:

everyone spoke of his plans, asked about Lenin's views, and made proposals for future work and correspondence. We were all thinking about Russia and speaking about trifles. At last we put on our furs and resumed our journey.

" We travelled in sleighs, day and night, three hundred versts along the Enisseĭ. Lenin had wrapped my mother and me closely in our furs and at every halt came attentively to see if we had not frozen in the interval. He himself travelled without a fur coat and assured us he was quite warm; he merely kept his hands in a muff, and in thought was already in Russia where a great work awaited him.

" At Ufa we were welcomed by our friends. Lenin spent a few days there; then left mother and me in the care of our comrades and himself went on towards Petersburg. In Ufa he visited a bookshop and had a conversation with the bookseller, in which his voice sounded weaker than I had ever heard it; it was an impression I could not forget.

" Now his real work was beginning, and I quite understood that he did not wish to stay in Ufa, but to live near Petersburg. He settled in Pskov, where some of his friends lived, and began to weave the threads of the organization which was to link up with the homeland the Russian newspaper he had planned to publish abroad."

" While Lenin in Pskov was building up the future organization of the Russian Social Democratic Party," Krupskaia goes on, " I remained in Ufa, did translations, gave lessons, and lived as best I could. At that time the Social Democratic Party in Ufa was split into two camps, of which I was considerably more in sympathy with one group than the other; it included about a dozen people and was led by a certain Iakutov. He often came to see me, borrowed books and argued about Marx, and told me that he was not afraid of exile, for he could not be ruined anywhere. Iakutov was a splendid

conspirator, especially as he hated fine talk. In the
year 1905 he was elected president of the Republic then
formed in Ufa. After the victory of reaction he was
executed. At the moment he was suspended on the gallows, all the prisoners in the cells of the Ufa prison burst
into revolutionary songs, and swore to avenge his death.

" During my stay in Ufa I came into close contact
with the workers, and did my best to enlighten them
politically. I also made friends at this time with a metal
turner, a nervous, temperamental individual, who introduced me to the life of the workers of Ufa. He later
went over to the Social Revolutionary Party and
finished up in an asylum.

" I was also often visited by the consumptive book-
binder, Krylov, whose speciality was the making of
books with secret compartments. He told me a great
deal about the life of compositors, and this information
was afterwards used in Lenin's *Iskra*. Ufa was at that
time the centre where all those who had been sent to
Siberia assembled; the returning exiles also mostly
stayed some time in the town. We succeeded at that
time also in establishing a connection with Martov,
who was living in Poltava, and who supplied me with a
lot of revolutionary literature."

At the beginning of 1900, then, Lenin returned to
European Russia, resumed his propagandist tours, and
collected men everywhere who, like himself, were
working for revolution; in 1901, along with Martov and
Potresov, he founded the journal *Iskra* (*The Spark*),
which was to play such a great part in the future of the
revolutionary movement in Russia. The motto of this
paper was Pushkin's utterance on the Decabrist rising:
" From sparks will burst forth flame." In *Iskra* Lenin
obstinately championed his radical point of view and
defended the necessity of creating an organization of
" professional revolutionaries," on the ground that the
fight for freedom required not amateurs at this craft,
but professionals, technicians.

[Lenin soon found himself obliged to leave Russia; in the year 1902 he gave a course of lectures at the Paris " Academy for Social Sciences," in which he explained in detail to his small audience what he could do with the wealth of Russia if power were in his hands.] Even then he emphasized the necessity of settling accounts ruthlessly with the Tsar and the nobility, and also with the landowners and manufacturers, and of making use of terrorism for this purpose. During his stay in Paris, he and his wife lived in great penury an almost ascetic life.

In 1903 he took part in the second Congress of the " Social Democratic Labour Party." At this Congress the Party split into two sections, the Bolsheviks, or majority, and the Mensheviks, or minority. Here Lenin's characteristic intransigence was already in evidence: on a point of quite subordinate importance he broke ruthlessly with many of his best friends. [Henceforward war against all supporters of any compromise whatever was to be a constant feature of Lenin's revolutionary activity: he mercilessly persecuted any opportunist interpretation of Marxist thought and any deviation from his Marxist system.] He also tried to prove to each of his opponents that his theories were absolutely bound to lead to reaction. [On this occasion Lenin gained a reputation for incredible arrogance, for aiming at absolute tyranny, even for lack of intelligence.]

Lenin himself once made a collection of the unfavourable criticisms of himself made by his party comrades. He stated that he had been called " autocratic, bureaucratic, formalist, centralist, one-sided, pig-headed, narrow, suspicious, and unsociable." Trotskiĭ, too, later his closest fellow worker, could not on that occasion have enough of attacking Lenin: " At the Second Congress of Russian Social Democracy, this man with

F

all his native energy and talent played the part of
destroyer of the Party. . . . Comrade Lenin mentally
reviewed the membership of the Party, and came to the
conclusion that he, and he alone was the iron hand. . . .
Comrade Lenin turned the modest Council into an
all-powerful Welfare Committee, in order that he
himself might take over the part of Robespierre the
Incorruptible. . . ."

Lenin did not fail to answer Trotskiĭ: in public utterances and published works as well as in his private
letters to Gor'kiĭ, he expressed his aversion for his former
friend and styled him an empty *poseur*; even as late as
1918 he wrote, over a pseudonym, it is true, a bitter and
ill-natured article on *The Cult of the Revolutionary
Phrase*, which was aimed at Trotskiĭ.

[In the years that followed his assumption of the
leadership of the Bolshevik group he carried on intensive
propaganda for his ideas. In May 1905 the Third
Congress of the Social Democratic Labour Party of
Russia took place in London and was attended only by
Lenin's followers. In his speeches at this Congress he
made a violent attack on the " illusions of Parliamentarianism," and supported the idea of a revolutionary
dictatorship of workers and peasants.]

Previously, very little information was available about
Lenin's first foreign sojourn; it was not till Nadezhda
Krupskaia's recently published memoirs appeared that
the details of this important period in Lenin's development became known.

I quote below several passages from Krupskaia on
Lenin's experiences in the years from 1900 to 1905, in so
far as the information is new:

" Just before he went abroad Lenin nearly went to
prison again: he had come from Pskov to Petersburg,
where he met Martov; he was discovered by police
spies and arrested. In his waistcoat were found two
thousand roubles and various revolutionary documents
written in sympathetic ink. Luckily Lenin had taken

the precaution to write fictitious accounts with ordinary
ink on these papers, so that the gendarmes never thought
of examining these accounts more closely and holding
them over a flame. Thus nothing could be proved against
him, and they had to release him after ten days' detention.
He then made a journey to Ufa to say good-bye to me.

"After about a week he left Russia. He wrote to me
regularly in books containing secret communications.
It appeared from his accounts that the founding of the
paper was not proving such a simple matter as he had
expected, as special difficulties occurred in the negotiations with Plekhanov.

"Lenin's letters from abroad were generally short and
indicated a mood of dissatisfaction. They almost always
ended with the words: ' I will tell you everything when
I see you again.' For a time I received no letters at all,
and impatiently waited for the end of my term of exile.

"At last I was free again and I travelled to Moscow
with Mama to Lenin's mother's. I was very fond of her,
for she was very tender and kind. Later, when we were
living abroad, she never wrote to Lenin alone but always
joint letters to both of us. Lenin was devoted to his
mother. He often said that she had an iron will, or else
she could hardly have survived Alexander Ul'ianov's
terrible end. Lenin certainly inherited his energy from
his mother and also that sensitiveness of feeling which
enabled him to understand every man through and
through.

"While he was still in exile, in 1887, Lenin once read
in a Moscow paper of the death of a Maria Ul'ianova; he
became deathly pale and said to his companion: ' I have
just learnt of my mother's death! ' It was not until later
that he learned that it was another Maria Ul'ianova who
had died.

"Lenin's mother had had a very unhappy life: her
eldest son was executed, one daughter died, and her
other children were almost permanently in prison.
When Lenin was ill in 1895 she hurried to him at once,

prepared his meals, and nursed him devotedly. Also when he was arrested she was immediately on the spot, waited for hours in the office of the detention prison, and smuggled in clandestine letters to the prisoner.

" After I reached Moscow on my way back from Siberia, I first took my mother to Petersburg and then proceeded abroad, first to Prague, where, as I believed, Lenin was living under the name of Modrachek. I had telegraphed to him, but found no one at the station. A little uneasy, I took a cab, had my trunk put on it and went to find Modrachek, who lived in a tenement house in the working-class quarter. I ran up four flights and knocked, the door opened and a fair-haired Czech woman stood before me.

" ' Modrachek? ' I asked in embarrassment.

" ' No, he is my husband! '

" Mrs. Modrachek looked at me and then cried:

" ' Ah, you must be the wife of Mr. Rittmaier who lives in Munich. I forwarded all the books he sent to us to you in Ufa! '

" I then spent the whole day with Mr. Modrachek. I told him about the Russian movement, and he gave me an account of the Austrian; his wife showed me her needlework and regaled me with Czech dumplings.

" I went on to Munich and appeared there wrapped in furs, while all the other ladies were already wearing thin clothes. I left my trunk at the station and sought out Mr. Rittmaier, whose house turned out to be a beer-house. I went up to the bar, where a fat man was standing, and asked hesitatingly for Rittmaier. I felt instinctively that I had again come to a wrong address. The man replied: ' Rittmaier? That's me! '

" I replied in perplexity: ' No, it is my husband! ' We stared at each other bewilderedly until Rittmaier's wife appeared and exclaimed: ' Probably it is the Mrs. Maier who is expected from Siberia. Please come with me! '

" She took me across a court to an apartment and

opened the door; behind a table sat Lenin. In my
excitement I forgot to thank the hostess and shouted to
Lenin: ' You wretch! why did you not write to tell me
where to find you? '

" ' What *do* you mean? Not write? I have been
going to the station three times a day! Where have you
come from? '

" It appeared later that the man who was to forward
Lenin's letters had neglected to do so, and so I remained
without news. It was a pure chance that I met Lenin
in Munich; he might just as easily have started for
London in the interval.

" Lenin, like Martov and Potresov, had decided to
live under a false name in Munich. They did not wish
to bring suspicion on Russian workers coming to
Munich, and thought it would be easier to correspond
with the comrades in Russia under a false name. So
Lenin lived under the name of Maier, with Mr. Rittmaier, the proprietor of the beer-house, who was a
staunch social democrat.

" He had a sparsely furnished, modest little room
where he led a bachelor life. He usually took his mid-
day meal with a German lady, who generally gave him
porridge and similar messes. He made his own tea
morning and evening; his supper consisted usually only
of tea and bread.

" He looked very anxious and troubled, for his affairs
were progressing more slowly than he had expected.
Besides Lenin, Martov, Potresov, and Vera Sasulich
were also living in Munich at that time. Plekhanov and
Axelrod had demanded that the paper should appear
somewhere in Switzerland under their direction. They
set no special value on Lenin's ideas, and did not foresee
what a great part *Iskra* was to play in organization.
Lenin continued to take the standpoint that his paper
must appear somewhere removed from the great
emigrant centres, because only in this way would it be
possible to maintain permanent connections with Russia.

Although we were in exile, we were better informed about events in Russia than our comrades at home, and were able to work energetically from abroad for the labour movement in the Empire of the Tsars.

" Lenin bought a passport from a Bulgarian, entered me on it as his wife under the name of Maritza, and then rented a room with a working-class family. I took over the editorial secretaryship of *Iskra*.

" It gave me a great deal of work. Letters from Russia were sent to different addresses in German towns; the German comrades then sent the whole correspondence on to a Doctor Lehmann and he forwarded it to me. We had no regular transport connection with Russia, and had therefore to try to get our paper over the frontier in trunks with false bottoms through the agency of stray travellers. These trunks were then delivered to specified addresses in Russia, where our comrades removed the contents and distributed them among the various organizations. We were also in touch with agents in Paris, Berlin, Switzerland, and Belgium, who told us of people likely to transport the prohibited literature to Russia.

" Our most active assistant in Russia was the Petersburg worker Babushkin, a personal acquaintance of Lenin. He travelled through the Russian industrial towns, sent us regular reports, and generally maintained relations with the comrades. Many revolutionaries from Russia also came to visit us in Munich, among them Noskov, the representative of the Northern Union; Peter Struve also visited us.

" Grave differences had already arisen between Lenin and Struve: Struve had by that time already left the Social Democratic Party and gone over to the Liberal camp. Violent quarrels took place, and Lenin in the end refused to have anything more to do with Struve. With great difficulty I managed to bring about a meeting, which was most dramatic: Lenin called Struve a renegade and made fun of him, with the result that

Struve abandoned us for ever. His wife, my old school friend, however, sent me a letter before she left, and a packet of sweets.

" After my arrival in Munich we lived with a German workman's family. The husband, who was the bread-winner for six persons, lived with his family in the kitchen and one little room; but everything was scrupulously clean and the children were well brought up and neatly dressed. I decided to do the cooking myself, and prepared the food in our room and then cooked it on the common stove. Meanwhile Lenin worked at his book, *What is to be Done?*

" When he was writing, he first sat down at his desk and thought for a moment; then he stood up again, walked from one end of the room to the other and uttered his thoughts half aloud. Finally, he returned to his desk, seated himself, and wrote what he had spoken aloud.

" During our walks, Lenin used to explain his literary plans to me in a low voice; this gradually became a necessity to him, and we discussed almost all his articles before he wrote them down. We wandered through the magnificent country round Munich, sought out un-frequented places, and there Lenin developed his ideas to me. About a month later we had our own home in a tenement house in Schwabing; we had bought our old furniture for twelve marks, and thus began a new life.

" About one o'clock, immediately after dinner, Martov turned up regularly at our rooms. Thereupon began the so-called editorial council, during which Martov talked without ceasing. He jumped all the time from one subject to another, was informed about everything and knew everybody.

" ' Martov is the typical journalist,' Lenin frequently remarked. ' He grasps everything immediately, but he takes things too lightly.' Martov's help was absolutely indispensable to *Iskra*, for he did the bulk of the work.

" Lenin was so fatigued by these daily six-hour conversations that he could hardly write. Once he asked me outright to go to Martov and ask him not to come any more. Lenin desired that in future I should maintain the connection with Martov, inform him of all that was happening, and take over his contributions to *Iskra*. At first this new system seemed to answer, but soon it became clear that Martov could not live without discussions; he turned up again and began his endless arguments afresh. Later, when Dan came to Munich with his wife and children, Martov spent his days with him.

" In October we went to Zürich to form an alliance with a revolutionary organization there, but we did not succeed in reaching an agreement. Our stay in Zürich was most pleasant: we all lived in the same hotel and were together nearly all the time. I remember a conversation we had with Plekhanov in a coffee house; there was a hall next to it, where armed workers fought with shields. Plekhanov said with a smile: ' One day we too will fight like that.' But during our homeward journey he corrected himself gravely: ' No, no, it will not come to armed warfare.'

" When we returned to Munich again Lenin sat down at his desk and finished his work, *What is to be Done?* It was at that time that the first serious differences of opinion arose about *Iskra*: Plekhanov rejected a programme drawn up by Lenin, and this led to misunderstandings. Axelrod took refuge behind headaches and stayed away from the discussion. Meanwhile, we had also learned that *Iskra* could no longer be printed in Munich, because the owner of the printing works refused to take the risk. We were thus compelled to move. Plekhanov and Axelrod proposed Switzerland, while the others wished to continue their work in London.

" Afterwards we thought of this Munich period as a bright spot in our emigrant life; the next years of exile were considerably harder to bear. During our stay in

Munich no serious differences arose, for then we were all animated by the same idea, the founding of an All-Russian newspaper and the creation of a new revolutionary organization. This unanimous enthusiasm inspired a kind of joyous carnival mood in all of us in those days.

" We had really scarcely observed public life in Munich at all; we went to a few labour meetings, but found them uninteresting. In Munich we also took part in the first May Day festival permitted by the authorities; the police required that the gathering should not take place in the city itself, so great bands of German social democrats proceeded to one of the suburbs, and spent the day in an inn with copious drinking of beer. This May Day festival truly did not suggest a demonstration.

" We lived in strict seclusion and held aloof even from the German comrades. Now and again we saw Parvus, who lived in Schwabing not far from us with his family; on one occasion Rosa Luxemburg visited him and met Lenin on this occasion.

" We now proceeded to London, taking Liége on the way. The town was in a state of great excitement. A few days before the soldiers had fired at striking workers. Universal excitement and anger were plainly visible in the proletarian districts; we looked at the People's House, and remarked that the masses assembled there could if necessary easily be cut off and captured. From Liége we went on to London.

" There was a thick fog on the day of our arrival in the English capital, but Lenin's face was animated and he looked with intense curiosity at this stronghold of capitalism; he forgot that day all his disputes with Plekhanov and his other colleagues on the editorial board.

" We were met at the station by Alexeev, a colleague who lived in England. He was our guide in London, since it was soon evident that we were completely helpless there. We thought we had mastered the English tongue because we had translated a fat book from

English into Russian in Siberia, but in London we found that no one understood what we said. We often got into awkward situations, which made Lenin decide to learn English as quickly as possible. For this purpose we attended as many meetings as we could and often went to Hyde Park, where speeches were usually to be heard. Soon afterwards Lenin discovered two Englishmen who wanted to study Russian and gave him English lessons in exchange.

" Meanwhile Lenin explored London eagerly; it is true that he did not go to the British Museum, because there was only one museum he liked to visit, the Revolutionary Museum in Paris. In order to study London he went all over the city on the top of a bus, and often walked with me on foot through the working-class districts, in the dirty lanes where pale-faced children played.

" Lenin was always drawn to places where the workers assembled; for this reason he liked to visit the public reading rooms, of which there are a great number in London. It was then that Lenin formed the plan, which he realized later, after the Bolshevik Revolution, of introducing similar reading rooms in Russia.

" He also frequently visited popular restaurants and churches. In England, after the service, a sort of discussion is held in the church, in which workers also take part; Lenin used to look in the newspapers for announcements of such church meetings, and seldom missed an opportunity of attending. Once we also went to a social democratic church, where a worker read the Bible and explained that the flight of the Jews from Egypt symbolized the flight of the workers from the realm of capitalism into that of socialism. After the sermon the whole congregation rose and sang an anthem: ' Lord, lead us from capitalism into the realm of socialism! '

" We also visited the Church of the Seven Sisters where the social democratic young workers used to assemble. A young lad gave a lecture there on municipal socialism, and declared that he had been fighting for the socialist idea since he was twelve.

" As our custom was, we frequently visited the outskirts of the city. We went particularly often to Primrose Hill, because the fare was the cheapest; it cost only sixpence. The cemetery where Karl Marx is buried is near there, and on each of his expeditions to this neighbourhood Lenin used to visit the grave of this great apostle of socialism, and spend a considerable time there in deep reflection.

" As my mother was going to join us soon, we decided to rent two rooms and do our own housekeeping; English food did not suit us and was besides too expensive. In London no documents are required from foreigners, and so Lenin took the name of Richter; our landlady took us for Germans. Soon Martov and Vera Sasulich also arrived and settled near us. While Lenin spent whole days in the British Museum reading room, I dealt with current correspondence with Martov's assistance; the dispute with Plekhanov had been temporarily adjusted.

" Soon after this, Lenin went for a month to Brittany where his mother was living, because he wanted to see the sea. He had an extraordinary love of the sea, and could watch the play of the waves for hours; the sound of the sea soothed his nerves. After his return to London he met many supporters and organized the revolutionary party. Soon afterwards Plekhanov also came to London and was followed by Baumann, Krochmann, and Blumenfeld, adherents of our movement who had escaped from prison at Kiev.

" In the beginning of September Trotskiĭ also appeared in London. He had escaped from Samara. But as Plekhanov had no confidence in him Trotskiĭ soon left again. When Lenin, who would gladly have protected Trotskiĭ, sent one of his articles to Plekhanov, the latter replied: ' I do not like your new friend's pen.' Lenin retorted: ' Perhaps you do not understand his style, but every man can live and learn, and I think that this man could be very useful to our movement.'

" In March 1903 Lenin proposed that Trotskiĭ should join the editorial board of *Iskra*, but this plan failed owing to Plekhanov's opposition. Trotskiĭ then went to Paris, where he appeared successfully at various student meetings.

" Our party now resolved to leave London and settle in Geneva; Lenin was the only one to oppose this plan, but he was outvoted. These dissensions worried him to such an extent that he was attacked by a nervous malady; at that time we had not enough money to send for a doctor, all the more so because English doctors charge very high fees. For this reason the workers are very seldom treated by a doctor; they confine themselves to all sorts of domestic remedies.

" In April 1903 we left London for Geneva. Lenin was in a high fever during the voyage, and had to go to bed as soon as he arrived. For a fortnight he was very ill, and was only gradually able to resume work.

" We hired a little house in a working class-quarter in Geneva; our whole premises consisted of a kitchen with a stone floor and three little rooms; we used our book boxes for furniture. The kitchen served as a reception room, and there was always a crowd of people there.

" We had decided to call a congress of delegates, and a new arrival turned up nearly every day. We discussed our programme in the fullest detail with the delegates and heard their reports. Martov was continually at our house and conversed unceasingly with our visitors. Soon Trotskiĭ arrived, and supported Lenin's point of view with Plekhanov; the discussions between Trotskiĭ and Plekhanov mostly took place in the Café Landolt. The Russian workers frequently declared themselves for Trotskiĭ's views, which made Plekhanov beside himself with rage.

" The dissensions in the *Iskra* editorial board became so acute that the position was absolutely intolerable. It

came in the end to an open split, with Plekhanov,
Axelrod, and Sasulich on the one side, and Lenin,
Martov, and Potresov on the other. The work became
more and more difficult, but we kept on hoping that it
would be possible to reach agreement at the proposed
congress at Brussels. At this time Lunacharskiï also
came to Geneva and joined the editorial board. He
proved to be a model speaker, and Lenin took a great
liking to him. Every evening these two would sit in the
Café Landolt with a few other comrades of like views,
and discuss events in Russia and their own plans over
a glass of beer.

"In 1905 Russian publishers approached us for the
first time and stated that they were prepared to print
hitherto prohibited works in Russia. At the beginning
of October a plan for a journey to Finland was mooted,
but subsequent events caused Lenin to go direct to
Russia, while I remained in Geneva a few weeks longer
to clear everything up."

XI

Towards the end of the year the first revolution broke
out in Russia in connection with the unsuccessful war
with Japan. Lenin, though he had been exiled, contrived to return to Russia. At first, he carried on an
agitation in Moscow, in support of the Petersburg rising,
but soon the Central Committee of the Party forbade
him to take any active part in events because, as an
illegally returned exile, he was exposed to very great
danger. In these circumstances he was only once or
twice present, hidden in the gallery, at the meetings of
the Petersburg Soviet.

According to his friends' accounts, Lenin regarded
the Moscow rising in December 1905 as an event of the
greatest historical importance. While the street fighting

was still going on he collected reports, questioned those who had taken part in the fighting in the most minute detail, and tried in this way to form a clear picture of what was happening. Even after the collapse of the rising, he supported the view that this revolution, in which the Russian workers fought for the first time against the Tsarist army, was of supreme historical significance; this defeat was worth more than many other victories.

The collapse of the revolution led to the break-up of the Bolshevik Party by the Government. As the Party, however, secretly continued its activities, Lenin in 1906 was threatened with arrest and had to retire to Finland. During his stay there the little place where he lay hid was to some extent the headquarters of the Russian Revolution. On Saturdays and Sundays numerous workers visited him to ask his advice; the authorities were aware of this, but did not yet dare to take any energetic measures against Lenin so soon after the summoning of the Duma.

Lenin at that time collected all the extreme revolution-aries about him, and immediately attacked the Mensheviks, who had abandoned the revolutionary cause and were trying to confine themselves to activities permitted by law. With the idea that they must possess themselves in patience and wait, but meantime go quietly on with revolutionary agitation, the Bolsheviks decided to found a proletarian labour paper, but to publish it abroad and smuggle it secretly over the Russian frontier. Lenin was entrusted with this task, and he proceeded to Zürich in 1907 and then on to Geneva.

In 1908 the theoretical philosophical dispute about Bogdanov's 'empirio-criticism' arose; Lenin went to London to study philosophy, and then moved to Paris, where a Bolshevik conference took place in 1909. The following years up to 1912 were spent in theoretical and practical propaganda for his philosophical and political ideas.

To this period of exile belongs the interesting correspondence between Lenin and the novelist Maxim
Gor'kiĭ, in which the chief traits of Lenin's character are
revealed perhaps more clearly than in any other document, his inflexible courage, his unshakable faith in
ultimate success, and his dislike or rather his abhorrence
for any compromise with those who held different
opinions. In these years, the political position in Russia
was discouraging and hopeless, and the revolutionary
movement, under the pressure of reaction, was showing
increasing signs of collapse. Lenin's letters to Gor'kiĭ,
however, breathe unshakable confidence, and an
assured conviction that by new ways and new methods
the working class would one day be victorious.

" In Lenin's letters to Gor'kiĭ," says Kamenev, " you
will not find the fiery language, the lofty style of the
' historic personality '; they are simple, natural, often
jesting, but always practical, clear-sighted, and clear
from one end to the other, as though written in one
breath. As you glance through them you feel as plainly
as possible how great this work was, how mighty is the
spiritual power reflected in these letters. In Lenin, the
man and the mission were welded into one; it was
physiologically impossible for him to separate his
subjective standpoint from that of the revolutionary
movement: personality and revolution in him were
joined to form an indivisible whole. Nowhere nor at any
time could the smallest rift be discerned between the
personal interests of Lenin and the interests of the
historical process in course of evolution. This makes
Lenin's letters genuine documents for a new proletarian
culture, bred from struggle."

But while his friendship with Gor'kiĭ was thus
strengthened, his former supporters were becoming
more and more alienated from him. This went so far
that a Paris comic paper in jest offered half a kingdom
to any person who could name a fourth Bolshevik to
keep Lenin, Zinov'ev, and Kamenev company. For his

relations with Gor'kiĭ were personal rather than political; Gor'kiĭ has never been a Bolshevik in the true sense of the word.

In the year 1912 Lenin went to Galicia and established at Cracow a kind of central office for the Bolshevik movement in Russia: the chief leaders of Russian Bolshevism frequently visited him there to receive his instructions. He was surprised by the world war in Belii-Dunaets in Galicia. He used to go every day on his bicycle to the post office at Poronin; several of his comrades were staying there and he discussed all the events of the day with them and played chess in his leisure time.

After the outbreak of the world war Lenin was arrested as a Russian spy on information supplied by the Austrian police. He rode along the railway line every day on his bicycle and used sometimes to read the newspapers there, which gave rise to a suspicion that he was spying out the line, if not meditating an attempt at wrecking it. Lenin's friends were extremely alarmed at his arrest, and strained every nerve to prevent his being handed over to the Austrian military authorities. They were well aware how summary were the sentences of the military courts at that time and how rapidly their sentences were executed, and, therefore, how extreme was the danger which threatened their leader. They telegraphed to Victor Adler at Vienna, informing him of the position and begging him to take immediate steps for Lenin's release.

Victor Adler immediately approached the then Austrian Prime Minister, Count Stürgkh, and explained to him that the arrest of Lenin would inevitably lead to exasperation against Austria among the Russian workers, while, on the other hand, it might be most advantageous if the radical revolutionary were allowed to work unmolested. These arguments induced Count Stürgkh to order the immediate release of Lenin, and that was the end of that episode. Lenin, however, felt uncomfortable in Austria

after that, and decided to move to Switzerland; after
some difficulty with the Austrian authorities he finally
succeeded in doing so towards the end of 1914.

He then settled down in Zürich, where he lived in a
little room in a workman's house, with his wife, Krupskaia, who was his faithful companion on all his travels.
She was Lenin's staunchest fighting comrade, at once
his wife and his secretary. " This woman," says Klara
Zetkin, " with her absolutely puritanical simplicity, her
hair smoothly combed back and tied in a simple knot,
with her cheap plain dress, was the image of a Russian
working man's wife." And even when her husband was
reigning in the Kremlin as an all-powerful dictator, she
made no change either in her dress or her mode of life,
and avoided anything which might look like official
dignity. In addition to her share in Lenin's work, she
devoted herself chiefly to the advance of national
education and instruction, in which field she has done
very valuable work.

Lenin spent the years from 1915 to 1917 in Switzerland. He took part in the many socialist conferences
which were held in this neutral State. He made himself
conspicuous at the Zimmerwald and Kiental conferences in particular, by advocating sabotage and armed
rebellion to put an end to the war. Undisturbed by the
hail of attack and suspicion, the allegations that he was
a traitor who wanted to sell Russia, Lenin urged the
view that it would be an advantage for the Russian
proletariat if Tsarism suffered a military defeat in the
world war, because this would result in the social
revolution.

XII

In February 1917 the Revolution in Russia prophesied
by Lenin actually occurred. The people repudiated the
intolerable wastefulness at Court, the Army and Navy
mutinied, and a few days later the Tsar was dethroned
and the democratic republic proclaimed. Lenin tried
to get to Russia as soon as possible. This proved to be
difficult, however, for the Entente States refused him a
passage. But he had contrived in the interval to procure
a forged Swedish passport, and tried to proceed to
Russia through Sweden along with a few friends.
Suddenly one of the comrades put forward the objection
that none of the alleged Swedes could speak a word of
Swedish. Lenin actually thought for a moment of pretending to be deaf and dumb on the journey, but this
plan was immediately given up on account of the serious
dangers it involved.

Then came the famous journey through Germany in
the " sealed coach." The German social democrats of
the Left Party, Karl Liebknecht in particular, undertook
the necessary negotiations with the authorities and
secured sanction for Lenin to pass through Germany.
This journey was later extensively used to brand Lenin
as a paid agent of the German Government, but there
is no doubt that Lenin's vindication of himself was quite
true, and that the way through Germany was chosen
by the Bolsheviks purely on grounds of expediency.

During the journey through Germany and Finland
Lenin was all the time afraid that he would be arrested
by the provisional bourgeois Government after his arrival
in Petersburg. He was all the more astonished, therefore, to find great crowds of workers on the station at
Petersburg, who gave him a tempestuous welcome. In
spite of this, it was a long time before he gave up his
suspicions, for he was sceptical enough to recognize
that public ovations were of scant value. During the

first period of his stay in Petersburg he used to say nearly every day: "They have not locked us up to-day, but it will come to-morrow."

On the very evening of his arrival, while still on the steps of the station, Lenin delivered his first revolutionary speech and called for the dictatorship of the proletariat. On his way through the streets of Petersburg he had again and again to mount the roof of an armoured car illuminated by searchlights, and address the masses which thronged about him.

On 7th April Lenin published his Bolshevik programme in *Pravda*. He demanded the repudiation of annexations, the transference of political power to the proletariat and the peasantry, the replacement of democracy by dictatorship, and the abolition of the police, the army, and the bureaucracy. He called for the nationalization of all land, the dissolution of the banks, and the taking over by the State of the control of industry and the rationing of food supplies.

In the early summer Kerenskiĭ, Prime Minister of the bourgeois Government, under pressure from the Western allied powers, decided on a new offensive in Galicia; this strategic movement failed and ended in a military catastrophe, which seriously impaired the prestige of the new Government in Russia and strengthened the position of the Bolsheviks. On 3rd July a military revolt broke out in Kronstadt, but this time the Government was still able to subdue the insurrection. Kerenskiĭ issued a warrant for the arrest of Lenin, Zinov'ev, Trotskiĭ, Kamenev, Lunacharskiĭ, and other Bolsheviks.

Lenin and Zinov'ev had, therefore, to hide as quickly as they could from Kerenskiĭ's police; they decided, with the help of a comrade, to retire to a village in the neighbourhood of Petersburg and live in a hayrick. Both revolutionaries for a time shared the life of the agricultural workers there and even took part in cutting and bringing in the hay harvest. On this occasion Zinov'ev was once nearly discovered when he was out shooting: a forester surprised him, confiscated his gun, and asked him to account for himself. As the Government had offered a reward of two hundred thousand roubles for the capture of Zinov'ev and Lenin, the situation was more than critical. But the comrade who was concealing the two of them, interposed and declared to the forester that Zinov'ev was a Finn who did not understand a word of Russian. Whereupon the forester desisted from asking for further details and let the matter rest.

When the weather began to get colder, Lenin and Zinov'ev decided to cross to Finland, where their movements would be less restricted. They were provided with forged papers in the character of workers in the neighbouring Sestroretsk munitions factory; they shaved, cut their hair, and fitted themselves out with wigs. Then a comrade photographed them and pasted the photographs on the forged papers, and in this way they succeeded in crossing the Finnish frontier.

During his stay in Finland Lenin was concealed for a time, under the name of Ivanov, in the house of the Chief of Police at Helsingfors who had Bolshevik sympathies. This seemed to him the best way to secure himself against the pursuit of the Kerenskiï Government. Even in this hiding place he worked zealously. He procured Russian papers every day and organized a secret postal service through the agency of a railway official.

The Chief of Police went to the station every day and bought all the newspapers which had arrived from Petersburg. Lenin studied and worked on these till late in the night, and in the morning he nearly always had an article ready for despatch to Petersburg. Only a few of the Bolsheviks living in Helsingfors, among them Smilga, knew of Lenin's presence in the town. Smilga saw Lenin frequently and gave him information about the temper of the garrison and the working class.

But as events in Russia were approaching a crisis,

Lenin did not remain in Helsingfors but moved to Viborg, nearer the Russian frontier. For this purpose the Chief of Police had to provide him with a forged passport as well as a wig and make up. They discovered a theatrical barber who, after lengthy negotiations, promised to deliver a grey wig next day. Thus in a different suit with false hair and painted eyebrows Lenin proceeded to Viborg, whence he soon after pressed on to Petersburg.

In October 1917 Lenin finally returned to Petersburg. On 24th October the Revolution broke out for the second time, and the Bolshevists occupied the telegraph office and the Neva bridges. Next morning, 25th October in the Russian and 7th November in the Western European calendar, the Central Post Office and the State Bank fell into the hands of the revolutionary soldiers. The Government troops went over to the rebels in crowds, by noon Kerenskiï, the Prime Minister, had fled and the news of the overthrow of the Provisional Government got abroad. Lenin showed himself in public, called a meeting of the Soviet, and delivered a speech in honour of their victory.

An eye-witness has described the impression which Lenin made on his audience at his first public speech in Petersburg. A short thick-set man came on to the platform. While storms of applause echoed through the hall, he smoothed his hair with both hands, as if he still wore the wig which but recently had helped him to escape from his pursuers. When the noise had subsided Lenin began to speak in a clear voice, sometimes becoming slower. At the beginning of his speech he kept both hands buried in his pockets, but suddenly he drew out his right hand and began to use it to underline the meaning of his words with vigorous gestures. After a short time the left also emerged, and he now illustrated the flow of his thoughts with both hands. At the moment when his speech reached its climax, he threw his whole body back, stuck his hands in his waistcoat, and began to make curious movements with his body.

On the evening of the same day the Winter Palace, the last refuge of the Provisional Government and the troops which had remained faithful to it, was stormed by the revolutionaries. Lenin was now master of Russia. Next day he was elected President of the Council of People's Commissars.

Immediately after the Bolsheviks assumed supreme power Lenin had a telephone conversation with the fortress of Kronstadt. This conversation, which was taken down in shorthand, forms one of the most interesting documents of revolutionary days. After Lenin's secretary had got the connection with Kronstadt, the telephone was answered by a man who introduced himself as a social revolutionary.

" Lenin wishes to speak to you, in the name of the Revolutionary Government," said the secretary.

" Good, what does he wish to communicate to us ? "

Lenin himself took up the receiver at this point: " Are you empowered to negotiate in the name of the District Committee of the Army and Navy ? " he enquired.

" Certainly," was the answer from Kronstadt.

" Are you in a position to send a large number of mine-layers and warships to Petrograd immediately ? "

" I will ask the Commander of the Baltic Fleet to come to the telephone ! "

" We need," explained Lenin, " as many bayonets as possible, but only soldiers who are heart and soul with us. How many such can you locate ? "

" Five thousand. We can despatch the troops to Petersburg at once."

" With the most rapid means of transport possible, how soon can you guarantee the arrival of the military forces ? "

" In twenty-four hours at most," was the answer.

"Have you the necessary food and equipment at your disposal?"

"Yes. We have plenty of foodstuffs. There are three hundred and fifty-six machine-guns here and some batteries of field artillery which we can place at your disposal."

Lenin appeared delighted: "Then I request you, in the name of the Republican Government, to despatch the troops at once. You may know that a new Government has been formed. How was this news received by the Kronstadt Soviet?"

"With great enthusiasm."

"Then," ordered Lenin, "please see that the infantry regiments, adequately equipped, are started immediately."

This remarkable telephone conversation closed with the assurance that this would be done at once. Next day the Kronstadt troops arrived in Petersburg according to programme, and were henceforward one of the most trustworthy supports of Lenin's new Government.

Trotskiï gives an interesting account of Lenin's behaviour in the Petersburg days immediately following his victory. "From the instant that the Provisional Government was declared to be overthrown, Lenin, both in small things and great, acted as 'the new Government.' We had no machinery, no contact with the provinces, the bureaucracy was obstructive, there was no money and no army. But Lenin issued orders, decrees, and commands in the name of the Government. Needless to say, he was farther removed than most from any superstitious veneration for formalities. If, however, he was to unite the work coming from above, from the abandoned or obstructive Government offices, with the productive activity coming from below, this tone of formality and decision was necessary, the tone of a Government which at the moment was still floating in the void, but which to-morrow or the next day must become a power and must appear as such from the

outset. This formality was also necessary for disciplin-
ing our own people. Little by little the threads of the
apparatus of Government were spun over the boisterous
element, the revolutionary improvisations of the proletarian troops. Lenin's office and mine were at opposite
ends of the Smolny cloister; the corridor uniting—or
rather separating—us was so long that Lenin in joke
proposed that we should maintain communication by
bicycle. We were telephonically connected, and besides
sailors ran backwards and forwards and brought me
Lenin's famous minutes, little scraps of paper containing
two or three vigorous sentences, with the important
words underlined several times and ending with a
question. Several times a day I went along this inter-
minable corridor, which was like an ant heap, to take
part in a consultation in Lenin's room."

The weakness of the new machinery of Government
was seen most clearly when the German attack began.
" Yesterday we were still firm in the saddle," said Lenin
at that time, " to-day we are hanging on by the mane.
But it is a good lesson. This will have a good effect on
our damned Oblomovism. Those who want to escape
from slavery must take firm hold and organize. It will
be a good lesson, if only the Germans do not overthrow
us first."

Trotskiï's reports show that Lenin was well aware of
the dangers which threatened his life at that period.
" What do you think? " he once unexpectedly asked
Trotskiï, " do you think that Bukharin and Sverdlov
will be able to manage things alone if they kill you and
me? "

" What's that you say? They won't kill us," Trotskiï
answered jestingly.

" God knows! How can you tell? " said Lenin with
a laugh.

Meanwhile, under pressure of the German offensive,
the peace negotiations of Brest-Litovsk had begun, in
which Trotskiï took part in the capacity of leader of the

Russian delegation. He refused the harsh peace conditions of the Central Powers, whereupon the Germans declared the armistice at an end and resumed their advance.

At this juncture Lenin, in opposition to all his followers and friends, decided to accept the German terms, to have " peace at any price," in order to save the Revolution from the German bayonets.

XIII

Soon after this Lenin proceeded to transfer the seat of government from Petersburg to Moscow. This time also there were bitter differences of opinion before he could carry his point. His friends objected that it was a kind of desertion of the colours to abandon Petersburg, the city of the Revolution, and the Smolny Cloister, the symbol of Soviet power. Lenin, however, flew into a rage and was quite beside himself when he heard such remarks. " How can people decide the fate of the Revolution with sentimental nonsense? If the Germans take Petersburg with a rush and find us there, the Revolution is lost. But if the seat of Government is in Moscow, then the fall of Petersburg is merely a severe loss. How can it be possible that you do not grasp, do not understand this? And further. If we remain in Petersburg, then we are making its position more dangerous, for it is as if we were challenging the Germans to capture it. But if the Government is stationed in Moscow, then the temptation for the Germans to march on Petersburg is enormously diminished. . . . Why do you babble of the symbolic meaning of the Smolny. The Smolny is the Smolny because we are in it. Once we are in the Kremlin, all your symbolism will be transferred to the Kremlin ! "

Finally, Lenin carried, or rather enforced, his views, and the Government was transferred to the Kremlin in Moscow. Lenin, with his wife and sister, moved into a small apartment in the building formerly occupied by the Court of Appeal, where he worked from sixteen to eighteen hours a day.

One of Lenin's party friends, G. Sorin, gives a vivid description of the dictator's methods of work in the Kremlin at that period: " He sat in his office and screwing up his eyes tried to question the hundred and one comrades about the feeling among the masses. He did it in such a way that the person who was being questioned did not know what he was driving at. Only in this way was it possible to get objective, and not too favourably coloured, reports.

" Then he compared the result of these interrogations with the conclusions drawn from the thousands of reports; then he added the two statements and multiplied the total by some plan on the agenda, in order, after subtracting about a dozen of his own and other people's mistakes, to examine the whole thing again for the tenth time. After finally asking the People's Commissariat for the Food Supply about the coming potato harvest, he gave his decision:

" ' They seem to be all right. But if they are all right, the matter must be carried out exactly at any price. It is necessary to supervise the carrying out, to supervise it most carefully.' "

In the summer of 1918 the social revolutionary, Dora Kaplan, made her attempt on Lenin's life. For several days he hovered between life and death, but he made a rapid recovery and was soon able to resume the direction of the affairs of the State. This was the more urgently necessary, as at that time the political position of Soviet Russia was becoming visibly worse. Almost all over the country risings had taken place and counter-revolutionary armies had been formed. The opponents had to be defeated one after the other in stubborn and bitter fighting, before the Bolshevik regime was at last firmly established in Russia.

Meanwhile, the economic situation had become difficult and even menacing. The strict blockade instituted by the other powers, combined with the resistance of the peasants to requisitioning, had brought about such a shortage of food that hunger and misery prevailed in the whole of the Soviet State, especially in the industrial centres.

It was at this point that Lenin dared to take one of his boldest steps, the entirely unexpected transition to the " new economic policy " from the system of " militant communism " previously in force. This truly statesmanlike decision to make a complete break with the methods of compulsory communism, without doubt saved the Soviet regime from certain ruin. Nevertheless, this sudden right-about-face on Lenin's part roused the greatest opposition among almost all his followers, and in those days many prominent leaders of the Bolshevik Party regarded this *volte face* of Lenin's to a greater or less degree as a betrayal of the supreme principles of communism.

Lenin in no way troubled about objections of this kind and did not let himself be diverted from carrying out his new plan. By again recognizing private property, granting concessions to foreign undertakings, encouraging trade and stabilizing the currency he, overnight as it were, changed the whole social system and the economic structure of the Soviet State.

In a few months the deserted streets took on fresh life, the old shops opened again, foodstuffs appeared in the markets, and economic commerce with Western Europe and America, which had been completely suspended for many years, began to revive. Lenin had in mind a kind of State capitalism, which was to form a transition stage on the way to complete communism; this hope had to compensate him for the fact that, since the introduction of the " new economic policy," economic life in Russia was undeniably approximating more and more closely to the methods in force in capitalist countries.

This bold decision suddenly to replace the existing communist organization of trade and industry by a capitalistic system, is certainly one of the most amazing examples of Lenin's capacity for adapting himself to the conditions of the moment, and not shrinking even from actions which were bound to make his loyalty suspect even in the eyes of his followers. As in other similar cases, here too he did not hesitate for a moment to confess his mistake and to replace a method which had proved itself erroneous by one entirely different.

XIV

All through his life Lenin had always the courage to stand alone and to offend his best friends, if his ideas did not agree with theirs. " It was characteristic of Vladimir Il'ich," says Pokrovskiĭ, " that he never hesitated to take the responsibility for every step even if the fate not only of himself and his party, but of the whole country might depend on it. Almost all his movements were initiated by himself alone at the head of a tiny group, because always only very few could be found bold enough to go with him. This was most clearly shown during his propaganda for an armed rising in the years 1904 and 1905, when this man, who went about in a tattered coat, ruthlessly declared war on the omnipotent power of the Tsars. I still remember the attitude of the bourgeois professors towards this appeal; they never uttered the word ' comrade ' without a sneering smile, as if it meant an utter blockhead.

" But Lenin neither feared mockery nor shrank from the overwhelming magnitude of the task he had set himself, nor was he afraid of the consequences of his appeal for bloodshed. When the first attempt failed, he did not lose heart. There were many who, after the December days of 1905, declared that the only thing for Lenin to do was to put a bullet through his head. But he had not the faintest intention of doing any such thing. This man, who but recently had been advocating an armed rebellion, suddenly recommended his followers to devote careful study to the shorthand reports of the sessions of the Imperial Duma, thereby exposing himself to ridicule not only from the bourgeois, but also from his own party comrades. The result was that at that time there was hardly a single person who did not consider Lenin an impotent weakling.

" But later events proved that participation in the Duma was the best means of continuing to carry on revolutionary propaganda. Lenin rightly saw in the Socialist section of the Duma a mouthpiece for the working classes, and recognized that, in existing circumstances, nothing could be done without this instrument. But to profess his faith in parliamentarianism of this kind required extraordinary political courage, certainly greater courage than was needed for preaching armed rebellion."

Lenin never had any fear of isolation. " I shall perhaps be alone," he said once in Switzerland, " but I shall never be turned aside from my opinions; I shall never cease to champion them and follow the straight line. Zinov'ev relates how Plekhanov once made fun of the young social democrats, of whom Zinov'ev was one, for their devotion to Lenin: " You are still following him, but his way is such that in a few months he will only scare the monks in their orchards. Lenin is done; once he breaks with us who are experienced, his day is over." When the young men told him of this remark Lenin said with a laugh: " We don't count our chickens till autumn. We will fight and see whom the workmen will side with!"

Immediately after the Revolution Lenin came into sharp conflict with his comrades on account of his demand that the Constituent Assembly must be dissolved. Untroubled by the objections which sprang up in all quarters, he had demanded that the Constituent Assembly must be immediately despatched home and the new elections postponed. On this occasion he was outvoted in the Council and had to give in in the end, but he kept shaking his head and exclaiming that they would all pay dearly for this mistake.

At the time of the Treaty of Brest-Litovsk, too, Lenin was in opposition to all his party friends. He clearly recognized the impossibility of going on with the war and insisted on the acceptance of the German ultimatum, though everybody about him violently opposed him and declared that it was impossible to capitulate to the Germans.

In Radek's opinion Lenin's greatness consisted in his capacity for making quite fresh decisions from day to day, and immediately rejecting any formula which had proved to be a hindrance. On one occasion, when someone tried to oppose one of his motions by appealing to a socialist party dogma, he shouted furiously: "You are worse than hens. A hen has not the courage to cross a chalk line, but it can at least justify itself by pointing out that the chalk circle was drawn by somebody else. But you have drawn your own circle and are now gazing at the chalk line instead of seeing reality!"

As a proof of Lenin's unerring perspicuity, his followers quote his philosophical dispute with Bogdanov. Pokrovskiĭ says: "At that time, we clasped our hands and declared in amazement that only his idleness abroad could have induced Lenin to devote himself so earnestly to trifling problems of this kind. It was a critical moment, the Revolution was beginning to flag, and a radical alteration of former tactics was under discussion.

But instead of devoting his attention to all these problems Lenin had buried himself in libraries, spent whole days there, and finally wrote a philosophic work. But later events justified him in this case also, for this seemingly unnecessary theoretical work became the intellectual foundation of Bolshevism."

XV

Still another trait was particularly characteristic of Lenin and contributed greatly to his ultimate success. That was his deep kinship with the working people, with the proletarians and peasants. It was entirely practical. Lenin's closest fellow workers are unanimous in testifying to his capacity for making the most trifling troubles of the workers his own, studying them on the spot, and worrying about the best way to relieve them. Bukharin says that it almost seemed as if an extraordinary sixth sense enabled Lenin to " hear the grass growing under the ground, and the thoughts in the workers' minds." He would listen patiently and with the closest attention to a peasant, or a soldier, or a worker. A chance conversation with an old woman made the true feelings of the peasants clearer to him than hundreds of official reports. He had the special gift of talking to everybody in a way which made them tell him frankly and unreservedly of all their slightest doubts, needs, and desires. He did not meet the workers and peasants as the proud head of the State, but as a comrade in the real sense of the word, as a sincere personal friend. Everything he said and did was for the masses and calculated for its effect on the masses. He always tried to ensure that his words could be understood in the most remote villages. This spiritual contact with sections of

the Russian people about whose weal or woe no previous
Russian statesman had ever troubled himself, brought
Lenin close to the masses and won him unlimited
popularity among the whole population.

Personally, too, Lenin felt a strong disinclination for
any kind of luxurious living. He wanted his way of life
to be as little different as possible from that of the
proletariat. During the terrible famine year of 1919 it
was a great worry to him that people would send him
food from all over the country, as he thought he had
no right to eat more than any of his comrades. He
generally distributed all the foodstuffs he received to
sick and starving proletarians. Once he invited Gor'kiĭ
to lunch, remarking, " Have lunch with me, I've been
sent smoked fish from Astrakhan." Then he wrinkled
his brow, took Gor'kiĭ aside, screwed up his eyes, and
said: " People send me food, as to a master. If I do
not accept the parcels, I insult the donors. But I find
it very unpleasant to accept food when the people
around me are hungry."

He was very fond of talking to workers and peasants
and testing the success of every measure by means of
such conversations. He pumped these people to find
out all they knew, and, on the other hand, in all his
measures he considered the effect which his new decisions
would have on the simple people. " When Lenin had
to solve a great problem," says Radek, " he did not
think in abstract historical categories, he did not puzzle
over ground rent or surplus value, nor over absolutism
or liberalism. He thought about living men, the
peasant Sidor from Tver, the workman from the
Putilov Works, or the bobby on the street, and tried to
imagine how the decisions in question would affect the
peasant Sidor or the workman Onufri."

Amongst the collected official documents written by
Lenin is a bundle of short letters, each of which contains
an order in favour of some ordinary man. One directs
that a certain worker is to be supplied with food, in

another Lenin asks for new clothes for one workman or tries to provide a house for another, or medical treatment for a third. Every one of these orders is accompanied by a statement giving the exact and detailed reasons for its issue.

Lenin also read all the letters sent to him, devoting particular attention to those from peasants. " They are real human documents," he used frequently to say when he received a communication of this kind from a peasant; " no official report could throw so much light on the situation." He often made exhaustive enquiries about the writer, whether he was a rich or a poor peasant, and what was his attitude to things in general and to Bolshevism in particular. Rykov, the People's Commissar, relates how Lenin, during the food crisis, used to send for quite simple peasants and hold long and exhaustive conversations with them in order to get an exact picture of the position and the possibilities of improving it.

His capacity for getting into immediate touch with men of the people and putting himself on their level was not confined to Russia. Once when on a visit to Gor'kiĭ at Capri, he used to talk a great deal with the fishermen there, although he did not understand a word of Italian. The fishermen liked him very much, because they found his laugh sympathetic. An old fisherman used to say of him: " Only an honest man can laugh like that." When Lenin returned to Russia, the fisherman used to ask Gor'kiĭ: " What is Signor Lenin doing? Has the Tsar arrested him yet? "

The English workers, too, who got to know Lenin at the London Conference in 1907, said that no other socialist leader appealed to them as Lenin did. When they were asked for their views on Plekhanov, one of them said: " Plekhanov is our teacher. He is a gentleman. But Lenin is really our comrade! "

Lenin had undoubtedly a genius for organization. His extraordinary ability in this direction was perhaps most clearly shown by the way he contrived to create

H

collaborators for himself, to attract a whole staff of
politicians, administrators, soldiers, and diplomatists, to
whom he communicated the science of government.
He chose about a thousand men from proletarians and
intellectuals entirely inexperienced in statesmanship, and
put the whole administration in their hands. In this
connection he also contrived cleverly to attach even
political opponents to his service if he needed them for
their special abilities. He made generals of people who
had not the faintest knowledge of military affairs,
handed over to them army commands, and sent them
to the front against the counter-revolutionary armies.
He appointed journalists as ambassadors, and sent them
on diplomatic missions, and handed over to a handful of
peasants and workers the organization of complicated
financial and administrative tasks.

And the miracle worked. The improvised com-
manders-in-chief won victories, the new diplomatists
succeeded in concluding favourable agreements with the
European powers, and the home administration under
the new regime functioned at least no worse than it had
done under the Tsars. Lenin clearly had a sure eye for
putting the best men in the right posts and for training
them besides.

XVI

Thus he succeeded in bringing his new state into
being with quite new men. For the Soviet Republic
is actually an entirely original political creation without
any forerunner or prototype whatever in the history of
the world. A passing episode of the revolutionary days
of 1905, the calling of a workers' council in Petersburg,
was enough to suggest to Lenin the conception of an
entirely new political form, to give him the idea of a

Soviet Republic. All the other revolutionaries had striven for some form of the parliamentary system. Lenin was the only one to decide to give up parliamentarianism altogether and democracy along with it, and to base the dictatorship of the proletariat on the council system. Whatever we may think of the system, the fact that he was able to carry this idea into practice, and to organize a State of a hundred and fifty million inhabitants on the council principle in a few years, almost in a few months, must be acknowledged to be a marvellous and almost incomprehensible achievement of organization.

It is not surprising that Lenin's health could not permanently keep pace with the colossal burden of work resting on his shoulders. After forcing himself to go on working for months in terrible physical suffering, he was at last obliged to retire from direct management of the State, and to exchange the Kremlin for the quiet sanatorium at Gor'kiĭ where, in the end, he died, with his right side paralysed.

Lenin's illness, according to the account of his wife, Nadezhda Krupskaia, began towards the end of 1921: " The exact point at which Lenin began to be seriously ill is difficult to fix, for his indisposition developed very slowly and only gradually undermined his strong constitution. He himself troubled very little about his illness.

" In March 1921 the doctors examined him and pronounced him to be sound. At that time neither his nervous system nor his internal organs were affected. But as he complained continually of headaches, and was extremely fatigued, it was proposed that he should take a few months' leave and go to Gor'kiĭ. Soon after this, at the beginning of May, the first symptoms of an organic injury to the brain appeared. He had a stroke which resulted in general weakness, loss of speech, and paralysis of the right foot. These symptoms lasted for three months.

" Later there were other similar attacks; they occurred periodically in the course of May, June, and July and lasted from half an hour to two hours. Under careful treatment, however, Lenin's condition improved so much during the summer that, in October, he was able to resume his former activities even if only to a limited extent. In November he delivered three great political speeches; but in December the attacks recurred, and, finally, on 16th December, led to paralysis of the right hand and the right foot. Henceforth he had to keep his bed.

" In January and February 1923 Lenin's health changed now for the better, now for the worse. In February he could still dictate political articles, but on 9th March paralysis of the whole right side occurred, which made speaking almost impossible.

" In the middle of May, in view of the fine weather, Lenin was moved to Gor'kiĭ, where he remained till his death. At first his condition improved a little again, but in the second half of June he became worse. At that time he suffered especially from insomnia.

" In the second half of July a period of slow but steady improvement began. He was taken out every day in a bath chair; his spirits were good, he ate well, and was able to sleep. He even began gradually to walk without assistance. In the beginning of August it was possible to undertake experiments for restoring his speech, which were continued almost up to his death.

" In September Lenin could go up and down stairs again without assistance, walk about the room, and go for daily motor drives in the forest. The paralysis of his speech was considerably less, and he began to take part in public life again. He read the papers daily, drew attention to articles which interested him, and caught up with everything very quickly. With great difficulty he set about learning to write with his left hand.

" At the beginning of the sunny winter days he often went sleighing in the forest, and during these expeditions he was good-humoured and seemed in excellent spirits. At Christmas, a tree was decorated for the village children; Lenin took part in the Christmas festivities, was in wonderful spirits, and saw to it that the children enjoyed themselves thoroughly.

" We all believed that his health was improving surely if slowly. But after this brief period of apparent recovery, the catastrophe occurred at six o'clock on the evening of 21st January 1924. A serious attack, lasting nearly an hour, resulted in an almost complete loss of sensation and muscular contraction. At ten minutes to seven his temperature was 108, and he died of paralysis of the breathing centre of the brain."

The post-mortem carried out by a board of Russian professors revealed general arterial sclerosis with particularly serious deterioration in the blood vessels of the brain. Obviously, Lenin was a victim of overwork.

One of the doctors who took part in the post-mortem said later that it was not surprising that Lenin died; the really incomprehensible thing was how he lived so long. Obviously, the arteries of his brain were already largely hardened and decayed at the time when he was still reading the newspapers and taking an interest in politics. Only a man of almost incredible will power could have carried on any kind of intellectual activity under such conditions.

It was Lenin's death which first made Europe understand his real greatness. Up till then he was still treated in the foreign Press as a " bandit " and a " German spy "; but now opinions began gradually to change. More and more voices were heard calling attention to Lenin's true significance. Soon after his death the views of foreign politicians, authors, and scholars on the dead Russian leader were solicited for a book to be published in memory of him. The replies received testify to the change which had taken place in the interval in the opinion of Europe. Not only did social democrats like Karl Kautsky or Otto Bauer express

themselves in words of the highest appreciation and call
him a proletarian leader and teacher of genius; similar
words of appreciation came from the bourgeois camp
too. Thus Painlevé wrote that he admired the extraordinary vital will-power, energy, and force of Lenin;
Herriot also stated that, in spite of all the difference
between their political opinions, he had always been
captured by Lenin's unusual gifts as a statesman, by his
energy, his resoluteness, and his all-round education.

"Lenin," said Thomas Mann, "was undoubtedly a
phenomenon of the century, a human organism of new
democratically titanic dimensions, a powerful combination of the 'will to power' and asceticism, a great pope
of the idea, full of world-destroying fanaticism. He will
be remembered along with Gregory, of whom the heroic
poem says: 'Life and teaching were not in discord with
each other,' and who himself said: 'Cursed be the man
who holds his sword back from bloodshed.'"

Romain Rolland prefaces his opinion with the words:
"Lenin, the greatest man of action in our century and
at the same time the most selfless." The great English
scholar and writer, Bertrand Russell, again, declares
that the death of Lenin has deprived the world of the
one truly great man of the age: "We may take it for
granted that our century will go down in history as the
century of Lenin and Einstein, the two men who
succeeded in completing a colossal synthetic work.
Lenin seemed a destroyer to the bourgeoisie of the
world; but what made his greatness was not his destructive activity. He was a harmoniously creative mind, a
philosopher, a practical systematizer. . . . On me he
makes the impression of an absolutely sincere man
totally devoid of egoism. I am convinced that he was
concerned only with social aims and never with his own
power. I believe he would have been ready to stand
aside at any moment if by so doing he could have
advanced the cause of communism. . . ."

Bernard Shaw expresses himself to the same effect,

saying in his characteristic paradoxical way that the day will come when Lenin's statue will be erected in London alongside that of George Washington. Washington was in his time slandered in the English Press in the same infamous fashion as Lenin is now.

Many simple Russians for long refused to believe in Lenin's death, and soon numerous legends sprang up which maintained that Lenin was only pretending to be dead in order to be able to control the administration of his successors. One of these legends tells that Lenin rose suddenly one day from the lunch table, sent for the doctor, and asked him: " Can you arrange matters so that it will seem that I am dead? "

" Certainly," said the doctor, " but why do you want it? "

" I want to see," explained Lenin, " what will become of Russia if they think me dead. At present they shove everything on to my shoulders and make me responsible for everything."

" Very good," said the doctor, " we will announce that you are dead and lay you in a glass case from which you can see everything that goes on around you."

" Excellent, doctor! But it must be kept a strict secret. Besides you and me, only my wife must know."

Soon after, it was announced to the people that Lenin was dead. The people lamented and mourned for him, and his comrades laid him in a storeroom which they called the mausoleum.

Lenin lay here for a day, a week, or a month until he was sick of the glass cage. Finally, one night he rose quietly and went out of the mausoleum by the back door into the Kremlin, where a meeting of the People's Commissars was in progress. The sentries let him by, as he carried a pass, and no one recognized him, for he had pulled his hat down over his face.

So he listened to the deliberations of the People's Commissars, then turned away contentedly and lay down in his glass case again. But next night he rose again and went to a factory. There were only a few workers there on night work, and Lenin talked to them and asked them if they were satisfied with the Government and their life.

The third day he went to the station, took a train and journeyed to the distant villages to see if things were right there. It was not until he had convinced himself that things were still going his way among the peasants also that he went quietly back to Moscow and laid himself in his mausoleum again. No one knows exactly how long he will continue to lie there pretending to be dead. But one day he will rise again and appear among his comrades.

XVII

But the greatness of Lenin's political work in its entirety can be really understood only if it is regarded as the continuation and crown of an historical process: for Lenin, who dug the grave of Tsarism, was, however singular it may sound, the real executor of the political testament which Peter the Great left to Russia. He himself was quite conscious of this, and often called the Tsar Peter his political ancestor. In this connection it is interesting to note that he actually opposed any change in the name of the city of Petrograd, with the remark that Peter the Great was the first revolutionary to sit on the throne, and that his memory must be held in honour by Bolshevik revolutionaries also.

In fact, Peter the Great was the first to attempt to bridge over the yawning gulf between Russia and Western Europe, and to make his empire into a modern, civilized state. Since then, the whole political and cultural development of Russia has stood in the sign of these " Westernizing " tendencies, which, though at

first confined to the Court, later spread to the widest
circles. Once Peter the Great had faced Russia with
the question of deciding whether she was to follow the
path of European civilization, or preserve intact her
Eastern character, this problem swayed almost the whole
of the eighteenth and nineteenth centuries.

Although the Tsar himself understood by Europeanization only the introduction of Western sources of
power, an ever greater number of men later saw in it
the one way to social liberation and release from the
yoke of Asiatic despotism. Just when Alexander Herzen
had clearly formulated these hopes for the first time,
the opposite point of view also began to gain ground,
sponsored at first by the brothers Kireevskiĭ. In the
'sixties the Russian public was already split into two
great hostile camps, " Westerners " on the one side and
" Slavophils " on the other. The efforts of the Westerners did not reach a decisive stage, however, till the
moment when the Russian social democrats adopted
their views, and proclaimed that Russia could be
Europeanized and dovetailed into the cultural development of the West only through the proletariat. That
was the first emergence of the idea that the Europeaniz-
ing of the Russian Empire was the historic task of
Labour.

The opposite Slavophil tendency was at first represented by the " Narodniki," the national Socialists, but
later by the social revolutionaries. Even the Narodniki
acknowledged the necessity for a social reformation, but
they wanted to carry it through without European
support, entirely with the aid of the forces latent in the
Russian peasantry. In their view, the Russian peasant
communes actually contained the purest primitive form
of socialism; thus the hopes of the Slavophils were
wholly set on the Asiatic-Russian element in the
peasantry.

Beginning in the 'sixties the differences between the
socialists and the Narodniki became more and more

acute until any alliance between the two parties was impossible; all the attempts which were then made, in spite of this fact, to bring about a union between them, proved vain.

Lenin accomplished the great work, and brought about a reconciliation between the Western and Eastern trends of thought, between country and town. In this sense the "Republic of the Workers and Peasants," Lenin's most personal work, was much more than an empty phrase, for it was nothing less than the first solution of a century-old problem.

Even the split between Lenin's section and Social Democracy, which was complete in 1903, had its cause in the different sides taken on this problem. The Mensheviks (the social democrats) represented the view that the proletarian revolution was only possible in a country with a highly developed capitalist industrial system; in backward and semi-feudal Russia the dominion of the nobles must first be replaced by the bourgeoisie, then a strong capitalistic class must arise before the proletariat could begin to play its historic rôle. The task of the Socialists, in the Menshevik idea, must first be to support the bourgeoisie in their fight against the nobles, and thus accomplish the liberal revolution; this was the preliminary condition for the ultimate success of socialism itself. By this way of treating the question the Mensheviks were automatically forced into a fighting alliance with the bourgeoisie, who faced West, and who were not indeed without sympathy for Socialist ideas.

Lenin had fought this Menshevik view with the utmost energy; he was of opinion that socialism must follow directly on feudal lordship, and that any alliance with the bourgeoisie was pernicious and objectionable. He was convinced that the Marxist principles were immediately realizable, and he directed his energies exclusively to adapting them to Russian conditions. In this bold sacrifice of his whole world-image to the political expediencies of the moment, as he saw them, he even rejected the inviolability of the strict Marxist creed; this had to be exactly adapted to the immediate demands of the political situation. Lenin, the " practical Marxist," determined that this was the real essence of historic materialism, whose " dialectical " principles, in his view, pointed directly to the adaptation, as occasion required, of theory to political practice.

Lenin had made it his task to discover the forms of the class-war best suited to Russia, independently of the views of Western Social Democracy, which regarded a period of capitalism and middle-class domination as one of the main preliminary conditions for the ultimate rule of the proletariat. This conception might suit Western Europe, but it was not, in Lenin's opinion, applicable to Russia, where no adequately developed industry existed, and where, therefore, the road to socialism, by way of evolutionary development through concentration of capital and middle-class organization, could not be followed. The only way possible for the proletariat to attain power, Lenin was convinced, was by violent upheaval, by revolution; in no other way did it seem possible for Russia to make up for the enormous start of the highly developed industrial West.

Lenin's real work, therefore, lay in this " correction " of Marxism which, in his view, was necessary to adapt it to Russian conditions, and in the establishment of a new revolutionary programme, which no longer had much in common, fundamentally, with the socialism of the West. This " Leninism " naturally had to find support in forces different from those of Western socialism, since it could not tolerate leaving the liberation of the country from its feudal overlordship to a bourgeoisie ripening for the task, but was resolved itself to carry it through immediately without their help. In contrast to the Mensheviks, Lenin thus sought his allies outside the ranks of the westward-facing intelligentsia, and, as a result, came to look for support to the Asiatic peasantry. The rural population has from earliest times formed an overwhelming majority of the inhabitants of Russia, and thus promised an infinitely stronger reserve than the numerically insignificant bourgeoisie. In alliance with the enslaved Russian peasantry, the battle would be carried on simultaneously against feudalism and the bourgeoisie, so that, after both these opponents had been finally overcome, the joint proletarian rule of workers and peasants might be established.

Therefore, it was Lenin's main endeavour to strengthen this alliance between peasants and workers, which he regarded as the best guarantee for the permanence of proletarian rule in Russia. This also explains the very cautious and mild way in which, as dictator, he always dealt with the peasantry, and why he wooed the favour of the rural districts, although he thereby incurred sharp criticism from his party colleagues.

·Lenin, the originator and the proclaimer of the ruthless use of violence, always showed the most friendly spirit in dealing with the demands or protests of the rural population. " Lenin always held the view," says Voronskiĭ, " that there should be no violent interference with peasant economy or the communal administration in the rural districts; and that we should rather try to train the peasants by friendly methods and through good example, for we are in many respects the pupils of the peasants, and not their teachers." And because he was attempting to make the peasants the travelling companions of the Russian worker, Lenin wished to create an alliance whose foundations should be more firmly laid than those of any other association whatever. He was of opinion that the Russian proletariat is not a self-contained phenomenon of the great cities, as it is in Western Europe, but that, as it came from the peasantry, that rural past is still part of it. Therefore, the fraternal union between workers and peasants should merely define, in a political sense, the connection which, from the beginning, has existed in Russia between the factory and the country.

By the union of the urban proletariat and the rural population Lenin actually succeeded in bringing about a compromise between the " Western " and " Slavo-phil " sides, and in giving a strong peasant national note to the proletarian movement. Henceforward, the Marxist doctrine was no longer to be exclusively the concern of the urban proletariat, but rather the concern of the whole people.

Whereas, then, the endeavours at Europeanization of the Russian social democrats and the westward-facing bourgeois intelligentsia had earlier been aimed merely at a very slender section of the population, they could for the future, under the Bolshevist regime, be extended to the great masses of the peasants, and thus to the whole nation. By the inclusion of the peasantry in the pro-letarian revolution, the peasant himself must be prole-tarianized, and, therefore, at the same time " Western-ized "; Lenin hoped in this way to be able to complete the historical process begun by Peter the Great. The eruptive force of the Bolshevik Revolution, however, should not only weld into a unity the Russian working class and the peasantry, but also Russia and Europe, and thus draw the old Muscovite Empire into the civilization of the rest of the world.

This adoption of Western civilization, in Lenin's view, was to find expression mainly in the technification of Russia. From the moment he attained to power one of his chief cares was to advance Russian technology, still so backward, to the utmost, and to substitute immediately for the mediaeval methods of work and organization, which were particularly marked in Russian agriculture, the most modern achievements of European and American technique. " The Russian," he ex-claimed, "is a bad worker compared with the progressive nations. This could not be helped under the Tsarist regime and under the influence of serfdom which had not then been completely overcome; but now it is above everything necessary that the Soviet State should set the nation the task of 'really learning to work.' The Soviet Republic must, at all costs, adopt all that is valuable in the progress of science and technology. The realization of socialism will come into being through the union of our revolutionary organization with the very latest advances of capitalism."

Lenin exerted himself zealously to introduce modern technical resources into Russia, agitated for the use of motor ploughs and threshing machines among the peasantry, and concerned himself especially with the electrification of the whole country. He sent for American, German, and English workers and engineers, in order that they might spread a knowledge of their technical methods and way of working all over Russia. Russian agriculture was to be fitted out with the most modern resources at one blow, the peasants were to be accustomed to replacing their ancient ploughs by complicated machinery. The great Russian cities, especially Moscow, were also, as it were over night, to be transformed into a kind of mechanized " Super-Chicagos "; skyscrapers of cement, glass, and iron were to rise in place of the former modest century-old buildings.

An Institute for the Investigation of Human Labour Power was founded in Moscow on the direct initiative of Lenin, which, under the direction of Gastev, was to devote itself, on the lines of Taylor's investigations, to the normalizing and systematizing of the human movements necessary for every labour process, and to produce in this way workers with specialized training for their occupations. But what distinguished this work of Gastev from the studies of Taylor or Ford was the almost religious fervour which his disciples, if not Lenin himself, brought to these experiments. They hoped that they would produce a new and more valuable human life. More and more frequently voices were heard proclaiming that the world of the future would

belong to the completely mechanized machine man.
He would be the first really to enjoy, unhindered by any
disturbing agitations of the soul, the blessings of the
new forms of life. Lenin himself expected at the very
least an important rationalization of all labour processes
in Russia, and, accompanying this, an increasing
superiority of the Russian over the Western European
worker. He vigorously insisted on the improvement and
further development of Gastev's work and regularly
received reports on its progress.

Not last in novelty in the achievements of this remarkable man was the fact that he immediately proceeded,
with dry objectivity, to the execution of his idea, to
practical proof " in conformity with the theories of
historic materialism." The Bolshevik historian Pokrovskiĭ was not mistaken in pointing out that the prud-
ence which considered only practical performance was
just that which distinguished Lenin fundamentally
from all former revolutionaries: while all other reformers have freely indulged in " rhetoric," Lenin was the
only one who was not content with " grand words," but
went on to " action."

Pokrovskiĭ extols this " practical " sense in Lenin
with positively religious enthusiasm: " There was
above all his enormous capacity to see to the root of
things, a capacity which finally roused a sort of superstitious feeling in me. I frequently had occasion to
differ from him on practical questions, but I came off
badly every time; when this experience had been
repeated about seven times I ceased to dispute, and
submitted to Lenin, even if logic told me that one
should act otherwise. I was henceforth convinced that
he understood things better, and was master of the
power, denied to me, of seeing about ten feet down into
the earth." Pokrovskiĭ, therefore, holds that Lenin can
be compared only with two personalities in recent
history, Cromwell and Robespierre; but Robespierre,
in the end, introduced the cult of a higher being without

being influenced by any considerations but personal motives, whereas Lenin never carried out a measure except for purely objective reasons. As for Cromwell, he was only a pitiful and weak man, ruled by the crazy idea that God himself commanded his actions; from this idea alone proceeds the completely unrevolutionary spiritual constitution of the English reformer.

In this way Pokrovskiĭ arrives at the conclusion that Lenin is the only true representative of progress in the political history of mankind, and he tries to fortify this statement by numberless proofs; all these examples seem to show convincingly how little Lenin let himself be influenced by mere theories, and how strictly he always contrived to pursue only practical aims.

Special emphasis is naturally laid again and again on the practical significance which is inherent in the introduction of rationalistic methods of labour and organization in Russia, and also in the materialistic and collectivist culture which has been the goal of Bolshevik endeavour.

Lenin's friends and partisans do not, however, see in his interest in electrification, wind-motors, and motor-ploughs the only proof of his wonderful understanding of practical problems; they rather see in his whole programme the systematic continuation of the traditional Russian policy of Europeanization with the only practical means possible at the moment. Even the notion that the future of the socialist order of society should not be left to a tedious process of evolution, but adapted to the specific Russian conditions and forced on by a revolutionary upheaval, is, in the opinion of Lenin's adherents, the complete expression of a true " Realpolitik."

XVIII

If we are to believe the Bolsheviks to-day, we should think that here certainly it is a question of the dawn of a paradisaical future, not in the form of a Utopian dream, such as all Messianic reformers have hitherto striven for, but rather the practical and tangible precipitation of the golden age.

And yet never perhaps in the history of mankind has freer play been given to the Utopian arts of illusion, bedazzlement, and misdirection, and it is precisely in the work of Lenin that Utopia has surpassed itself, in its appeal to the faith of credulous humanity on behalf of wind-motors, dynamos, and automatic machinery. It is true that the scientific organization of production and human labour, the introduction of electric light into the villages, the systematic organization of energy, are the highest expression of a rationalistic, materialistic philosophy of life; it is true that all these machines, motors, and plant are the tools which rationalism uses in its practical manifestations.

And yet all these things, all these wind-motors and dynamos, together with a rationalist industrial system and the psycho-technical organization of labour, become fantastic Utopian visions, dissolve into symbolical forms of crazy irreality, immediately they are brought into contact with present-day Russia. In Europe all these things are entirely natural, nay, everyday phenomena of economic life, since they are merely the adequate expression of a general technical development based on civilization, the appropriate working tools of the Western European. But if these products of a specifically Western stage of evolution are transplanted into a world, like the Russian, where all the necessary conditions are lacking, then these tools and appliances, in themselves practical and rational in the highest degree, suddenly

I

become senseless and useless playthings in the hands of
visionaries.

The romantic and fantastic nature of Russian Bolshevism is thus shown in the much extolled deviation
from Western European socialism, which sees the
dominance of the proletariat as the final product of a
natural process of evolution in a ripening civilization.
However splendid Lenin's bold attempt to leap over the
development of centuries, and, for " practical " reasons,
to proceed directly from feudal overlordship to the
dictatorship of the proletariat, may seem at the first
glance, a closer consideration shows that Lenin was, in
truth, a typical Utopian, while Western socialists,
although not abandoning their idealistic aims, have
always represented a practical programme directed
towards a definite end.

It must be admitted that this Utopia of Lenin's, which
works with the ideas, " rationalism," " reality," and
" systematized industrial organization," is very skilfully
contrived, so that its fundamental error is not to be
discerned at the first glance. Lenin maintained that the
practical realization, and, thus, the justification of the
Marxist theory, consists precisely in the dialectical
adaptation of the theory to conditions of reality, in this
particular case to Russian conditions. From this he
inferred that Russia, in order to arrive at the ardently
desired " mechanistic world of proletarian dominion,"
need not imitate the course of evolution followed in the
West, but must go its own special way. The fallacy
which is concealed in this " logical argument," and the
exposure of which leads to the very opposite result from
that desired by Lenin, is now plain. For an acute
observer sees immediately that that statement of Marxism that the theory is only justified if it is adapted to
actual reality, leads to a result which is diametrically
opposed to that of the Bolsheviks; they should have
considered the undeniable fact that mechanization and
technification have been conditioned in the West by

historical necessities, but not in Russia, which, being centuries behindhand, must, in the true sense of the Marxist theory, first pass through an industrial and capitalistic phase of development before ultimately arriving, by way of accumulation of capital and State capitalism, at the dominion of the proletariat. Adjustment to actual conditions should consequently have led to a recognition that economic life must first show some primitive form of organization before a comprehensive rational industrial system can be thought of; agriculture, too, could only in the course of a long period of development gradually pass from the simplest methods of work to higher forms in order finally to reach ultimate freedom from all physical burdens with the complete mechanization of labour.

This " revolutionary jerk," this " leap " over centuries, betrays the romantic Utopian spirit of Bolshevism and makes of the organic products of Western civilization, so nicely adapted to their ends, fantastic and nonsensical alien bodies in a world which has remained essentially of the Middle Ages. It was from this violent grafting of two fundamentally different forms of culture on each other that there arose that entirely peculiar, extraordinary, and new phenomenon, the world of " romantic rationalism," of the " mechanical Utopia," that chain of inner contradictions which forms the least harmonious characteristic of Bolshevism in all its manifestations. The more the " rationalism " and the " Realpolitik " of the Bolsheviks are emphasized, the more clearly evident becomes the romantic core of the whole phantasmagoria. Lenin, the great Utopian, could, it is true, see necessity clearly, but he lacked all insight into reality, as represented by the actual conditions of the time. It is in this lack of any understanding of the realities of his own time that his romanticism lies; it is here that we must seek for a solution of the extraordinary riddle of Bolshevism, for the explanation how an attempt to re-shape the world by purely practical means, in a

way adapted to the end in view, could lead to results so
utterly opposed to all common sense, so grotesquely
abstruse.

XIX

Even Lenin's admirers and partisans, whose attitude
to him was otherwise almost uncritical, could not completely ignore this great deficiency in the character of
the reformer. Trotskiĭ's statements in his memoirs of
Lenin are particularly noteworthy on this point.
Trotskiĭ tells how, in Lenin's theses belonging to the
beginning of 1918, it is several times stated that *some
months were still required* before socialism could be put
into full effect in Russia. " These words," remarks
Trotskiĭ, " seem quite incomprehensible now. Has
there not been a slip of the pen? Did he not mean some
years or even decades? No, there is no slip of the pen;
other declarations of Lenin to the same effect may be
found. I remember quite clearly how, in the earliest
period, Lenin often repeated to the Council of People's
Commissars that we should have established socialism
in six months and be the mightiest country in the world.
The Left Social Revolutionaries, and not they alone,
raised their heads in astonishment and perplexity and
looked at each other in silence. It was a system of
suggestion: Lenin was teaching us all henceforward to
judge everything not from the point of view of the final
goal, but in the perspective of to-day and to-morrow.
He was using here, too, the method of sharp contrast
peculiar to himself: yesterday we were still speaking of
socialism as the ultimate goal, to-day we must think,
speak, and act as though it could be realized in a few
months. Was this then merely pedagogic tactics? No,
it was something more. To pedagogic pertinacity must

be added one thing, Lenin's strong idealism, his tautly braced will, which reduced the stages and compressed the course of time in this sharp change from one epoch to another. He believed what he said. This fantastically brief period of six months, in which he believed he could bring socialism into effect, is as characteristic of Lenin's mind as his realistic method of dealing with every worry of daily life. This deep and unshakable faith in the mighty possibilities of human development, for which any price in sacrifices and sufferings could and must be paid, was always the mainspring of Lenin's thought."

This violent romanticism, this incredibly bold attempt to realize at one blow the century-long dream of his country, is what made Lenin the leader of Russia; it is the real secret of his greatness. This man, too, is of that race of dreamers which alone up to now has given humanity its great pioneers. However soberly the new Gospel might preach of utilitarianism, of clean aprons, of turbo-generators and wind-motors, still it was a Gospel, an advancing epitome of a great national longing.

Wells, the English creator of technical Utopias, called Lenin the " dreamer of electrification," and thereby hit the nail on the head: his dream was for Lenin the starting-point of all his actions, even though the dream was a dream of technology.

When Lenin first proclaimed his teaching, the power of the Tsars seemed still unshakable. Socialism then existed only in debating and reading circles, and there was neither a true Russian proletariat nor its antipodes, a highly developed industry and a powerful capitalism. The left wing of the socialists, to which Lenin belonged, consisted of a few men who carried on the greatest part of their political activity from exile, from foreign countries or Siberian prisons. Lenin's own life alternated between Siberia and Switzerland. And yet he proclaimed the success of the social revolution and prophesied the rule of the communist proletariat in

Russia with the unshakable certainty of a dreamer. Everything which he undertook then and right up to his death was inspired by this somnambulistic certainty that in a short time the communist proletariat would have won to dominion.

The doctrines of modern socialism are in the main based on the theories of Karl Marx, the profound German scholar, on ideas for the understanding of which the deepest study of general scientific and economic problems is necessary. But the country in which the Russian, Lenin, set out to prove the correctness of this social and philosophic doctrine was Russia, in which an overwhelming majority of the population could neither read nor write, and was still largely at a cultural stage of the most primitive superstition. Only a dreamer could have embarked on the attempt to make comprehensible to this mass of men, who believed in the miraculous power of ikons, devils, and witches, a scientific theory for the understanding of which comprehensive many-sided technical knowledge and a strictly trained mind are necessary. In order to establish the chief preliminary conditions for permeating the whole population with the Marxist theories, one of Lenin's first cares as dictator was to make illiteracy a thing of the past in Russia. But here, too, he had no comprehension of the time necessary for this: within a few weeks a mighty organization was to be set up for the study of modern pedagogic methods, educational institutions were to be established, courses started, and propaganda trains with school books got ready. Very soon after the start of these feverish preparations, which were to lay the foundation for the Europeanization of Russia, Lenin was proclaiming with the " confidence of a clairvoyant " that by the tenth anniversary of the Soviet Republic in 1927 " illiteracy would be completely liquidated," and in the whole of Russia there would no longer be a single person unable to read or write.

Before the eyes of Lenin, the dreamer, even in the

earliest days of the Revolution, floated the vision of a Russia which was not only to reach the Western European level of culture and civilization, but even to surpass it. While civil war was still raging, and the Bolshevist sphere of influence was still confined to the district around Moscow, Lenin had before his eyes the electrification of the whole country down to the most remote villages. He had heard of the stupendous results achieved by the electrification of agriculture in Germany, France, and North America; besides, he saw in the lighting of the peasant villages one of the chief conditions for any cultural development. Therefore Lenin treated electrification as one of the most urgent tasks of Soviet Russia; as early as the disturbed times of the civil war, in the midst of the utmost revolutionary confusion, an electrification commission was appointed, and, ever since, this problem has been a standing item on the agenda of Soviet Congresses.

In the country of waste of time, of complete apathy, among men like those depicted with such extraordinary vividness in Goncharov's novel *Oblomov*, with the aid of a bureaucracy of truly Oriental laziness, Lenin decided to create a super-American system of labour organization in which not a grain of energy should be wasted. In Russia, among Russians, he desired to organize human labour in accordance with the latest scientific methods; he established an Institute for the Psychotechnical Investigation of Human Labour Power; he caused a " League " to be founded to utilize time down to the last second; each of his ideas, each of his attempts was a Utopia, a dream.

XX

He died without having lived to see his hopes and aims realized, and he left the country in a state of extraordinary confusion. The powerful influence, the mighty onset to form a new world were arrested half-way to the goal, and created a fantastic between-world which, by its divided nature, must certainly be numbered among the most peculiar cultural and social phenomena in history. A cross between Asiatic indolence and lethargy and extreme Americanism, between the muzhik and the mass man, now represents the new Russia; the country is now dominated by an apposition of bastard forms, chaotically jumbled together.

This lack of harmony is even more marked in the whole ideology of Bolshevism, as created by Lenin, than in external things. In spite of its indisputable magnificence, the whole conception of a new humanity which Lenin tried to realize and partly succeeded in realizing is vitiated by a profound inner conflict which penetrates right down to the roots.

Lenin's whole life is a proof that he honestly desired the liberation of humanity, that his work was the result of a profound sense of kinship with the dispossessed masses and a sincere endeavour and a serious, ardent longing to put an end to poverty and misery. But the means by which he tried to carry out this liberation were cursed by that mediaeval despotic spirit from which Lenin, even in his loftiest flights, could never quite free himself.

Even in the act of abandoning ourselves enthusiastic-ally to the wide perspectives revealed in so many of Lenin's words and deeds, we are always immediately conscious again of the stuffy atmosphere of a mouldering out-of-date mental attitude, in which freedom seems possible only through slavery and new rights only through loss of rights. In such moments we hear in

Lenin that world of Russo-Asiatic slave-mentality which seems to have vanished almost without leaving a trace from the whole moral development of Western Europe. Lenin, the prophet of a new free humanity, never quite succeeded in rising above this reactionary spirit of violence, hate, and suppression of all opinion opposed to his own.

From Lenin's own friends and disciples, we know that his whole mind had been inflamed with hate ever since the execution of his brother, to such an extent that during the last years of his exile abroad his bitterness made visible changes even in his features: " As soon as you met him," says Zinov'ev, " you could observe in Lenin a deep, unquenchable hate, which as it were shook a clenched fist in the face of the bourgeoisie. Even his face was changed in the course of time by this secret fury."

Hate was Lenin's element. Just as he knew no other means of dealing with political opponents but *écraser*, " crush them," so for him the hate-laden cry of the enemy was " the most beautiful music." In the most difficult moments of his fight for power he was fond of repeating the lines which he uttered on the eve of the October Revolution:

" Kind words are no praise for us,
The hate-laden cry of rage is our only delight."

According to Zinov'ev, these lines are thoroughly characteristic of Lenin, " the whole of Lenin is contained in them."

From the old empire of the Tsars he created what was in design the most modern State in the world, the Soviet Republic. But the machinery which moves, dominates, and preserves this State is the old despotic machinery of the past with its army and police, its prisons, executions, and sentences of banishment.

Lenin introduced a splendid new educational system to eliminate illiteracy, but inherent in this system from the very outset was the objectionable feature that it aimed merely at training a subordinate class of Soviet bureaucrats and half-educated agitators. Instruction was so designed that no one could ever exceed the allowance of knowledge and education officially permissible for the moment, so that the subjects of the proletarian state would never run the risk of being roused to reflexion by an improperly large stock of knowledge. While Lenin on the one hand fought against illiteracy, on the other he suppressed free science, banished from Russia countless scholars whose views seemed to him politically dangerous, and subjected all theoretical research to a strict " Marxist revision " which recalls the Inquisition.

Lenin was one of the first to introduce into Russia the modern economic theories of scientific socialism, the doctrines of Karl Marx and Friedrich Engels. But his interpretation of Marxism, in spite of his continual appeals to strictly scientific thought, cannot hide the school of which it is the product. Even as an adherent of historic materialism and as a statesman, Lenin still remains the true Russian terrorist of the Bakunin type. Even Zinov'ev, Lenin's reverential biographer, cannot deny the inner kinship of this modern Marxist with the old romantic terrorism: " Comrade Lenin by temperament belonged entirely to the first generation of terrorist revolutionaries, to that glorious host of warriors whose names still shine like glittering stars. . . ." Axelrod, too, who together with Plekhanov founded the Socialist labour movement in Russia in the 'eighties, used to call Lenin an " anarcho-terrorist." The Swiss social democrats also blamed him for corrupting the labour movement with his " Russian anarchism."

The appearance of Lenin at such a decisive moment in its political and intellectual development was certainly of the greatest historical importance for Russia herself. But it must not be overlooked that Lenin's importance remains confined chiefly to the Russian world.

Lenin himself was sometimes conscious of this entanglement in the old traditions of Russian terrorism. His cry " How can you carry out a revolution without executions? " was a manifestation of his incapacity to get free of the mental world of romantic anarchism, as was his complaint that it was " a hellishly hard task " to execute people, " ruthlessly to split skulls open," while the ultimate political ideal was, on the other hand, the fight against all violence. The fact that Lenin, even in his boldest dreams of a future class-less world without hate or oppression, could see no other way of attaining his end but naked brute force, is the most profoundly tragic thing in his peculiar destiny. If freedom had meant more to Lenin than " a bourgeois prejudice," he would be remembered in history not only as an extra-ordinarily resolute and successful revolutionary, but also as one of the greatest liberators of humanity.

A SELECTION FROM LENIN'S LETTERS FROM SIBERIA AND FROM EXILE

To Potresov.

Shushensk, Minusinsk District,
2nd September 1898.

I duly received your letter of 11th August together with the list of books and the *Journal of Social Legislation and Statistics*. The article of the " well known national economist," obviously Struve, seems to me extremely interesting and excellently worked out. The author had a rich store of material at his disposal; he seems to possess more talent for journalism than for economic writing. The *Journal* is an excellent paper, and I will certainly subscribe to it next year. I should be very glad to receive an English periodical, and should like to ask your advice about it, as I am not well informed as to which English papers are interesting. . . .

I press your hand,

Yours,

VLADIMIR UL'IANOV-LENIN.

Shushensk, 27th April 1899.

I was very glad to have your letter of 24th March, which at last broke your obstinate silence. I have a quantity of things to talk about in my mind, especially as there is no one here with whom I can discuss literary subjects at length. . . . There is only Martov in my immediate neighbourhood. He takes everything really to heart, but even with him I cannot talk very much, because here too this damned distance gets in our way.

I shall begin with the subject which is uppermost with me at the moment, Bulgakov's article and your review of it. I was uncommonly glad to find that you agree with me in principle; the editorial board obviously don't. This contribution of Bulgakov's, which repelled you, makes me positively furious. However often I read the article, I cannot understand how Bulgakov could have written such an absurd and discourteous article. I am also puzzled by the attitude of the editorial board in allowing such a violent attack on Kautsky, and merely trying to save themselves with the curt notice " We do not associate ourselves with the views of the author." Like you, I am convinced that the public will be bewildered if they are told in a work by an authority that Kautsky's views are entirely wrong. Kautsky is completely misrepresented in it. A man with party-political experience and conscious of his responsibility to all his comrades and their programme would never dare to take the field against a writer in this way. But Bulgakov seems not to feel any responsibility. . . .

I read Kautsky's work before Bulgakov's article appeared, and I maintain that Kautsky says the exact opposite of what Bulgakov ascribes to him. I sent my first contribution, *Capitalism in Agriculture*, to the editor a fortnight ago, and am now going to write a second on Bulgakov's article. I am afraid, however, that Struve will refuse it on the ground that it is too long. . . . Tell me your opinion, and whether you think Bulgakov's article can be left unanswered.

This new critical tendency in Marxism, as represented by Struve and Bulgakov, seems to be altogether highly suspicious, nothing but phrases and criticism of dogma without any definite results. I have also written a reply to Struve's contribution on *Markets*. The Elizarov sisters tell me that this reply is to appear in the *Scientific Review* and that Struve intends to publish a rejoinder.

Bulgakov's remarks against the catastrophic theory without any mention of Bernstein seem to me very singular. I have ordered Bernstein's new book, but am doubtful whether it will be sent to me. I have only read articles on the subject in the *Frankfurter Zeitung* and in *Zhizn'*. . . . I have come to the conclusion that I have misunderstood Bernstein's articles: he lies to an impossible extent and must therefore be buried, as the author of the *Contributions to the History of Materialism* expresses it in his open letter to Kautsky. . . .

I press your hand. Write often if you are not too lazy. Who else can I get news from?

With very kindest regards, .

Yours,

VLADIMIR LENIN.

To Plekhanov.

London, 28th July 1902.

MY DEAR GEORGIĬ VALENTINOVICH,

I am sending you a hundred marks for travelling expenses, and should be glad to know whether you intend to stay here for two or three months or whether you only want to make a short trip. At the time you are coming to London, many of our comrades from Russia will be there.

Your last letter to me was addressed to France, which I had already left. I have, therefore, not yet received this communication. I press your hand warmly and am looking forward greatly to seeing you again soon.

Yours,

VLADIMIR LENIN.

London, 8th August, 1902.

MY DEAR GEORGIĬ VALENTINOVICH,

Yesterday we had a visit from Comrade Vladimir Krasnokha, a member of the Petersburg Association for the Emancipation of the Working Classes, whom we had been expecting for a long time. He also knows that old friend who handed over the money to you. Above all tell this old friend Lepeshinskiĭ that he should come to London, as we need him urgently for the general discussion. Our mutual friend will be here only for a week or a fortnight. . . .

K

I give you another point to consider. Almost all the Russian labour leaders are stationed in Switzerland, at Montreux. Our guest, provided with recommendations from our Russian friends, is also going there. I think it would be better if he made your acquaintance first and if you spoke to him in Geneva before he meets the Russian friends at Montreux.

Consult the old friend about the matter and decide where you wish to see the stranger and let me know quickly. . . . Are you sure that your address is quite safe and that my letters cannot fall into the hands of un-authorized persons?

I press your hand warmly.

Yours,

VLADIMIR LENIN.

To Axelrod.

London, 19th August 1902.

MY DEAR PAVEL BORISOVICH,

I have just learned by telegram that Columbus has paid you a visit. A thousand greetings to our old friend! I enclose a letter for him. He will surely rest a little first and then come to us with Noskov.

Plekhanov writes that you must go to Munich to the Congress of the German Social Democratic Party. I quite agree, and I do not think that the others will have any objection, although I have not yet spoken to them. Write at once and tell me if you need money for the journey. I do not know where we shall get it, as we have only about a hundred roubles left in the cash box, but we will find it somehow. I will send Plekhanov's message to Leo Deutsch. How is your health? Did you have a long enough holiday in summer?

With kindest regards,

Yours,

VLADIMIR LENIN.

To Plekhanov.

London, 19th December 1902.

MY DEAR GEORGII VALENTINOVICH,

I have received your letter and hasten to reply to it. You are working at a pamphlet then? I am very glad of that. We could publish some articles in *Iskra*. It would be desirable if a number could appear next week, so that we could reply to the attacks of the social revolutionaries in good time.

I cannot judge whether a journey to Brussels is necessary. We have money now, as five thousand francs have come from America, and thus, if necessary, we could finance the journey. Koltsov could represent you temporarily, but not permanently, as decisive steps will have to be taken eventually.

In Petersburg our workers and also some representatives of the intelligentsia have been arrested. Lepeshinskiĭ is confined in the fortress and threatened with Siberia. I expect fresh news from the committee of organization soon.

With kindest regards,

Yours,

VLADIMIR LENIN.

London, 10th January 1903.

DEAR GEORGII VALENTINOVICH,

Please give the enclosed letter to Mrs. Lubov Axelrod. It is very urgent and important, so I beg you to send it to her immediately after you have read it yourself, in case you are not likely to be seeing her. If the people from Rostov come to Geneva, please tell them to hurry. How is it with *Zhizn'*? . . . With regard to money and printing, we must have further details. I should also like to ask your advice about my lectures at the High School in Paris. I have been invited to speak there, but the company of Chernov, Filipov, and Turganov is not to my taste. On the other hand, our

people in Paris write telling me I should give the lectures as it is very important. What do you think?
Yours,
VLADIMIR LENIN.

London, 28th January 1903.

MY DEAR GEORGIĬ VALENTINOVICH,
I am sending you an article of Trotskiĭ's and a statement from the committee of organization. Will you please return both as quickly as possible. The statement of the committee of organization must be preserved as a very important document. We must come to a decision about Trotskiĭ's article, as we have already a quantity of articles against the social revolutionaries in store; we must consider whether we are not overdoing it. We shall, of course, have to use Trotskiĭ's article, for this brief work is a reasonable answer to a stupid attack. On the other hand I should like to put Potresov's article aside, as it is no answer. Please consider matters and let me know your decision.
With kindest regards,
VLADIMIR LENIN.

London, 5th February 1903.

DEAR GEORGIĬ VALENTINOVICH,
I have received your article and letter. I cannot yet say which number the article will be published in. I am very glad that you are working at an article on the alleged friends of the proletariat. The reports that it is no longer possible to transport *Iskra* through Austria are founded on an error. So far everything is going splendidly and the consignments are being smuggled through Austria by three ways. . . . I press your hand warmly.
Yours,
LENIN.

Paris, 2nd March 1903.

I am proposing to all the members of the editorial board that Trotskiï be accepted as a member with full rights. I do not think that a majority is enough for co-option; a unanimous decision is desirable. We urgently need a seventh member, if only for voting, as six is an even number.

Trotski has written a contribution for almost every number of *Iskra* for some months past. In addition, he reads papers and has great success with his audience. We need him urgently for articles and notices on problems of the day.

Trotskiï is without doubt a man with exceptional qualities, of firm and vigorous character, who will certainly make his way. As a translator and popular writer he could also be of great use. We must attract young workers, encourage them and in this way spur them on to greater zeal. You yourself know how much we suffer from a lack of people of this kind. Only remember how difficult it has been to find a contributor for translation work. We also lack popular literature, for which Trotskiï would also be very suitable.

Of course there are also reasons against him, his youth, the possibility of his returning to Russia soon, and his sensational style.

But Trotskiï would not be put in an independent position, but merely work as a member of the board. There he will acquire the necessary experience and the party instinct. There is no doubt he has considerable knowledge at his disposal, and experience will come with time. It is certain that he can work when he likes. It is necessary to co-opt him in order to ally him strongly to the editorial board.

If we accept him as a member with full rights, he will certainly not leave Paris so soon; but even if he goes away, his connection with us as an organizer will be no drawback, but a pure gain.

The defects in Trotskiï's style are not important;

they can soon be altered. For the moment he takes all corrections in his work quietly if not with pleasure. I, therefore, suggest that all six members of the board should vote on co-opting Trotskiĭ. I would regard any postponement of the decision as inconvenient and annoying, for I know that Trotskiĭ is discontented in any case and thinks that we do not take him seriously because of his youth.

But if we do not accept him on the board, he will take it as a personal unfriendliness and will return to Russia. That would annoy me very much.

LENIN.

London, 15th March 1903.

I have received your letter. Your paper, *The March Ideas*, is splendid, but the article must be in my hands by 25th March at latest. We are already impatient for it. I am now writing a popular pamphlet entitled " *To the Peasant Proletariat*," which is specially intended for the peasantry. In it I try to explain the nature of the class war in the rural districts and to give concrete details of the four classes of the village population. What do you think of this plan? In Paris I became convinced that such a pamphlet might dispel certain of the suspicions of the peasants. . . .

I press your hand warmly. Yours, LENIN.

London, 10th April 1903.

I have been ill these days and could not answer your letter before. The stranger has gone. I do not know whether he will succeed in arranging the affair. Why do you not write about my pamphlet? Please have the work set up at once, as it is important to bring it out soon. We can then leave the proofs to those who take an interest in such things.

I press your hand warmly. LENIN.

To Noskov.

London, 4th August 1902.

DEAR BORIS NIKOLAEVICH,

You complain about our agent, a sore subject with me also. You declare that we set about the choice of agents much too lightly; I am well aware of this myself, but that is just the tragedy of our situation. We are not in a position to overcome certain hindrances in our work. . . . Take a hand yourself in the work of discovering suitable agents! Is there a sufficient number of people in Russia prepared to come to our assistance? I know that such people do exist and that the number is increasing. But it all goes on so slowly and with so many interruptions that one begins to be nervous. Believe me, I have lost all confidence in our assumptions, our avenues of approach, and our plans, and I am afraid it will all lead to nothing. We must supervise all these agents in their work and be continually on the watch to see that our ideas are circulated in Russia. It is our misfortune that we have much too small a number of capable organizers at our disposal.

It is as we write in our books: there is a mass of men, but no men. We must find a way out as soon as possible, for time presses and the number of our enemies is increasing.

With regard to your journey to London, you will have to go to Zürich first. What is making you feel ill? Would it not be a good thing if you got out of harness for a bit? What do you think of the Marxist writer, Sanin? Various people have told me about him, but it does seem to me that he is no worker; he is much too unruly!

I clasp your hand.

Yours,

VLADIMIR LENIN.

To Plekhanov.

London, 14th December 1902.

DEAR GEORGIĬ VALENTINOVICH,

It is long since I had any news of you. . . . We must again publish more frequently sharp attacks on the Petersburg Committee, the Moscow Committee, and many other people. The friendly committees should bind themselves to send detailed reports on local movements once a month.

We organized a successful evening here on Saturday last. The proceeds are not yet known exactly, but they will probably amount to from three hundred and fifty to five hundred francs. That represents a great success, for the socialists and the Federation boycotted us. Have the thousand francs from America arrived? As for the incident of the embezzlement of the money, that is a great shame and scándal! In what town did the donor pay in the amount? Does he know the person to whom he gave the money?

With kind regards,

Yours,

LENIN.

London, 19th December 1902.

MY DEAR GEORGIĬ VALENTINOVICH,

If you have decided to go to Brussels to take part in the Conference, please write at once and telegraph about the money. Levenson, the manager of the printing works where *Iskra* is produced, threatens to withdraw, as he is embroiled with Lalaiants, who has now been appointed director. I asked Lalaiants in a letter to arrange the matter, but will you also help me to appease Levenson and hint to Lalaiants that he should treat him more carefully. I am sending the first part of Kautsky's pamphlet to the printers, as well as a popular article on the life of the soldiers. The matter of transport to Russia is in a bad way. It is a real misfortune.

With kindest regards,
                              Yours,
                                        LENIN.

To Maxim Gor'kiĭ.

                              Geneva, 9th January 1908.

DEAR A.M.,

I arrived here with my wife a few days ago. We both caught cold on the journey. We are settling in here as best we can, but as at present it is supposed to be going to be only a short stay, it is not very comfortable. Your letter gave me great pleasure. It would be fine to come to Capri. I will certainly get free sometime and visit you then; for the moment it is unfortunately impossible. We have come here with a commission to found a newspaper, to move the *Proletarian* from Finland; it is not yet finally decided whether we shall fix on Geneva or some other town. Haste is necessary in any case, for the new arrangement will involve a lot of work. But if only it could be possible to visit you in spring or summer when the enterprise is well on its way. When is the weather quite particularly nice at Capri?

How is your health? How do you feel? Are you working easily? When I was passing through Berlin someone told me that you and Lunacharskiĭ had made a tour through Italy, devoting special attention to Rome. Did you like Italy and did you meet many Russians?

I believe it will be best if I visit you when you are not busy on important work, so that we can go walks and talk together.

.Have you received my book, the first volume containing my collected articles of twelve years? I had it sent to you from Petersburg.

Kindest regards to M. Fëdorovna. Au revoir.
                              Yours,
                                        N. LENIN.

My address is: M. Vl. Ul'ianov, c/o Küpfer, 17, Rue des Deux Ponts, Geneva.

                                    15th January 1908.

DEAR A.M.,
        I have just received your express letter. It would be deuced fine if I could come to you at Capri. You paint everything so gloriously that, by God, I feel that I must set out; I will also try to dig out my wife. It is only the time I am still not sure of. For the moment I must devote myself entirely to the *Proletarian*, put it firmly on its feet and get the work going at any cost. That will require a month or two at least, but it is absolutely necessary. Then in spring we will come to you to drink the white wine of Capri, see Naples, and talk with you. . . .
        M. Fëdorovna has a whole lot of commissions from me to-day:
        1. She absolutely must visit the Secretary of the Union of Seafaring Officials and Workers (there must be such a union!) about the ships which maintain connections with Russia.
        2. She must ask him from where the steamers go, where they go to, and how often. The man absolutely must find us a weekly transport. How much will it cost? He must also give us the name of a trustworthy person (are there trustworthy Italians?). Do you want an address in Russia (say in Odessa) to which you can deliver the paper, or is it possible for you to deposit small quantities provisionally with some Italian host in Odessa? That would be very important for us.
        If M.F. is unable to undertake all this herself, to find it all out, explain, and supervise it, she should put me into direct communication with this secretary, and we will then apply to him by letter.
        The whole matter is urgent. We hope to be able to

bring the *Proletarian* out here in two or three weeks, and we must see that it is despatched immediately.

Now, au revoir at Capri. Only keep well for us, A.M.!

Yours,

V. Ul'ianov.

13th February 1908.

Dear A.M.,

I really think that many of our differences of opinion are nothing but a misunderstanding. Of course I never thought of " driving out the intelligentsia," as the stupid syndicalists do, or of denying its importance for the proletarian movement. There can be no difference of opinion between us on these problems. That is my firm conviction, and since it is not possible for us to meet at present, we must make a beginning immediately with the joint work. Work will bring us most easily and surely to complete agreement.

I wanted to answer you last time about Trotskiĭ, but I forgot. We decided from the beginning to ask him to co-operate in the *Proletarian*, and wrote him a letter to that effect; in accordance with a common agreement we drew up the letter as the " editorial board of the *Proletarian*," because we wanted to give the whole business an official colour. (I personally carried on a violent fight against Trotskiĭ; at the time when he was a Menshevik, we were at daggers drawn.) I do not know whether Trotskiĭ took offence at this form; in any case he sent us a reply not written in his own hand, in which the editorial board is informed " on behalf of Comrade Trotskiĭ," that he is obliged to refuse his co-operation on account of pressure of work.

In my opinion this is a pose. He behaved like a *poseur* at the London Party Conference also. I am not sure whether he will go with the Bolsheviks.

With a hand clasp,

Lenin.

16th March 1908.

DEAR A.M.,

How tiresome that my journey to you has fallen through! I have received an answer from Brussels, and there would be no obstacle in the way here, but I have neither money nor time and I cannot leave the paper in the lurch.

From the fact that you have provided yourself with a goat I conclude that your spirits are good, your mental constitution sound, and your life normal. With us things are somewhat out of tune. I am rather annoyed with A. Al.[1] I am neglecting the paper on account of my passion for philosophy. To-day I am studying an empirio-criticist, and am swearing like a trooper. To-morrow I shall read another and curse like a bargee. And Innokentiĭ rightly blames me for neglecting the *Proletarian*. Things will not go right.

Well, it can't be otherwise. Time brings counsel!

It would be splendid if you could write for the *Proletarian* without interrupting your great work.

I press your hand and beg you to give my kindest regards to A.V. [Lunacharskiĭ] and M.F.

LENIN.

16th April 1908.

DEAR A.M.,

I received your letter to-day and make haste to answer it. It would be useless, even harmful, for me to come. I cannot and will not deal with people whose aim is to advocate a union of scientific socialism with religion. The time for " pamphlets " is past. It is absurd to dispute and useless to wear down one's nerves. Philosophy must be kept separate from party affairs. The decision of the B.Z. also makes this incumbent on us.

I have already sent an extremely formal declaration

[1] Bogdanov. Note by Kamenev.

of war to the printers. Diplomacy is no longer appropriate here—of course I am talking of diplomacy in the good, not the bad, sense.

" Good " diplomacy on your side, dear A.M. (if you also have not been converted to God) must consist in keeping our joint affairs apart from philosophy.

Conversation on subjects other than philosophy would for the moment lead to nothing and be unnatural. But if these other matters have really nothing to do with philosophy, if thus the *Proletarian* were to ask for an interview with you now, then I might come (I do not know where I am to get the money, there are difficulties there now), but I repeat, only on condition that I need not talk either philosophy or religion.

I will come to you without any conditions as soon as I have leisure and my work is done, so that I may have a talk with you.

I press your hand warmly,

Yours,

L.

My kindest regards to M. F-na. She is not championing God?

19th April 1908.

DEAR A.M.,

I have received your telegram and am sending you my refusal to-day or early to-morrow. I repeat once more that it is in no case permissible to mix up literary controversies about philosophy with the cause of the Party (and thus of the section). I have already written to this effect to Anatol Vasilevich, and I repeat it for the benefit of all the comrades in order to avoid all misconceptions and wrong conclusions to which my refusal to visit you might be liable. It is our duty to work together as before for the cause of our section; our policy during the revolutionary period proved the right one for each of us, and we are, therefore, bound to defend it with the Party and to carry it out. We can only do that if we are all united both in the *Proletarian* and in other Party work.

If A wants to attack B or B A on account of his philosophical views, that must be done separately, that is, without harm to the cause.

I earnestly beg you and the other comrades not to put a wrong interpretation on my refusal to come to you. I ask your forgiveness, but it is not possible for me to get away in view of the whole position of things and the state of the editorial work.

I send all a warm handclasp.

Yours,

LENIN.

We are expecting the promised article on the strike in Rome from Anatol Vasilevich as soon as possible.

We expect support for the *Proletarian* from all the writers. We have all to bear the responsibility towards any Russian who is dissatisfied with the paper.

A. Al. should look about for money with all his might. The people in Russia are howling about the lack of money.

3rd January 1911.

DEAR A.M.,

I have been intending to answer your letter for a long time, but the exacerbation of the dissension here (a hundred thousand devils take it!) has always prevented me.

And I would so like to talk with you. . . . With regard to Tolstoï, I entirely agree with you that the hypocrites and scoundrels will make a saint of him. Plekhanov, too, is furious about the fraud and angry about this toadying to Tolstoï. On this point we are at one. . . .

It is certainly very regrettable that they are beginning to beat the students; but with Tolstoï neither " passivism " nor anarchism, neither *Narodnichestvo* nor religion can be allowed to pass. . . . In Germany there is a perfect model of an opportunist periodical, the *Sozialistische Monatsheft*. In it gentlemen like Schippel and Bernstein have for long been shrieking about the international policy of revolutionary social democracy and declaring that this policy is leading to " distress among sympathetic people." That is a dodge of opportunist rascals, my friend. Order this periodical from Naples and get someone to translate the articles for you if you are interested in international politics. You are certain to have opportunists of this kind in Italy—it is only Marxists that are lacking in Italy, which is that country's misfortune. . . .

I was shocked when I read your final remark: " My hands are shaking with cold." Those miserable houses at Capri! But that is terrible. We have actually steam heating which warms the house very well, while " your hands are freezing." You shouldn't submit to it.

With a warm handclasp.

Yours,

LENIN.

I have received an invitation to Bologna to visit the school there (twenty workers). I have refused because I don't want to have anything to do with these " progressives." We will bring the workers back to our side.

Cracow, 1st August 1912.
Cracow, Austria, Zwierzyniec, 218.

Vl. Ul'ianov.

DEAR A.M.,

I have received your letter and also that of the Siberians. My address is no longer Paris as you can see from the above.

I am not quite clear what party you want to drive me out of, not the social revolutionary?

No. Joking apart, you have got into a bad habit, a middle class and bourgeois way of dismissing people with: " You are all fighting cocks. . . ."

The bourgeoisie, the liberals, and the social revolutionaries, who never deal with " great problems " seriously, but trot one behind the other, make pacts, and go on in the old grooves with eclecticism, are always crying out about the dissensions and discords in social democracy. That is the exact difference between all of them and social democracy: the fight between the individual social democratic groups comes from deep roots of thought, whereas with them even the differences are varnished over on the surface, while inside they are empty, petty, and superficial. Never at any price would I exchange the vigorous fighting of the various tendencies in social democracy for the togged-up emptiness and poverty of the social revolutionaries and their partners.

With a warm handclasp,

Yours,

LENIN.

P.S.—Greetings to M.F.

P.S.—In Russia an exalted revolutionary mood prevails, nothing short of a downright revolutionary mood. For we have at last succeeded in establishing a daily newspaper, *Pravda*, which is due not least to the conference (in January), which the idiots barked at so loudly.

Undated.

DEAR A.M.,

. . . There is a ferment in the Baltic Squadron! A special delegate sent by the Sailors' Assembly visited me in Paris (this is confidential). There is no organization—it's enough to make one weep! If you have any connections in officers' circles, you must do all you can to accomplish something. The mood of the sailors is bellicose, but perhaps they will all perish again. . . .

You want to know why I am staying in Austria. The C.C. has established an office here (this is confidential). We are taking advantage of the neighbourhood of the frontier. Petersburg is not so far away, we receive the Petersburg papers three days after publication. It is also much easier to send contributions to the Russian papers from here, so that co-operation is going better. There are fewer controversies here, that's on the plus side, but there are no good libraries, which is on the minus side, for it is difficult to work without books.

With a warm handclasp.

Yours,

LENIN.

Greetings to M.F.

Undated.

DEAR A.M.,

I received a communication to-day from the editors of *Pravda* asking me to inform you how very glad they would be to have your permanent co-operation: "We would offer Gor'kiĭ twenty-five kopeks a line, but are afraid he would think it an insult."

In my opinion there is nothing whatever insulting about such an offer. No one could think that your co-operation is influenced in any way by monetary considerations. It is also well known that *Pravda*, a labour paper, which usually pays two kopeks a line, or more often nothing at all, is not in a position to offer tempting rates.

But there is no harm in the contributors to a proletarian paper receiving regular payments, even if they are modest ones. The circulation now amounts to from twenty to twenty-five thousand copies, and it is time to be thinking of regular business with paid contributions. What harm could it do if gradually all the people who write for labour papers were to earn some money?

What then can there be to take offence at in this offer?

I am sure that the fears of the Petersburg editors are unfounded and that you will take this proposal in a comradely spirit. Perhaps you will write a few lines either to the editor direct or to me. . . .

I press your hand warmly and wish you good health above everything. Kindest regards to M.F.

Yours,
LENIN.

Undated.

DEAR A.M.,

It is long since I have had any news of you. What are you doing? Are you well?

To-day I received No. 187 of *Pravda* with the subscription form for 1913. The paper is in difficulties. The circulation dropped considerably in the summer, and is picking up again only very slowly, so that there is a deficit. Meanwhile even the payments to two regular contributors must be suspended since the position is extremely serious.

We intend to carry on increased propaganda among the workers in order to secure subscriptions. We want to raise money in this way to improve the position of the paper and build it up. Otherwise there would be no more room left for articles after the sessions of the Duma start.

I hope that you will also take a share in the propaganda work for gaining subscribers in order to improve the circulation again. But how? If you had a fairy tale or something else suitable, an advertisement about this would have a good propagandist effect. If you haven't, will you please at least promise me by letter that you will send in some manuscript in the near future, in 1913. Finally, a few lines of a letter from you to the workers, pointing out the importance of active help (subscriptions, propaganda, meetings) for the labour movement would have an excellent influence.

Whatever you decide on, please write either direct to the editor of *Pravda* (Ianskaia 2, St. Petersburg) or to me here (Ul'ianov, 47, Lubomirskiego, Cracow).

It will probably not come to war. We remain here temporarily in order to " turn to advantage " the mad hate of the Poles for Tsardom. . . .

We are fighting " against the stream." If you represent revolutionary agitation among the masses, you have now to fight against a large number of " also-revolutionaries." . . . Among the mass of the working classes there is undoubtedly a revolutionary atmosphere, but the new democratic intelligentsia (including the labour intelligentsia) with revolutionary ideology increases but slowly, remains backward, and cannot join us for the moment

Kindest regards.

Let me have a few lines.

Yours,

LENIN.

P.S.—Greetings to M.F. I never hear from her now.

Undated.

DEAR A.M.,

Dear friend, what are you up to? You are suffering from overwork, over-fatigue, and neuralgia. That is a fine state of affairs! You should be able to lead a regular life at Capri, especially in winter when the stream of visitors must have slackened. Have you let yourself come to this because no one is looking after you? Really and truly, this is very wrong. Pull yourself together and observe an exact regime—I really mean it! It is absolutely unallowable to want to be ill these days. Have you embarked on night work? When I was at Capri, they were always saying that it was I who brought disorder with me, and that before my arrival you went to bed betimes. You absolutely must try to recover and begin a strict way of living.

As to the doctrine of the material and its structure, I entirely agree with you that we must write on the subject, and that this would be a good remedy for the poison " which the inchoate Russian soul absorbs." But you are wrong in calling this poison metaphysics. It should rather be called idealism and agnosticism.

For the Machists actually call materialism metaphysics. At the moment a crowd of distinguished modern physicists are actually at work and in the act, in connection with the "miracles" of radium, the electrons, and the like, of trying to smuggle in the good God everywhere both in his crassest as well as in his most subtle form, in the guise of philosophic idealism.

As for Piatnitskiĭ, I am for going to the courts. There is no sense in making difficulties here. All sentimentality would be inexcusable. The Socialists are by no means opposed to appeal to the courts. We are for the utilization of legal forms. Marx and Bebel appealed to the courts against their enemies in the socialist camp. One must know what is to be done, but must do it in any case. Piatnitskiĭ must be condemned without more ado. If anyone reproaches you about it, spit quietly in his face. Only hypocrites could attack you on this account. It would be quite unpardonable if, out of fear of the courts, we were to give in to Piatnitskiĭ and let him go unpunished.

Well, I have chattered a lot to-day. Write and tell me about your health. Yours,

LENIN.

25th July 1913.

DEAR A.M.,
I have made up my mind to write you again and again, but have had to put it off from day to day on

account of my wife's pending operation. This finally took place the day before yesterday and the patient is already improving. The operation proved rather difficult, and I am very glad we were able to get Kocher to do it.

Now to business. You write that you will be in Berlin in August. What part of August, the beginning or the end of the month? We intend to leave here on 4th August. We have tickets by Zürich, Munich, and Vienna and shall stop in all these towns. (It may be that the Doctor will not let us start on the 4th, in that case we shall postpone it.)

Can we not see you somewhere. It would be on your way to come by Berne, Zürich, or Munich? . . .

I press your hand warmly and wish you the best of everything, especially good health on your journey. Please answer at once.

Yours,

LENIN.

Address Herrn Ul'ianov, 4, Gesellschaftsstrasse, 4 (Svizzera), Bern.

30th September 1913.

DEAR A.M.,

. . . What you tell me about your illness makes me very uneasy. Are you doing right to remain at Capri without any medical treatment. There are excellent sanatoria in Germany (at St. Blasien, for example, close to Switzerland) where affections of the lungs are completely cured. They get complete cicatrizations by fattening up the patients and then accustoming them systematically to cold. They harden them and send them off vigorous and capable of work.

But you want to travel from Capri to Russia in winter. I have grave misgivings that this may injure your health and lessen your powers of work. Are there good doctors in Italy? Do please come to a doctor of the first rank in Switzerland (I can procure names and addresses) or in Germany. Devote yourself vigorously for two months to treatment in a good sanatorium. It is inadmissible to be ill, to endanger your powers of work and waste State property uselessly. . . .

Write and tell me of your plans and how your health is. I earnestly beg you to take your cure seriously in hand. Really and truly it is quite possible that you can be quite healthy again, and it would be wicked and criminal to neglect your illness.

Yours,

LENIN.

Undated.

DEAR ALEXEÏ MAXIMOVICH,

. . . The news that you are allowing yourself to be treated on new lines by " a Bolshevik," even if it is only an ex-Bolshevik, makes me profoundly uneasy. Heaven protect us from " comrades " in general as doctors, but Bolshevik doctors! Truly in ninety-nine cases out of a hundred, comrades are perfect " asses " as doctors, as a good medical man once said to me. I assure you, trifling apart, that we should always have ourselves treated by authorities of the first rank. To let a Bolshevik try experiments on you is appalling. The only other thing is supervision by Naples professors . . . if these professors are really capable. . . . One thing I urge on you. If you travel in winter, then at least make a trip to the distinguished doctors of Switzerland and Vienna. It would be unpardonable to neglect to do so. How are you now?

Yours,

N. LENIN.

Undated.

DEAR A.M.,

What are you really up to? It is simply terrible!
Yesterday I read in the *Rech'* your answer to the outcry
about Dostoevskiĭ and had begun to rejoice. But to-day
in the *Liquidator* I light upon a paragraph in your article
which was omitted in the *Rech'*. This paragraph reads:

" ' God-seeking ' must be deferred for a time (only
for a time?)—it is a useless occupation. There is no
sense in seeking for what does not exist. He who does
not reap, does not sow either. You have no God, you
have not yet (not yet!) created him. The world does
not seek gods—it creates them; we do not think out
life, we make it."

It appears from this that you are opposed to " God-
seeking " only " for a time." That you are only opposed
to God-seeking because you aim at replacing it by God-
creating.

Is it not horrible to think what you will come to in
this way?

God-seeking differs from God-creating or God-
making and other things of the kind, much as a yellow
devil differs from a blue. It is a hundred times worse
to preach against God-seeking, not in order to condemn
all devils and gods whatever (that ideological plague, as
any faith in God, however pure, ideal, and spontaneous,
must be regarded), but in order to give to a blue devil
preference over a yellow—that is a hundred times
worse than to say nothing at all on the subject. This
applies in the same way to all kinds of gods, to the
purest and most ideal and to the " created " as much as
to the " sought."

In the freest countries where an appeal " to democracy,
to the population, to public opinion and science "
would be quite useless, in such countries (America,
Switzerland, and the like) the people and the workers
are stupefied with the idea of a pure, spiritual Godhead,
which had originally to be created. Just because every

religious idea, every idea of any God, nay, all coquetting
with such thoughts, is an unutterable baseness, it is gladly
suffered, often welcomed even, by the democratic
bourgeoisie, merely because it is the most dangerous
baseness, the most vile infection. Millions of sins,
obscenities, crimes of violence, and infections of a
physical kind are easily unmasked by the masses; they
are, therefore, much less dangerous than the subtle
spiritualized idea of God, dressed up to the nines in
ideological costume. A Catholic parson who rapes girls
(I happened to read of one lately in a German paper) is
much less a danger to democracy than a parson without
priestly garments, without crude religion, an ideal and
democratic parson, who preaches the creation of a new
God. For it is easy to unmask the first parson, easy to
condemn and reject him. But the other is not so easily
disposed of, it is a thousand times more difficult to get
rid of him, and no feeble vacillating *petit bourgeois* will
want to sentence him.

And you, you who know the feebleness and weak
vacillation of the *petit bourgeois* soul, lead it astray with a
poison which is as sweet as sugar-candy and decked out
in all sorts of gay fopperies.

It is truly sickening.

Enough of that " self-reviling which with us takes
the place of self-criticism."

And God-creation, is not this the worst form of self-
reviling? Every man who occupies himself with the
construction of a God, or merely even agrees to it,
prostitutes himself in the worst way, for he occupies
himself not with activity, but with self-contemplation
and self-reflection, and tries thereby to deify his most
unclean, most stupid, and most servile features or
pettinesses.

From the social and not the personal point of view,
all God-creating is nothing but the tender self-contemplation of the dull *petite bourgeoisie*, the feeble
Philistine, the dreamy, self-reviling, doubting, and tired

bourgeois (as you were so kind as to say quite justly of
the soul—but you should have spoken not only of the
Russian soul but of the *petit bourgeois* soul in general,
for the Jewish, Italian, or English soul is no better—
they are all of the devil, equally vile; the *petite bourgeoisie* is base throughout; but this democratic philistin-
ism, which concerns itself with ideological contagion, is
trebly base).

I am reading your article again and trying hard to
understand how you could fall into this error, but I
remain bewildered. What does it mean?

Is this the remnant, an echo, of your " Confessions,"
which you yourself no longer approve?

Why make democratic mystifications for the reader
instead of distinguishing the *petit bourgeois* sharply from
the proletarian? The one, feeble, vacillating, tired,
despairing, self-contemplating, God-contemplating, God-
creating, self-reviling, feebly anarchist (a grand word!
and so on and so on)—the other full of ability, not only
brave in words, able to distinguish the " science and
publicity " of the bourgeoisie from their own, bourgeois
democracy from proletarian democracy.

Why do you do it?

A thing like that hurts a man devilishly.

Yours,
V. UL'IANOV.

To Smilga.

Viborg, 27th September 1917.

DEAR COMRADE SMILGA,

I take the opportunity of having a long talk with
you:

1. The general political situation makes me uneasy.
The Bolsheviks have declared war on the Government,
but the army is in the hands of the Government, which
is preparing systematically for conflict. What are we
doing meanwhile? Passing resolutions and holding

congresses, that is, wasting our time. The Bolshevik party at the present time is doing no decisive work to prepare the military forces for the overthrow of Kerenskiĭ.

Recent events only confirm my idea that we must equip ourselves for an armed rising; the political problem has now become a military one. I am afraid that the Bolsheviks are forgetting that and are lulled by the hope that a wave will sweep Kerenskiĭ away. This hope is very naïve, for we cannot reckon on chances. In my opinion it would be a crime if the proletariat, instead of preparing for an armed rising, were to set their hopes on a lucky dispensation of providence. Perhaps you could have typed copies made of this letter and pass them on to the comrades in Moscow and Petersburg.

2. Now for your own part. The only section of the military which is firmly in our hands is the Finnish regiments and the Baltic Squadron. You must use your high position, hand over less important work to your secretaries, and devote yourself entirely without loss of time to the military preparation of the Finnish regiments and the Baltic Squadron. We must assemble the most trustworthy soldiers in a secret committee, discuss everything with them in detail, supervise the whole movement ourselves, and collect exact reports about the strength of the troops in the neighbourhood of Petersburg, in the city itself, about the possibilities of transporting the Finnish regiments to Petersburg and also about the manœuvres of the Fleet.

We would be in a queer position if, in spite of all our resolutions and soviets, we were without military power. It is possible for you to assemble trustworthy and experienced soldiers, to visit Fort Ino on the Finnish border, and make an exact survey of the strategic position. We dare not in any circumstances accede to the desire of the Government and permit a transference of the revolutionary troops from Finland. It would be far better if we could use these regiments for the rising, and then, when we have seized power, bring the Soviet regime into being. As I read the newspaper reports, the danger of a German attack on Finland is practically nil, for the Germans have no longer enough coal to carry out a great naval action and set their transports in motion.

3. The Finnish Government must develop systematic propaganda among the Cossacks stationed in the country. Kerenskiï has had part of the Cossacks moved from Viborg and stationed in localities between Viborg and Terioki to isolate them from the Bolsheviks. It is urgently necessary that propaganda-sections should be formed from the best sailors and soldiers in Finland and sent to the Cossacks.

4. We must use for purposes of agitation the soldiers and sailors who are travelling to their villages on leave. They should evolve a regular system of propaganda in the rural districts. Your personal position is at the moment very favourable. You will be able to co-operate with the left social revolutionaries. This *bloc* will provide us with power in Russia and a majority in the Constituent assembly. Proceed at once to create this *bloc*, organize the preparation of revolutionary appeals, form agitation groups each consisting of two persons, a Bolshevik and a Social Revolutionary, and send them out to the villages. The social revolutionaries enjoy considerable prestige there, and it is, therefore, very lucky that with their help you can revolutionize the peasants.

5. In my opinion the battle-cry should now be " Power must at once pass into the hands of the Petrograd Soviet." The Petersburg Soviet will then hand the power over to the general Soviet Congress. Why should we lose three weeks and wait till Kornilov and Kerenskiï have made preparations for war? Finland can only gain advantage from the spreading of this battle-cry.

6. Once you gain mastery over Finland, a further important task devolves on you. You must organize the smuggling of revolutionary literature from Sweden, without which all talk of the International remains an empty phrase. It would be best to form an organization of soldiers on the frontier, or at least, if this is out of the question, to make it possible for a trustworthy man permanently to tour those districts, where I myself will take on the rest. . . . Perhaps it will be possible to do something with money. In any case and in all circumstances the affair must be carried through.

7. I think we must meet once to discuss everything thoroughly. You could visit me without losing even a day by so doing. If you come, make Rovio ask Huttunen, the deputy of the Finnish Seim, by telephone whether it is permitted to visit Rovio's wife's sister. Without this arrangement, it is possible that I might be away when you arrive. In any case, send me confirmation of the receipt of this letter, and inform me through the comrade who will hand this communication to Rovio. I shall in any case stay here until the post and transport are organized. You could be helpful to us by giving the railway officials envelopes for the Viborg soviet; our communications to Huttunen would be sent on in these envelopes.

8. Send me by the same comrade a signed authorization typed on the paper of the local committee to the effect that the president guarantees the comrade and asks all the soviets to give him their complete confidence and to support him as much as possible. The authorization should be made out in the name of Konstantin Petrovich Ivanov. I need it for all contingencies as unexpected conflicts and collisions may occur.

9. You perhaps possess the *Materials for Examination of the Party Programme*, the Moscow edition? Look for this pamphlet in Helsingors and send it to me by the same comrade.

10. Note that Rovio is an excellent man but lazy.

You must always be behind him and remind him of everything twice a day or he gets nothing done.

Kindest regards.

Yours,

K. IVANOV.

[Lenin's *nom de guerre*.]

GANDHI

Gandhi to Tagore :

" True to his poetic instinct, the poet lives for the morrow, and would have us do likewise. He presents to our admiring gaze the beautiful picture of the birds in the early morning singing hymns of praise as they soar into the sky. These birds had their day's food, and soared with rested wings in whose veins new blood had flown from the previous night. But I have the pain of watching birds who for want of strength could not be coaxed even into a flutter of their wings. The human bird under the Indian sky gets up weaker than when he pretended to retire. For millions it is an eternal vigil or an eternal trance. It is an indescribably painful state which has to be experienced to be realized. I have found it impossible to soothe suffering patients with a song. The hungry millions ask for one poem, invigorating food."

GANDHI

I

WHENEVER Gandhi travels through the country by rail in the poorest class, or, clad in his beggar's garments, staff in hand, wanders barefoot from town to town, from village to village, masses of people, often tens of thousands, gather around him, follow him, and wait patiently for a word from the Master's lips, or for the moment when he will grant them the sight of his face in accordance with the Indian custom of " Dharsan." They flock in great crowds to the railway carriage or the hut where Gandhi is, sing hymns in his honour and greet him with the national shout of triumph, " Mahatma Gandhi-ki-ii-jai! " If he spends the night in a village or in the open air, crowds make pilgrimages to him as to a saint. The Parsee priests in their fire-temples pray for his well-being; many Hindus regard him as a reincarnation of Shri Krishna and revere him as divine; countless popular prints on which Gandhi is represented as Shri Krishna are in circulation throughout the whole of India.

The English magistrate Mr. Lloyd, one of Gandhi's fiercest enemies, declared after his arrest that he must be buried alive in prison and no one allowed access to him, or his cell would soon become a Mecca for the whole world. How well founded this fear was is clearly shown by the description in an Indian paper: " In the evenings," this journal states, " the public assembled in large numbers at the Sabarmati Prison to do homage to their beloved leader; the masses stood before the prison as before a temple. When the bell rang to announce the hour of admission the sound was received with thrills of

M

joy. Then the crowd of pilgrims approached their revered Mahatma; some threw themselves at his feet, others touched him with awe, others again showed their respect only by profound salaams. Mothers laid their infants in his arms and old women touched the ground before him to show their devotion."

The people look on Gandhi as a saint; he is venerated in India as no other man has ever been. Although his birth and caste are not such as to seem likely to win prestige, since he is neither a Brahman nor a Kshatriya, but belongs to the Banya caste, nevertheless the most high-caste Brahmans bow reverently before him. "The whole nation follow him implicitly," says Rabindranath Tagore, "and for one reason only, that they believe him to be a saint. To see a whole nation of different races, of differing temperaments and ideals, joining hands to follow a saint, that is a modern miracle and only possible in India. The worst and most deep-rooted passions are soothed by the words: ' Mahatma Gandhi forbids it. . . .' I don't agree with Gandhi in many things, but I give him my utmost reverence and admiration. He is not only the greatest man in India, he is the greatest man on earth to-day."

It is not only the masses who feel Gandhi's spell; Indian intellectuals also speak of Gandhi as the "Mahatma." What this word "Mahatma," "great soul," means to the Hindu is also explained to us by Rabindranath Tagore: "The word 'Mahatma' means the liberated ego which rediscovers itself in all other souls, that life no longer confined in individual human beings, the comprehensive soul of the Atman, of the spirit. In this way the soul becomes ' Mahatma,' by comprehending all souls, all spirit in itself."

Anyone who would understand the greatness of Gandhi's influence must make himself familiar with the peculiar conditions prevailing in India. The population of the country consists of an immense number of stocks, races, and groups, widely separated ethnologically, who speak eleven different languages and belong to the most varied religions and sects. Seventy millions are adherents of Islam alone, and have for centuries lived with the Hindus in continual dissension and perpetual hostility.

By the ancient traditional caste system, the Hindu population of India is split into about eighty-four main castes and some thousands of subsidiary castes; all these castes are kept apart by the prohibition to eat together or to intermarry. For example, that potter who sits turning his wheel and making little crocks cannot form a marriage connection with his fellow artisan who stands at his work and produces large crocks. One-fifth of the whole population belongs to the caste of the " untouchables," the pariahs; they are treated as outcasts, whose touch, nay, whose glance or shadow even, pollutes every orthodox Hindu. The caste system dominates the population of India to such an extent that it reaches even the industrial proletariat: members of a higher caste never work at the same machine or the same bench as members of a lower caste.

Only the unique personality of Gandhi could have succeeded in bringing into one camp this Indian society thus split into innumerable castes and faiths, strictly isolated from each other, in overcoming apparently insuperable differences, and in bringing about a revolutionizing of century-old traditions perhaps unprecedented in the history of humanity.

He succeeded in winning the hearts of the Parsees, the rich Calcutta merchants, and at the same time in bringing over to his side the working classes, even the trade unions organized on Socialist lines. The whole nation, from the richest and most powerful down to the poor and disinherited, is under the spell of his words. If Gandhi speaks, all social and religious differences disappear, Brahmans and pariahs, Hindus and Mahommedans, Parsees and poor factory workers, for the moment at least, become brothers.

After one of the conferences of the " All Indian

Congress " at Ahmedabad, a great banquet took place with Gandhi as president, at which more than fifty thousand persons belonging to the most various castes and religions were present. In the face of all prejudices, Hindus of all creeds ate on that occasion with Mohammedans, Brahmans, and Parsees, with "untouchables," at the same table, often from the same dish. This meal had a powerful revolutionary and symbolic significance for India, since it was a sign of a great break with the past, of the beginning of a new historical epoch in the life of the country. Not long after this event Gandhi was appointed absolute dictator of India by the elected representatives of his countrymen.

When Gandhi was ill the whole country feared for his life: from the farthest provinces consecrated ashes were sent to him and holy water from the banks of the Ganges. In the temples the Brahmans held special intercessory services for the recovery of the Mahatma.

Later, when Gandhi's release from prison became known, the whole of India celebrated a great feast of rejoicing. In the towns and villages, the population announced the news with a flourish of trumpets; in the Hindu temples and in the mosques, thanksgiving services were celebrated; processions, in which the adherents of all creeds, those belonging to all castes and races, took part in brotherly harmony, marched through the decorated streets of the towns. Countless speakers addressed the crowds, declaring that Gandhi was a messenger of God sent to earth to destroy evil. The bazaars were shut, the industrial workers stopped work, and in the villages the rich gave banquets to the pariahs. Thousands of poor people were fed and clothed at the public expense. The blind and the cripples mustered and were presented with food, money, and clothing by their more well-to-do countrymen.

There is some truth in the assertion sometimes made that Gandhi is the real ruler of India. For all the pomp and circumstance of the Maharajahs and the English

Government at Delhi, for all the receptions and festivities they organize, the Indian people is in reality perhaps ruled less by the official Government at Delhi than by the influence of that frail little man in the garb of a pariah who, hunted through prisons and hospitals, has become eternally persecuted and harried. A bare prison cell, the ward of a hospital, the modest " Ashram," the home of the Mahatma in Ahmedabad, or a railway carriage, a poor stranger's hut, these are the real political headquarters of India. In Gandhi's immediate environment many important questions are still being decided which may represent the real destiny of the country.

This is still true, although apparently the " no co-operation " movement has been wrecked and the political life of India is governed by the " co-operation system." Even now, when Gandhi has retired from direct participation in the political struggles of the day in order to devote himself entirely to the organization of his economic movement, real decisions in India are unthinkable without him. His advice is still always asked at critical moments, and his is the deciding vote. As before, everything else that temporarily possesses authority fades before him; the renaissance and liberation of India are for all time inseparably bound up with the name of Gandhi.

When he lay ill in the hospital at Poona, C.F. Andrews, an English friend of the Mahatma, wrote of him: " Here lies the ruler of India, whose influence far surpasses that of the Imperial power. Long after the names of the Governors who now reside in the palaces at Delhi are forgotten, his name will still be honoured and exalted among the people, the memory of Mahatma Gandhi will be handed down for ever to their children by all the mothers of India, as the memory of one of the greatest, a saint and a redeemer."

Not even his greatest enemies could escape the influence of Gandhi's personality; even the statesmen who were his opponents speak of him with admiration; many of them, the Boer, General Smuts, and the Viceroys, Lord Reading and Lord Hardinge, were turned from enemies into sincere friends.

" Gandhi is more than a religious revivalist and a holy man," writes the English publicist Percival Landon, " he is a Mahatma, to whom almost divine attributes are ascribed; there is no one like him in the world to-day."

Even at the moment when Gandhi appeared before his English judges on a charge of incitement to disaffection against the authorities, the charm he exerts was felt in the whole court. The Indian poetess, Sarojini Naidu, Gandhi's faithful disciple, tells of the atmosphere which prevailed during the hearing of the case against the Mahatma: " Gandhi was in the eyes of the law a convict and a criminal; but when he entered, the entire court rose in an act of spontaneous homage. The judge treated him with the greatest respect, and at the end, after he had given his verdict, declared: ' I cannot refrain from saying that you belong to a different category from any person I have ever tried or am likely to have to try.' "

Like every significant political leader, Gandhi also of course has bitter enemies; but even the violence with which they oppose him is as much evidence of his greatness as the veneration of his disciples. A certain Englishman during his stay in India collected opinions on Gandhi from men of the most varied classes. " He is a God," was the reverent verdict of a Bengali stationmaster. " This man reminds me of the Apostle Paul," declared an English Government official; others again styled him a dangerous revolutionary, a visionary, an astute politician, or an unscrupulous agitator. " Whatever he is," says the English reporter in a note at the end of his collection, " he is no common man; be he saviour or wrecker, he arrests attention and demands a hearing."

The fame of the divine qualities of the Mahatma reached the most remote villages; legends formed round the figure of Gandhi. Sir I. C. Bose spoke with some of the aborigines of the hill country, the Bhils; they told him they had given up hunting altogether and were trying to live by agriculture. Their explanation was simple: the Mahatma had said: " Leave the forest in peace!" That was all. None of them had ever seen Gandhi; it was merely the legend of his goodness and wisdom, of his doctrine of " Ahimsa," " thou shalt not kill," which had penetrated to them. This was enough to make them loyally obey his command, and not only give up hunting, but decide for the future not to kill domestic animals. At first, they tried to sell their stock of cattle, but when they could not find purchasers, they sacrificed the whole of their wealth by letting the animals go free.

Prosper Bunarelli, of the New York *World Magazine*, tells of a conversation he had with a Hindu. In reply to a question whether he knew Gandhi personally he made a deprecating gesture and spoke " like one starting a holy thesis." " I do not know Gandhi personally. He is too great, too high." " That," remarks Bunarelli, " was the motive that sounded endlessly in his talk, an impassioned mystic reverence for the saint, which I gathered was the feeling of the millions of India, from the drudging labourers on rice plantations to the Hindu graduates of English universities. The figure of Gandhi appeared not that of an earthling of bread and salt, but of a holy one on a shining height, and recalled the ascetic who walks in penance and truth and behind whom trail worshippers by thousands."

Gandhi's South African comrade, J. Polak, also gives it up as hopeless to find words when he tries to describe the wonder of Gandhi. " You cannot say, this is he, or that is he. All you can say with certainty is that he is here, he is there. Everywhere his influence reigns, his authority rules, his elusive personality pervades.

This must be so, for it is true of all great men that they are incalculable, beyond definition. They partake of the nature of the Illimitable and Eternal, from which they have sprung and to which they are bound."

II

Gandhi, the Mahatma revered as a saint, is a little man of inconspicuous appearance in the sixties. " A shrimp of a fellow, as thin as a lath," is the description of Mr. Lloyd, the English official who had him arrested. His face lacks all beauty, and is peaky and sickly. He has a curiously shaped skull with very prominent ears and short-cropped hair slightly grey over the temples. Great brown eyes glow under his deeply furrowed brow; his delicate, thin upper lip is half concealed by a little moustache. His frail, slight body has become so weakened and exhausted by privation and sickness that, when he wants to address the people, he has to be placed on a high chair in the midst of the crowd that throngs about him; in this sitting position, feeble as a decrepit old man, he speaks to his disciples.

His speech is passionless, quiet, and measured. For this man, who has succeeded in revolutionizing the whole of India, like Lenin, that other great popular leader, lacks the usual oratorical gesture. He hardly ever moves his arm, hardly even a finger. The modulations of his voice are even, and his way of speaking sober and simple. He avoids all rhetorical ornament and detests all emotional appeal. " He appeals particularly to the intelligence of his audience," says J. Doke, " and he never abandons a subject before he feels that he has made it perfectly clear."

Gandhi himself has declared that he does not feel the slightest desire to win anyone over to his side until he has succeeded in convincing him that his views are right. The vague fine phrase is quite out of his line. He is deeply religious, but he does not shrink from rejecting the divine origin of the most ancient Hindu religious writings, if they fail to convince his reason. " My belief," he writes, " does not require me to accept every word and every verse in the sacred poems as divinely inspired. . . . I decline to be bound by any interpretation, however learned it may be, if it is repugnant to reason or moral sense."

Romain Rolland, in his excellent study of Gandhi, rightly stresses the fact that the Mahatma is the only one of the great prophets of the world who has never claimed to see visions and to receive revelations. " His forehead remains calm and clear, his heart devoid of vanity. He is a man like all other men." Gandhi himself has more than once energetically rejected the idea that he is a saint: " I have no special revelations of God's will. My firm belief is that He reveals Himself daily to every human being, but that we shut our ears to the ' still small voice.' I claim to be nothing but a humble servant of India and humanity. I have no desire to found a sect. . . . I endeavour to follow and represent truth as I know it." He has never hesitated for an instant to confess to being wrong: " I make no claim to superhuman powers. I am as subject to error as the weakest among us. My services have many limitations, but God has up to now blessed them in spite of the imperfections. . . ."

Before his arrest he wrote that he hoped that his disappearance and imprisonment would prove a blessing to the people: " In the first instance, the superstition about the possession of supernatural powers by me will be demolished. Secondly, the belief that people have accepted the non-co-operation programme under my influence and that they have no independent faith in it will be disproved."

The greatest and truest successes of Gandhi depend

not least on his absolute freedom from ambition, desire for fame, and exaggeration of his own powers. " Almost perfect selflessness," writes C. F. Andrews, " enables the Mahatma to see more truly and clearly than all other men and to realize his clear vision with unrivalled resoluteness."

His appearance and the clothes .he wears are in harmony with the simple modesty of his life. He usually wears only a loin-cloth of coarse hand-woven material, which covers his lean brown body from the waist to the knees. Only in the bad seasons does he sometimes throw a coarsely woven " kambal " cloth over his shoulders to protect him against the cold. He usually goes bareheaded and almost always barefoot. He appeared even before his English judge and actually before the Viceroy in this pariah's garb.

All reports speak of the persuasive effect of this modest, unassuming appearance in the garb of a beggar; his careworn face is lit up by his glowing brown eyes and his movements and his walk are witness to an inner distinction, an incomparable, easy, noble ardour.

He is no orator, and yet a whole nation blindly obeys his word. However excited the rabble may be, Gandhi can calm them with a single word, a single movement of the hand. It has happened again and again that he has appeared before an angry, excited crowd and checked by a few words a dangerous outbreak. " This shrimp as thin as a lath," Lloyd had unwillingly to confess, " carries three hundred and twenty million men with him. A nod, a word from him is a command; he is their god."

" He is, without doubt," says Gokhale, forerunner and teacher of the Mahatma, " of the stuff of which heroes and martyrs are made. Nay more. He possesses the marvellous spiritual power of turning ordinary men around him into heroes and martyrs."

At the end of a speech of Gandhi's, the masses crowd round him to kiss the hem of his garment or touch his feet. During that memorable meeting of the Mahommedan League in Calcutta at which the arrest of the Ali brothers was announced, the whole assembly burst into loud sobs when Gandhi rose to speak.

The content of his speeches is free from emphasis and exuberance. He speaks to the people quietly and gives them practical advice in simple words. Like Lenin, he too attends to every trifling practical detail. His arguments about the spinning-wheel, for example, are full of exact technical instructions about the proper methods of weaving, the most suitable quality of yarn, and the possibility of disposing of the goods produced.

Yet these sober exhortations of Gandhi produced results such as the most emotional appeals have seldom achieved. Hundreds of thousands of men and women of all ranks and castes responded to Gandhi's summons, and regarded it henceforth as their highest duty to spend a few hours every day at the spinning-wheel or the loom. For the great mass of the people spinning and weaving became a new way of serving God. The most distinguished and high-born ladies, who had previously worn nothing but *saris* made of the finest Japanese silk or muslin, with the enthusiasm of faith threw away their foreign-made garments, and wrapped themselves in coarse khaddar that they wove themselves. As in the times of the great Emperor Kabir, the old spinning-wheel was brought out again in the magnificent palaces of the Indian princes, in the houses of the Brahmans, and also in the miserable huts of the pariahs; princes of royal race as well as outcasts sat at handlooms and spinning-wheels, in order to provide India with cloth and make it independent of imports from abroad.

But Gandhi's fame spread also into the abodes of despair and poverty: hundreds of girls from the brothels of Lucknow and Barisal gave up their occupation to devote themselves to the work of spinning; even the convicts in the prisons began to weave and spin. Never before had the people of India been able to unite in enthusiasm for an idea; the spinning-wheel all at once became a national and social symbol of the highest significance, the symbol of the union of all Indian creeds, races, and castes.

When Gandhi declared that the wearing of foreign materials was a sin, and asked the people not only to get rid of all foreign textiles, but also to destroy them, the people, faithful to the words of their leader, proceeded with the greatest enthusiasm to erect pyres on the public squares of the great cities and to burn ceremoniously innumerable bales of English cloth. Rich and distinguished merchants brought the most costly materials from their warehouses, women of the people dragged their daughters' trousseaux and threw them on the flames; in Bombay alone in one day about a hundred and fifty thousand pieces of valuable cloth were publicly burned.

Wherein lies the colossal power of Gandhi's personality? Percival Landon asserts that his nature has something almost divine in it, and that his voice has a note of detachment, remote and immaterial, which lends uncanny force to his speech. Gilbert Murray, again, says that Gandhi's whole manner irresistibly diffuses harmony, " a certain indefinable suggestion of saintliness."

III

Like Lenin, this great popular leader is also by no means an unapproachable fanatic: his glance, his features, his whole bearing radiate a wonderful peace, the joyous radiant peace of a man whom external events have no longer any power to touch. His quiet gaiety is particularly characteristic; all his biographers emphasize his charming child-like smile.

" This exalted gaiety of his nature," says Rabin-dranath Tagore, " is in him and never deserts him even in the hardest struggles." When the news of his imminent arrest became known and his friends and disciples, anxious about their Mahatma, hastened to say farewell to him, he cheered them all by his " sprightliness and abundant joy." For each of his friends he had a loving word or a joke; right up to the moment when the police official came up to him he played with the children as if he were a child himself and " spread the contagion of his lightness and happiness all around."

A report in an Indian paper of the proceedings against Gandhi describes the entrance of the accused into the court: " The Mahatma came into the room with a light step, and his smile shone on the whole assembly. He displayed an exalted gaiety, even a festive joy, as if he were coming not to his trial but to a wedding."

Once his friends visited him in the Sabarmati prison; they found him sleeping on the ground, his tired head resting on a bundle of khaddar. When he awoke there appeared on his face that " beaming smile with closed lips, so familiar to all who know him." He chatted and laughed with his visitors and was full of " the untroubled joy of a schoolboy at the beginning of the holidays." In his letters from prison recurs the cry, " I am as happy as a bird."

His attitude to everybody is friendly and polite, so that even his bitterest enemies feel compelled to take an equally affable tone. It is significant enough that, at the end of the proceedings at which Gandhi was sentenced to six years' imprisonment the judge gave the Mahatma a friendly nod, whereupon he, with his hands folded before his face, bowed and smiled in equally friendly fashion.

His way of living is extremely simple and in no way different from that of the poorest pariahs. His chief food is earth-nuts, plantains, lemons, dates, a little rice or goat's milk; he never has more than two meals a day, at sunrise and sunset. He drinks no alcohol, tea, or coffee; he sleeps on a piece of coarse woven cloth spread on the bare floor of his room, with a bundle of khaddar or books for a pillow. Whenever possible he sleeps in the open air, preferably wrapped in a cloth on the bare earth.

During his student years in England Gandhi made an attempt to adopt, as far as possible, the European way of life and social customs. He himself relates the difficulty he found in learning to tie his tie, how impossible it was for him to keep time at his dancing lessons, and how his violin playing, which he took up on the advice of his friends, was a complete failure. He soon recognized how useless all these efforts were, so he sold his violin and gave up his dancing lessons and his study of French. His appearances in society were as a rule marked by great shyness and uncertainty: the presence of several people confused and frightened him. Once when he was offered meat at a social function he remembered his religious oath which obliged him to be a strict vegetarian, and rose from the table, left the assembly, and from that moment relinquished all attempts to make himself into an English " gentleman."

After that, he spent several years in South Africa in the fight to free his fellow countrymen who were groaning under the weight of injustice; there he led a completely ascetic existence, and, under the influence of Ruskin and Tolstoï, tried to found a colony of men ready to lead the simple life. He bought land, built houses on it, and turned it into a settlement in which Indian immigrants could live quietly and peacefully as a self-contained community. All the inhabitants of this settlement, " Phœnix," which he even then called " Ashram," the place of peace, were to form a sort of spiritual brotherhood without any distinction of rank. Each one had to cultivate his plot with his own hands, and Gandhi himself in his leisure time was very fond of taking part in agricultural work. Naturally, the establishment and maintenance of this colony involved great personal sacrifices of a material kind, so that Gandhi, previously a well-to-do man, was almost reduced to beggary by his expenditure on Ashram.

He founded a similar Ashram in India, though it was limited to his family and his most intimate pupils. This is his Satyagraha-Ashram, a few miles from the town of Ahmedabad, on the banks of the Sabarmati.

Here the Mahatma lives in the midst of his nearest relations and his pupils, who have all, like him, taken the vow of poverty, and strive, by strictest asceticism, to arrive at a knowledge of truth.

" We are a band of humble, unlettered workers," says Gandhi with his native modesty, " knowing our own failings, striving to understand them still further, and undoubtedly intent upon finding the truth and wanting to live and die for it."

The living rooms at Ashram, which consists of several low buildings, contain only the most indispensable and primitive furniture; for all those who live in this house have taken a vow to divest themselves of everything which is not absolutely necessary to maintain life. They all feel themselves obliged to renounce all superfluous property.

" I suggest," declared Gandhi, " that we are all thieves in a way if we accept anything which we do not need for our own immediate use. It is a fundamental law of nature that nature produces enough for our wants from day to day, and if only everybody took enough for himself and nothing more, there would be no pauperism in this world, there would be no man dying of starvation in this world. . . . I do not want to dispossess anybody. But, so far as my own life has to be regulated, I dare not possess anything I do not want. So long as three millions of people have to be satisfied with one meal a day, we have no right to anything more. It is our duty to undergo voluntary starvation if necessary in order that all the poor may be nursed, fed, and clothed. . . ."

The mode of life of Gandhi and his family is entirely in accordance with this vow of poverty. The walls of the rooms are bare and unadorned; the only pieces of furniture in the Mahatma's study, in which he works and receives visitors, are a shelf of books and a little low desk. Here Gandhi sits at work, mostly with his legs folded beneath him, on a cloth spread on the ground. Besides the simple, coarsely woven khaddar cloth which he wears as clothing, his only possessions are two similar cloths; both he and his wife have given their whole property to the poor.

Gandhi's wife, Kasturbai, whom he married at the age of twelve, has ever since shared her husband's life of toil and privations with admirable loyalty. She is a little woman with a slight, almost childish, figure; her face, with its serious, almost austere, expression, is the index of a strong and yet kindly soul. She, like Gandhi, wears only hand-woven garments, of simple red-bordered khaddar; she too wanders like her husband through the villages and towns of India, working in conjunction with many of her young women disciples for the introduction of the hand loom or the freeing of the pariahs.

In South Africa, too, she was a courageous comrade to her husband in his struggles: when the Indians in the Transvaal, in response to Gandhi's appeal, voluntarily went to prison in crowds, she was one of the first to go and spent three months there. At the time when her sons were arrested for participating in the nationalist movement, and she was overwhelmed with expressions of sympathy from all parts of the empire, she circulated a le ter of thanks in which she said: " Only two of my sons are in prison, while thousands of the sons of our Indian mothers are there. I have no right to shed tears of grief when so many young men have been torn from their beloved mothers."

The sons of the Mahatma are also their father's faithful disciples: in the speech of the young Devandas Gandhi before his judge could be heard the voice of the Mahatma. When he was charged with having taken part in the movement against English rule he cried: " I declare that I am guilty in the sense of the charge. Whatever I have said or done was deliberate; I was fully conscious of my responsibility and I beg for the maximum legal penalty."

IV

Gandhi dwells in his Ashram, surrounded by his family and his closest disciples. In obedience to their vow, all the inhabitants of the house reduce their food to the minimum, and refuse any dish which is not absolutely necessary to physical maintenance. Gandhi has expressed the view that the man who controls his palate can easily master his other senses; moreover, the preparation of most articles of food and drink involves profound misery and exploitation for other people: " If we could see with our own eyes the shameful treatment meted out to the workers on the coffee, tea, and cocoa plantations, then we would freely renounce for ever the enjoyment of these beverages. In fact, if we troubled about the preparation of our foodstuffs as a whole, we should feel reluctance in eating nine-tenths of them."

Gandhi's ascetic doctrines also lay on all the inhabitants of Ashram the obligation to observe complete chastity, " chastity even in thought." Married couples are admitted to Ashram only if they promise to give up their former relations and live henceforth as brother and sister. In Gandhi's view, complete abstinence in thought, word, and deed is necessary to the attainment

N

of spiritual perfection; marriage should bring man and
wife only spiritually into relation and make them friends,
and this harmony of souls should not be disturbed by
sexual relations. The man who can abstain from all
sensual desire, loses all fear of death and departs from
life with a smile on his lips; the man who thus lives
and dies is a true man, of him alone can it be said that
he has not wasted his life.

These views of Gandhi remind one strongly of
Tolstoï's teaching; it is known, too, that the reading
of Tolstoï's writings had a powerful influence on Gandhi.
Thus, for example, the Russian novelist, in the epilogue
to the *Kreutzer Sonata*, declared that he knew " no
other sin " which involved consequences as frightful as
" sensual love." In his novel he tried to prove that " all
evil results solely from men and women using each
other as instruments of pleasure; from this comes the
hostility between man and woman." In his condemna-
tion of carnal love Tolstoï did not except marriage, for
" the marriage which is based only on sensual love is
also a sin." He, therefore, opposed the view that
marriage is a Christian institution, and declared that the
true and unadulterated teaching of Christ did not form
" a basis for the institution of marriage." He called
marriage " domestic prostitution," and thought that
it, like all other forms of sensual love, was a symptom
of the degeneration of the human race.

For these reasons Tolstoï insisted that the relations
between man and wife must be fundamentally altered
and transformed into brotherly and sisterly affection.
Unchastity in Tolstoï's eyes was a penal offence:
" Violation of the marriage vow must be punished at
least as severely as dishonesty in commercial life." He
indignantly attacks " the false interpretation of the
Church, by the aid of which marriage is to be approved
and the evil existing in life thereby justified." But he
also arraigns the artists who " have tried to idealize sin,"
and considers that their function is the very opposite

of this, to restrain men from the seductions of the senses: "Men and women should be trained in family life and by public opinion to feel, both before and after marriage, that love and the sensual excitement connected with it are not a poetically exalted, but rather a debasing and bestial state."

Gandhi preached to the whole nation the doctrine of Brahmacharya, by which he means abstinence from all sensual desire: "The mysterious power granted to us by God must be maintained by strict discipline, and transformed not only into physical, but also into mental and spiritual qualities. . . . We must keep the ideal of Brahmacharya constantly before us and try to approximate to it more and more to the utmost of our capacity. When little children are taught to write the letters of the alphabet, we show them the perfect shapes of the letters, and they try to reproduce them as best they can. Just in the same way, if we steadily work up to the ideal of Brahmacharya, we may ultimately succeed in realizing it." Gandhi confesses that he himself in earlier times repeatedly broke this commandment and always felt shame and repentance. For he himself, by Indian custom, was married at the age of twelve, and thus is personally acquainted with the grave physical and moral dangers of this early awakening of the senses.

Gandhi gives some account of this child-marriage in his autobiographical notes, and his description is a vivid picture both of this peculiar Indian institution and of his own deliverance from it. He tells us that the idea of his impending marriage hardly means more to a boy than a hope of fine clothes, a rich banquet, and the joy of thinking that " he will have a strange girl as a play-fellow." At the start, the young Gandhi tried to instruct himself in his rights and duties as a husband by means of popular explanatory pamphlets. He frequently came across, in these writings, the demand that married people must be faithful to each other all their lives, which soon roused in him a jealousy which was as baseless as it was violent. " I had," he writes, " no reason at all for doubting the faithfulness of my wife, but jealousy does not ask for reasons. I thought that I must know every step she took, and I forbade her to go anywhere without my permission. This sowed discord and dissension between us, since the restrictions I imposed were like imprisonment for my wife. Kasturbai was not disposed to submit to this without opposition; she insisted on going out whenever and wherever she liked. The more I tried to restrict her liberty, the less she troubled about my orders, and this made me more and more furious. Things came to such a pass that we two married children no longer spoke to each other. I now believe that Kasturbai was right. How could I expect a young girl not to go to the temple or visit her friends! Now I see it all clearly, but then I made desperate attempts to assert my marital authority."

The twelve-year-old boy continued of course to go to school even after his marriage; but during lessons he was bound to think continually of his young wife, and this longing of the senses began to demoralize him. Nevertheless, he was true to his sense of duty, even then strongly developed, during his studies; he believes that only this obligation to work saved him from grave physical and spiritual dangers.

For a long time he made vain attempts to teach Kasturbai everything he had learned himself, but here he struck against a deliberate resistance. In order to overcome it, the boy had recourse to unkindness and harsh compulsion; Gandhi adds in explanation that this strictness was an outcome of his love, as he wished to turn Kasturbai into an ideal wife and to absorb her life entirely in his own. His love for his wife also prevented him from succumbing to any temptation to be unfaithful, although some of his schoolfellows had made it a point of honour to break down his resolution.

According to Indian usage, Gandhi's wife almost always spent half the year apart from him, at her parents', a custom which, in Gandhi's view, is to some extent calculated to make up for the grave injuries caused by child marriage, and which saved him from an untimely breakdown.

Even his years in England made no change in Gandhi's jealousy and his efforts to mould Kasturbai forcibly to his ideas. Soon after his return discord again arose between man and wife, which went so far that Gandhi sent his wife back to her father. " I did not take her back," Gandhi says, " until I had made her utterly miserable. Later I recognized and deeply repented of the folly of my proceedings." These quarrels did not cease until husband and wife made up their minds to live in future like brother and sister.

Soon after this, Gandhi undertook to represent the legal interests of an Indian firm, and on their behalf made a journey to South Africa to conduct a case there. He was immediately caught in a vortex of political events, and was drawn into the fight for freedom for the oppressed South African Indians. When he recognized that his stay in South Africa would be longer than he had foreseen, he returned once more to India and fetched his family. Henceforth Kasturbai became her husband's faithful fellow worker in his political and social activities. Both developed into real comrades and fought together in enduring harmony for their great ideas of reform.

Looking back on his experiences Gandhi now thinks that these early mistakes taught him to prize all the more highly the benefits of Brahmacharya and to concentrate all his energies on a life of chastity. " Many people have told me (and I also believe it) that I am full of energy and enthusiasm and that my mind is by no means weak. Some even accuse me of rashness. There is disease in my body as well as in my mind; nevertheless, when compared with my friends, I may call myself perfectly strong and healthy. If even after twenty years of sensual enjoyment I have been able to reach this state, how much better should I have been if only I had kept myself pure

during those twenty years as well. It is my full conviction that, if only I had lived a life of Brahmacharya
all through, my energy and enthusiasm would have
been a thousand times greater, and I should have been
able to devote them all to the furtherance of my country's
cause and of my own. . . . We are born into this world
that we might wrestle with difficulties and temptations,
and conquer them; and he who has not the will to do it
can never enjoy the supreme blessings of true health."

In founding his Satyagraha-Ashram, Gandhi was
trying partly to give the Indian people an example of a
healthy and morally right way of living. In order really
to understand the strict rules which Gandhi has imposed
on the inhabitants of his Ashram, we must keep in mind
the fact that a widespread tendency to luxury and
indulgence and to sexual dissipation exists among the
Indian people, which often leads to grave dangers for
the national health. Therefore, it must have seemed to
Gandhi all the more necessary to set an example of
extreme abstinence, and thus to prove publicly the
possibility of an ascetic life for a whole community.
Gokhale, the teacher of Gandhi, and his predecessor in
the political leadership of India, had also set himself a
similar aim and partly realized it. He founded the
organization of the Servants of India with the object of
training the character of the Indian people and spiritualizing the political and physical life of the country.
Gandhi's Satyagraha-Ashram is thus directly related to
Gokhale's efforts, but Gandhi's methods are much more
radical.

In obedience to all these ascetic principles Gandhi
and his family and pupils at Satyagraha-Ashram lead an
extremely strict religious life, the impressive dignity of
which few could deny. Very early in the morning,
before sunrise, the Mahatma proceeds to one of the
terraces which open on the Sabarmati River, and in the
company of his disciples and pupils he performs his
morning prayer with the singing of spiritual songs.

These religious exercises, the recitation of sacred texts from the *Gitas* and the *Upanishads*, give a ceremonious beginning to the day, which is passed in ceaseless hard work and self-mortification; these prayers and ancient hymns always glorify the purity of the strictly ascetic life.

The Mahatma is particularly fond of the hymns of his native district, Gujerat; they consist of peculiar incessant repetitions of a few lines of poetry, which recall not so much music in the European sense as the ever-recurrent litany-like repetitions of the same sentence in the speeches of Buddha.

C. F. Andrews noted down the text of some of Gandhi's hymns; one of these, which is sung in the morning, runs as follows:

" The way of the Lord is open only to heroes, to cowards it is fast shut.

" Give up thy life and all that thou hast, so thou mayst assume the name of the Lord.

" Only he who leaves his son, his wife, his riches, and his life, shall drink from the vessel of God.

" For in truth, he that would fish for pearls must dive into the deepest depths of the sea and take his life in his hands.

" Death affrights him not: he forgets all the misery of body and soul.

" He who stands hesitating on the bank and fears to dive, gains nought.

" But the path of love is trial by fire. The coward shrinks back from it.

" He who dares the leap into the fire, attains to everlasting bliss."

Another similar hymn reads:

" Lord, preserve me from looking on things which arouse evil thoughts. It were better for me to be blind.

" Lord, preserve me from soiling my lips with impure words. It were better for me to be dumb.

" Lord, preserve me from hearing any word of slander and insult. It were better for me to be deaf.

" Lord, preserve me from looking with desire on any of those who should be my sisters. It were better for me to be dead."

Gandhi's favourite hymn glorifies the life of the " true Vaishnava "; this hymn was sung on the evening on which Gandhi departed from his friends to go to prison. " He is a real *Vaishnava*," says this psalm, √ " who feels the suffering of others as his own suffering. He is ever ready to serve, and is never guilty of over-weening pride. He bows before everyone, despises none, preserves purity in thought, word, and deed. Blessed is the mother of such a son: in every woman he reveres his mother. He preserves equanimity and never stains his mouth with falsehood, nor touches the riches of another. The bonds of desire cannot hold him. Ever in harmony with *Ramayama*, his body in itself possesses all the places of pilgrimage. He knows neither desire nor disappointment, neither passion nor wrath. . . ."

The old traditional words of this sacred song express perhaps better than anything else the spirit of Gandhi's life and teaching. He himself is the incarnation of all that which thousands of years ago was held up as the loftiest moral standard in these old Hindu songs.

Life at Ashram also obliges all the inhabitants to perform the roughest work; the pupils of the Mahatma, some of them men of very high caste, engage here even in " unclean " work like sweeping and cleaning, which in the Indian view is fitted only for pariahs. Most of the day is spent in the " charka " sheds attached to Ashram: there the Mahatma and his housemates sit at the spinning-wheel or the loom, all engaged in producing that white Indian khaddar, to which Gandhi looks for the economic and moral regeneration of his country.

About a mile from Ashram, but within visible distance, lies the Sabarmati gaol, the prison to which Gandhi was brought after his arrest on 10th March 1922. On that occasion he could declare with perfect justice:

" How should prison life and fare be a privation to me, since they could not possibly be simpler than the life and food I am accustomed to? " In truth, the migration from Ashram to the Sabarmati gaol did not involve any considerable change in his external circumstances. He simply continued his ordinary life there, with the one difference, that he, the much persecuted, could enjoy ✓ greater peace behind bolts and bars.

It is very characteristic that Gandhi employed his frequent periods of imprisonment almost exclusively in completing his literary education, and filled his involuntary leisure with reading. Books must have helped him over all the sufferings of his imprisonment; he himself tells us how the works of Carlyle, Ben Jonson, Walter Scott, and Lord Bacon, the writings of Tolstoï, Emerson, Thoreau, and Ruskin, together with the sacred books of India, especially the *Bhagavadgita*, took the place of the customary society of his friends, and shortened the endless hours of loneliness. " In prison I read many of these books for the first time. Usually I began in the morning with the study of the *Gita*, devoted the middle of the day to the Koran, and in the evenings read the Bible with a Chinese Christian."

Although Gandhi had felt a profound leaning towards Christianity since his youth and regarded Jesus as one of the greatest teachers of all time, his keenest interest remained always centred in the Hindu writings. The time of his confinement in Yeroda gaol was spent mainly in the study of the *Mahabharata*, which made a particularly profound impression on him in the original text; in addition, he also occupied himself with Mohammedan writings, particularly accounts of the life and fate of the Prophet and his companions. Sometimes he used also to read there one or other work of European literature, including the writings of the German mystic, Jakob Böhme. Gandhi later referred to this thinker with special emphasis, and in one of his lectures he quoted several sayings of Jakob Böhme.

According to his own account Gandhi studied Tamil
and Urdu with feverish zeal in Yeroda gaol, in order to
perfect his knowledge of the Indian languages. He also
read Sanskrit a great deal, to increase his knowledge of
that. He had drawn up a detailed programme of study
for the six years his imprisonment was expected to last,
and tried to make up as far as possible during the period
for all the reading that his tempestuous and hard-working
life had given him no opportunity for. " I used to sit
down," he said later, " to my books with the delight
of a young man of twenty-four, and forget my four and
fifty years and my poor health." He was able to carry
out only a small part of his programme, for he soon fell
ill and was again released on account of his dangerous
state of health; henceforward he was once again in the
centre of political events, and found no more time to
devote to literature.

V

Gandhi's continual search in all that he read and in all
religions with which he came in contact for the principles
of morality and truth, corresponds to one of the deepest
sides of his nature. The foundations of it were laid in
his upbringing and in his family traditions. Mohandas
Karamchand Gandhi, born in the year 1869 in Porbander
in the province of Gujerat, was brought up in an atmosphere of strict Vaishnavism. All his forbears belonged
to the Jain sect, and were distinguished for deep religious feeling and passionate craving for truth. Gandhi's
grandfather, a high financial official, incurred the dis-
pleasure of his prince and had to leave the court of
Porbander. The Nabob of Yanagadh received the
fugitive kindly; the latter, however, contrary to all
custom, held out his left hand in greeting to his new

master and declared boldly that, in spite of all the
injustice he had suffered, his right hand was still in the
service of the Prince of Porbander.

Gandhi's father followed almost the same career.
He too was a *dewan* or finance minister, and fell into
disfavour. He thereupon betook himself to Raikot,
where he rose rapidly in the favour of the ruler and was
loaded with presents. On one occasion, when the
English representative spoke disparagingly of the prince
in his presence, Gandhi's father at once took him sharply
to task. The all-powerful representative demanded an
apology, and when Gandhi's father categorically refused
to make one, had him arrested. But he did not get the
apology demanded, and in the end had to let the matter
slide.

One of the fundamental ideas of the Jain creed is the
commandment of *Ahimsa*, " thou shalt not kill," which
of course involves strict vegetarianism. As a schoolboy
Gandhi came for some time under the influence of
schoolfellows with atheistical views, and began to
despise the customs of his fathers as out of date and
absurd. In order to prove their emancipation from all
religious prejudices, the boys proceeded to buy meat
and eat it secretly. Gandhi relates how in the night
after the day on which he had eaten meat for the first
time he was tormented by nightmares as if a live goat
were bleeding in his inside; nevertheless he thought for
some time that he must give further proof of his emancipation. But being forced to explain, by various fibs and
evasions, his evident lack of appetite to his parents
proved so repugnant to him that, in order never again
to be obliged to tell a lie, he gave up eating meat and
withdrew from his " enlightened " companions.

Once the young Gandhi got into debt for buying
cigarettes clandestinely, and could think of no way out
but stealing a piece of gold from his elder brother.
Immediately after he did it, the boy repented; he could
no longer endure the state of lying and dishonesty to

which his behaviour had brought him, and decided in the end to compose a written confession and submit it to his father, then in bed ill.

His father glanced over the sheet of paper and tore it to pieces with tears in his eyes; this sight made Gandhi loathe all forms of lying and theft for the rest of his life. He tells us that it was only later that he understood that this simple form of pardon, granted him by his usually so strict father, was nothing less than pure *Ahimsa*.

In his autobiography Gandhi relates how, while he was at the Indian secondary school, he neglected to acquire a good handwriting, and how later in England this deficiency seemed to him disgraceful; but in spite of all his efforts he never succeeded in improving his handwriting.

Sometimes it was very difficult for the boy to follow the lessons, for he had lost a whole school year by his early marriage, and was supposed to make up for it rapidly by skipping one class. Geometry, in particular, caused him great difficulties, until at the thirteenth proposition of Euclid he suddenly grasped the nature of this form of knowledge and saw that it was merely a matter of the use of clear reasoning. After that geometry seemed simple and uncommonly interesting.

It also caused him much difficulty to penetrate the mysteries of Sanskrit, chiefly because this study mainly consisted in learning rules and words by heart. He found the language so difficult that he was once on the point of giving up Sanskrit and going over to the much easier Persian class. But his teacher reproved him and said that, as the son of a Vaishnava, it was his duty to learn the language of his forefathers. After that the boy applied all his energy to this study and finally acquired some knowledge of Sanskrit.

In the year 1887 Gandhi finished his course at the secondary school. After a short and not very successful attempt to attend lectures at an Indian university, he

Gandhi

proceeded, on the advice of an old Brahman who was on friendly terms with the family, to London to study law there. His devoutly religious mother would not give her consent until the youth had sworn before a priest to abstain, even when far from home, from wine, meat, and sexual intercourse.

Gandhi himself would rather have devoted himself to medicine, but his elder brother advised him that his father, who had died in the interval, had more than once expressed his dislike for this science and declared that a Vaishnava should not dissect dead bodies.

Leaving his wife and his recently born child, Gandhi went first to Bombay and there, after a considerable wait, finally embarked on the steamer which was to take him to England. As soon as he got on board, he found the first difficulties of intercourse with Europeans; shy and timid, he avoided meeting the other passengers as much as possible, and even took his meals in his cabin, especially as he did not know how to handle a knife and fork.

On his arrival in London he was soon overtaken by home-sickness and spent many sleepless nights in tears. He felt helpless and abandoned in the great city, friendless and unacquainted with the customs of the country, and suffered greatly from the difficulty of finding appetizing vegetarian food. Nevertheless, he was firmly resolved, once he had dared to make the journey, to remain in England for three years and bring his studies to a successful conclusion. After great trouble he finally succeeded in finding a vegetarian restaurant, and this seemed, at a moment when he was almost starving, to be a real dispensation of Providence.

A little later he joined a vegetarian association and took a certain part in its activities. It is interesting to learn that Gandhi, afterwards a great politician and popular orator, made his first public speech in a gathering of vegetarians in London and broke down miserably over it.

In addition to his legal studies Gandhi also devoted himself, partly owing to the influence of theosophists with whom he had become friendly, to reading religious writings. It was then that he read for the first time the *Bhagavadgita*. He also made the personal acquaintance of the theosophists, Madame Blavatskiï and Mrs. Besant and of their writings. He had also to thank one of his London friends for introducing him to Christianity, and he began at this time to study the Bible.

On 18th June 1891 Gandhi took his legal examination in London, and two days later he embarked on the ship which was to take him back to his own country. As soon as he landed he learned the sad news of his mother's death, which had been withheld from him till then.

A little later he settled in Bombay, where he became friendly with the poet Rajachandra. This friendship was of great consequence to him: Rajachandra, a jeweller, who devoted himself to poetry and mysticism, made a profound impression on the young Gandhi. The Mahatma later acknowledged that no other person had ever been able to give him such valuable aid in moments of spiritual tribulation. Gandhi says that he could not, however, regard his friend as his spiritual teacher, his " Guru," whom, indeed, up to the present, he has sought in vain.

" I believe," writes Gandhi, " in the Indian doctrine of the *gurus* and its importance for the spiritual development of every human being. In my opinion there is a great deal of truth in the belief that true knowledge cannot be acquired without a *guru*. In mundane matters an imperfect teacher may be tolerated; but when it is a question of the spirit we need a perfect guide. But in order to find such a one we must ourselves strive continually for our own perfection, for we only find the *guru* we deserve. Continual striving after perfection is the duty of every man and brings its own reward. The rest is in the hands of God."

Gandhi once declared that three moderns had made a

Gandhi

profound impression on him and captured his soul:
Rajachandra by his living influence, Tolstoï by his book
The Kingdom of God is within us, and Ruskin by his
Unto this Last.

During his residence in Bombay Gandhi tried to
establish himself as a barrister, and for a time devoted
himself zealously to his profession. Even here his love
of truth went on growing. This was so well known that
no one had the slightest doubt of Gandhi's sincerity,
and even his enemies had absolute faith in his word.
More than once during his legal practice he abandoned
his brief in open court on discovering that he had
received wrong information from his client. He never
undertook a case without expressly reserving the right
to withdraw if he discovered that he had not been told
the truth. Never in his whole life did he prosecute a
debtor, as he was convinced that debtors would pay
without this if they could and if they were honest men.

When Gandhi in 1908 was attacked and nearly
murdered by a fanatical Mohammedan, he refused to
prosecute his assailant or even to give evidence against
him. On the very day of the crime, when he lay bleeding
and seriously wounded, he issued an appeal to his
adherents and warned them to take no step whatever
against the assailant. "This man," he declared, "did
not know what he was doing. He thought that I was
doing what was wrong. He has had his redress in the
only manner he knows. I, therefore, request that no
steps be taken against him. I believe in him, I will love
him and win him by love."

The improbable happened. In the following year his
assailant wrote to Gandhi assuring him that all his
sympathies and his profoundest reverence belonged to
the Mahatma, and that he would do all in his power to
help Gandhi's ideas to triumph.

Gandhi has always regarded love as the only weapon✓
against evil. He has been attacked and assaulted three
times by the mob—once almost fatally—and left lying in

the gutter; but he was never angry with those who attacked him. He has been in prison four times, and there too he showed an unshakable amiability towards all the officials. Always, both in the fortress at Johannesburg and behind the bars of the gloomy Yeroda prison, he submitted without murmuring or complaint to all the rules and maintained the strictest discipline even in face of the most insolent demands of the prison officials. He also exhorted his fellow prisoners not to treat their warders as enemies, but as fellow men and brothers: " Our gentlemanly behaviour is bound to disarm all suspicion or bitterness on the part of our warders. Our own self-respect obliges us to obey the prison rules willingly."

Just as Gandhi had always, when free, refused to avail himself of any privilege whatever, so also in prison he would not accept any consideration not also granted to all the others who shared his fate. He asked his friends and adherents not to visit him in prison, because receiving visits was for him a privilege which he could neither claim nor accept. He regarded his imprisonment as a religious service to his ideas, and did not wish to lessen the value of his sacrifice by any alleviations or compromises whatever.

Even his opponents had to allow that every one of his actions was dictated by conscientious sincerity and entirely disinterested motives. The Bishop of Madras, in a public address, testified to Gandhi's moral superiority over his persecutors. " I frankly confess, although it deeply grieves me to say it," he declared, " that I see in Mr. Gandhi, the patient sufferer for the cause of righteousness and mercy, a truer representative of the crucified Saviour than the men who have thrown him into prison and yet call themselves by the name of Christ."

Rabindranath Tagore says of Gandhi: " His whole life is only another name for sacrifice." Tagore extols Gandhi as one who covets neither power, riches, nor

honour; his soul is perpetually anxious to give without
wishing for thanks; neither imprisonment nor threats
of death will ever daunt the steadfast mind of the
Mahatma.

VI

Europeans as well as Indians have often compared
Gandhi's fate with the Passion of Christ; many parallels
have been sought between the son of the Carpenter of
Nazareth and the " weaver of Sabarmati." Broomfield,
the English judge who reluctantly and almost against
his will had to condemn Gandhi, was more than once
compared with Pontius Pilate, and the later incarceration
of the Mahatma with the crucifixion of the Saviour.
Sarojini Naidu tells us that during Gandhi's speech for
his defence in court she was compelled continually to
think of Christ: " I realized now that the lowly Jesus
of Nazareth furnished the only parallel in history to this
sweet invincible apostle of India's liberty." European
papers also declared that Gandhi's behaviour in court
could only be compared with that of the Nazarene.

" A man who will live in history and in Heaven with
Buddha, Socrates, and Jesus! " Thus he is described
not only by his adherents, but even by men who strenu-
ously opposed his political system. Deshabandhu
Chitta Erjanjan Das, the second great leader of India,
who later, though of different political views, became his
successor, has also compared the Mahatma to Christ:
" If we want to find an analogy for Gandhi's demeanour
in court, we must go back two thousand years in
history, to the day when Jesus of Nazareth appeared
before his foreign judge, Pontius Pilate, to receive
sentence. Gandhi is beyond all question one of the
greatest men who have ever lived; the world has need
of him. And however the Scribes and Pharisees of our

day may jeer and mock at him, India will always hold his memory in reverence. . . .".

From distant New York comes the voice of a Christian minister, who from the pulpit compares Gandhi with Jesus: " If I believed in a resurrection," states J. H. Holmes, the leader of an American sect, " I would —I say it in all reverence—look on Mahatma Gandhi as Christ returned to earth. . . . I am not here thinking of the influence which the Nazarene, as Gandhi himself emphasized, exercised over him; I have in mind rather his whole mental and spiritual nature and the wonderful example of his life. The soul of the Mahatma is the soul of Christ: its inner simplicity and purity, its mystical trust in the eternal verities, the peculiar blend of humility and arrogance, the profound understanding and infinite sympathy, the boundless joy in sacrifice, the steadfast idealism, the love for and trust in man and God, all show that the spiritual powers of Jesus are again incarnate on earth."

One of the most decided traits in the character of the Mahatma is his boundless sympathy. Eye-witnesses relate how Gandhi more than once mingled with the lepers on the steps of the temple and in the dust of the streets, and wiped their ulcers with his garment, how, transcending all the rules of caste, he bandaged with his own hands the wounds of a savage. This true sympathy is the real explanation of the Mahatma's refusal of all the external joys of life: his asceticism has nothing in common with the egoistic absorption of the *yogis*, for his renunciation of all earthly goods and joys is not meant only to save his own soul, but is the expression of a deep, inner solidarity with all the disinherited and humiliated.

Gandhi's only garment is a loin-cloth of coarsely woven khaddar, because this is the garb of the poor. He dresses like a pariah so that no one in the whole country may be ashamed of his poverty before him, the Mahatma. Unfalteringly he takes on himself the lot of those who have to suffer the severest privations, in order by voluntary fasting to wipe out the guilt, the spiritual burden laid on his conscience by the compulsory fasting of the poor. Like Buddha, the suffering of the world has shown him the most appalling pictures. Once he had seen misery, he could never forget it, or seriously devote himself to any other idea than the problem of how to help the suffering.

Shattering personal impressions of his youth formed his whole mode of thought and decided his course of action for ever. " I was hardly yet twelve years old," says Gandhi, describing this great experience of childhood which was decisive for his whole future development, " when a scavenger named Uka, an untouchable, used to attend our house for cleaning latrines. Often I would ask my mother why it was wrong to touch him, why I was forbidden to touch him. If I accidentally touched Uka I was asked to perform the ablutions, and though I naturally obeyed, it was not without smilingly protesting that untouchability was not sanctioned by religion, that it was impossible that it should be so. I was a very dutiful and obedient child, but, so far as was consistent with respect for parents, I often had tussles with them on this matter. I told my mother that she was entirely wrong in considering physical contact with Uka as sinful."

It was then that Gandhi first became conscious of the injustice which was the permanent lot of the pariahs in India. In agony of soul he began to doubt the faith of his fathers, which demanded such inhumanity. He studied other religions, and for some time, as he himself confessed later, he wavered between Hinduism and Christianity. But finally he recovered his balance and recognized that for him salvation was possible only through the Hindu religion. But he continued always to regard the doctrine of " untouchability " as a " blot on Hinduism " and could never reconcile himself to the ostracism from the national community of so many fellow men. He came to the conclusion that untouchability was not an important part of true Hinduism. " I know no argument in favour of the retention of untouchability," he wrote, " and i have no hesitation in rejecting scriptural authority of a doubtful character in order to support a sinful institution. Indeed, I would reject all authority if it is in conflict with sober reason or the dictates of the heart. Authority sustains and ennobles the weak when it is the handwork of reason, but it degrades them when it supplants reason sanctified by the ' still small voice ' within."

With the boldness of a reformer he declares that if it could be proved to him that untouchability is really a fundamental concept of Hinduism, he would himself advise his country to go over to Islam or Christianity. But he is convinced that the outlawing of the pariahs is not a sanction of religion, but a later interpolation, a " device of Satan." " The devil has always quoted scriptures. But scriptures cannot transcend reason and truth. They are intended to purify reason and illuminate truth." He believes also in the divine authority of the Vedas, but points out that the letter kills, and the Spirit alone maketh alive. The spirit of the Vedas, which represents the teaching of pure divinity, the sum of all that is noble and brave, could not possibly demand the oppression and isolation of the pariahs.

How far Gandhi has deviated from the usual Hindu conception in this new interpretation can be seen with perfect clearness from a comparison with the book of *Manu*, the primitive Hindu code of religious laws. There in the first book it is stated: " Now Brahma, for the salvation of the world, created the four castes from the different parts of his body. From his mouth he created the Brahmans, from his arms the Kshatriyas (the warriors), from his thighs the Vaisyas (the merchants), and finally from his feet the Sudras (pariahs)." In the second book of *Manu* the following sentences occur: " May the name of Brahman bring good fortune

for all time, the name of Kshatriya be full of power, that
of Vaisya bring wealth, but that of Sudra be despicable!
Therefore the title of Brahman shall be connected with
prosperity, that of Kshatriya with protection, that of
Vaisya with wealth, and that of Sudra with slavery."
Further in the twelfth book of *Manu* it is specified in
detail that the castes correspond to the three " gunas,"
the basic elements of all existence; while, for example,
the Brahmans are the offspring of the *Sattvaguna*, the
luminous presence, the pariahs, on the contrary, like
the elephant, the tiger, and the wild boar, belong to the
kingdom of *Tamas*, the kingdom of darkness.

Gandhi, however, illuminated by the pure knowledge
given by sympathy, arrived at the sublime idea that the
calamitous fate of India was simply the consequence of
untouchability. Hinduism, by tolerating this sin, has
infected India with a moral plague and made her unworthy of freedom. " I have told them that our being
treated as social lepers in practically the whole world is
due to our having treated a fifth of our own race as
such. . . . We have driven the pariah from our midst
and have thereby become the pariahs of the British
Empire."

The Mahatma shows his fellow countrymen that all
the injustices and humiliations of British rule are nothing
compared to the injustice India has inflicted on the
pariahs: the breath, even the shadow of an untouchable
pollutes the members of a higher caste; the pariahs are
obliged to live apart from the rest of the people outside
the towns and villages; they may not use the public
wells, their children are excluded from the schools, they
are damned and accursed. " We are all guilty," cries
Gandhi, " of having oppressed our brothers. We make
them crawl on their bellies before us and rub their noses
on the ground. With eyes red with rage we push
them out of railway carriages. Has the English
Government ever inflicted anything worse on us? Indeed there is no charge that the pariah cannot fling

in our faces and which we do not fling in the face of Englishmen."

More than once Gandhi has declared that the liberation of India from the oppression of foreign rule will not be possible until the Indian people grant freedom and complete equality of rights to their own oppressed castes. √" It is idle to talk of the liberation of India, of ' Swaraj,' so long as we do not protect the weak and helpless, so long as it is possible for a single Swarajist to injure the feelings of any individual. We are no better than brutes until we have completely purged ourselves of the sins we have committed against our weaker brethren."

The desire to free the untouchables from their degrading position gave Gandhi no rest and became one of the leading ideas in his political activities. This thought occupied him unceasingly and so strongly that he once exclaimed that if he were to be re-born after death he would like to come into the world as a pariah, to share all their sorrows and sufferings, all the affronts levelled at them, in order to endeavour to free them from their miserable condition.

In his Ashram he is bringing up a little orphan, Lakshmi, the daughter of a pariah. This " little untouchable one " lives in the Mahatma's family as if she were his own child. " Lakshmi is not only the little pariah girl in the Mahatma's Ashram," says one of Gandhi's closest friends, " she is a symbol, a name for the seven hundred thousand brothers and sisters who are still regarded as unclean and untouchable in India."

In prison, too, Gandhi's thoughts were continually with the poor outcasts. It was not only that he asked for news of Lakshmi's health on every occasion, but that in his message to the Indian masses Gandhi once again through his wife begged them to banish untouchability from their midst, and to love even the pariahs: " Allow them to drink the water of your wells," he begged the people from prison, " take their children into your schools! Do not throw them the leavings from your

plates, do not insult them but treat them as free men!
It is the only way to make you yourselves free. . . .
Cleanse yourselves from all your sins; but what sin
could be greater than the refusal to touch a brother? "

Most of Gandhi's political activity was concentrated
on this truly great and stirring fight against untouchability. He personally approached the pariahs, became
their adviser and friend, and put himself at the head of
their movement. His great political plan of " Non-
Co-operation " embraces the pariahs also as brothers
with equal rights in the community in the fight against
foreign rule. He publicly appealed to the untouchables
to join the national movement under his leadership.
" If I invited the depressed classes to join the movement
of Non-Co-operation, I do so because I want them to
realize their strength." And he proclaimed to the
Hindus that the liberation of India would not be possible
until untouchability was overcome: " The Hindus must
realize that, if they wish to offer successful non-co-
operation against the Government, they must make
common cause with the untouchables, for non-co-
operation against the foreign oppressor presupposes
co-operation between the different sections forming the
Indian nation."

VII

Gandhi also interested himself in the fate of the
Indian prostitutes, his " fallen sisters," in the same way
as he had done for the pariahs. Here, too, it was a
personal impression that made him realize the suffering
of these fallen girls and made him their adviser and
protector. In Cocanda, in the Andhra Province, a
deputation of a hundred women from the Barisal

brothels sought him out to complain of their sufferings and ask his advice. " The two hours I spent with these sisters," he wrote later, " is a treasured memory to me." He was able then for the first time to observe the great misery of Indian prostitution, although the women could only convey to him in hints what this life really was. But Gandhi, as he says himself, was able to read the eyes of the speakers and understood more than the women dared to tell him: " I bowed my head in profound shame before these hundred sisters and their degradation."

He was nauseated and disgusted at the " infamous viciousness " which could bring man to " look with desire on his sisters and make them the prey of his lust. . . ." " All of us men," he declares, " must hang our heads in shame as long as there is a single woman whom we dedicate to our lust! I will far rather see the race of man extinct than that we should become less than beasts by making the noblest of God's creation the object of our lust. Of all the evils for which man has made himself responsible none is so degrading, so shocking, or so brutal as his abuse of the better half of humanity. The female sex is the nobler of the two, for it is the embodiment of sacrifice, silent suffering, humility, faith, and knowledge."

The painful impression which Gandhi received of the degradation of women through sensual desire is not the least part of the explanation of the moral rules, so surprising to a European, which he made first for himself and his Ashram, and then raised to an important duty for his whole race. He indignantly opposes the " false statement " that this " gambling in vice " has a necessary place in the life of humanity; and he also rejects with wrath the claim put forward to justify it, that prostitution has existed in India from time immemorial: " We are proud heirs to all that was best and noblest in the bygone age. We must not dishonour our heritage by multiplying past errors."

And Gandhi demands that every man in India must
guard and protect the virtue of every woman as if it
were his sister's honour. " *Swaraj* means ability to
regard every inhabitant of India as our own brother or
sister."

He also protests with the utmost firmness against the
other conventional usages connected with sexual life,
especially child marriage. " I loathe and detest child
marriage. I shudder to see a child widow."

He opposes all the claims made in favour of the
institution, especially the statement that child marriages
are connected with the sexual precocity of the Indian
people conditioned by the climate.

" I have never known a grosser superstition! I make
bold to say that the climate has absolutely nothing to do
with puberty. What does bring about untimely puberty
is the mental and moral atmosphere surrounding family
life. . . . The children are betrothed when they are
infants or even babes in arms. . . . The dress and
food of the children are also aids to stimulating the
passions. . . ."

Gandhi carries on an equally energetic warfare
against drunkenness and also against the tea and
gambling-houses and the opium dens. They, like
prostitution, are calculated to plunge the Indian race into
deeper and more fatal slavery and to increase its misery.

The Mahatma has been convinced a thousand times
by intimate experience of the extent of this misery; he
has repeatedly visited the famine districts and there
recognized that " misery and suffering have assumed in
India more appalling forms than in any other country
in the world." He has given a description of one of
these impressions, which he could never forget. It was
in Puri. The police superintendent took him to the
square before a temple where hundreds of men and
women were lying worn out with famine. " The lamp
of life was all but extinguished," says Gandhi, " they
were moving pictures of despair. You could count

every one of their ribs and see every vein. No muscles, no flesh! Withered wrinkled skin on their protruding temple bones; no light in their eyes. They seemed to have no other desire but to die, and they hardly troubled about the handful of rice handed to them. . . . They took the food, but almost gave you the impression that they could hardly bring themselves to eat it and go on living. This agonizing, slow, and lingering death of men and women, my brothers and sisters, is the most terrible tragedy I have ever witnessed. Their lot is an everlasting forced fast, and when they occasionally break it with a handful of rice, it almost seems as if they were mocking at our way of life."

Often and often in his wanderings through the Indian villages Gandhi saw the people, decimated by plague and cholera, wasting away destitute of all help. At least a tenth of the population, he wrote once, are half-starved, and the rest are almost all under-nourished. Even in the middle classes this under-nourishment has already made such strides that the infants no longer have enough milk. " Throughout my wanderings in India I have rarely seen a buoyant face."

Pictures of this misery pursue him ceaselessly, his one thought is how to help. He declares that he would be unworthy to bear the name of a human being if he did not place all his strength at their service. " India," he said on another occasion, " has more than an ordinary share of disease, famines, and pauperism. . . . We suffer under the triple curse of economic, mental, and moral drain."

This disgust at the prevailing poverty and misery led Gandhi to an idea which may be unique in the history of humanity. In view of this misery he recommended the whole nation to live a life of complete sexual abstinence. " Is it right for us," he cried, " who know the situation to bring forth children? We only multiply slaves and weaklings, if we continue the process of procreation whilst we feel and remain helpless."

" Not till India has become a free nation," this
mournful appeal goes on, " able to withstand avoidable
starvation, well able to feed herself in times of famine,
and possessing the knowledge to deal with epidemics . . .
have we the right to bring forth progeny." Gandhi
declares that every report of a child born affects him
painfully, since India in its present situation is not
capable of affording the necessary livelihood to the
population already existing. The Mahatma, therefore,
exhorts his followers not to bring any more children
into the world at the present time, recommending for
this purpose not artificial contraceptives but rigorous
self-control. He desires a reduction in the number of
marriages, and demands complete sexual abstinence of
all married couples. Thus his programme is nothing
more nor less than a self-chosen voluntary decimation of
the people of India: " In my opinion it is our duty at
the present moment to suspend bringing forth heirs to
our slavery. . . . I have not a shadow of doubt that
married people, if they wish well to the country and
want to see India become a nation of strong and hand-
some, well-formed men and women, would practice
perfect self-restraint and cease to procreate for the time
being. . . ."

Never perhaps since the days of Buddha has any heart
been so shaken by the sight of human misery. It was
thus this profound sympathy with suffering that determined the whole of Gandhi's thought and action, and
led him to active intervention in politics. As a barrister,
who had undertaken to conduct a case for an Indian
firm, Gandhi came to Pretoria, but direct acquaintance
with the needs and humiliations of Indian workers in
South Africa made him devote the next twenty years
of his life to the fight for these exploited and oppressed
countrymen of his.

For on South African soil Gandhi found hundreds of
thousands of Indians in a most melancholy situation,
which had grown up in the course of many decades.

About the middle of the nineteenth century the South African colonists, in their search for cheap labour, hit on the idea of engaging workers in India. Numberless agents induced the Indian peasants with alluring promises to conclude long term contracts with them, and to bind themselves to serve for several years in South Africa. The white colonists,• especially in the Transvaal and the Orange Free State, however, treated the Indian immigrants as slaves with no rights, shamelessly exploited the labour of these men existing under miserable conditions, and did their best, on the expiry of their contracts, to compel them to keep on renewing them on unfavourable terms. This end was served by a special system of laws, by which the Indians in South Africa were deprived of almost all civil rights; the racial pride of the whites was openly expressed in this legislation against the despised "niggers," and bands of terrorists completed the work of adding to the humiliations and persecutions which were the lot of the Indians.

Gandhi was forced to recognize with dismay that an area of the British Empire existed in which the Indians were treated as a despised and outcast race. He at once resolved to place all his energy at the service of his South African fellow countrymen; his political activity thus began, instigated by the sight of his fellow Indians exposed to persecution and oppression.

It was his sympathy with the oppressed that was the ultimate cause of Gandhi's fight against the English Government also: "The main indictment brought by Gandhi against the English Government," says C. F. Andrews, "may be summed up in one sentence, his accusation against England of oppressing the poor. The starved creatures, the living skeletons which Gandhi met with everywhere in India, had so stirred him that the thought of helping them gave him no peace day or night."

Andrews also states that Gandhi later, when his Non-Co-operation movement was in full swing, made a

proposal to the English Government that he would give
up the whole undertaking and co-operate with the
British authorities if they decided on an energetic
campaign against starvation in India.

Therefore, all the ideas which Gandhi made the basis
of his political system are rooted in his humanity, which
is so deeply bound up with the misery of his people, and
in his own heart-breaking experiences. " I have often
and often," says Andrews, " watched Mahatma Gandhi
in the heart of the great South African city of Durban,
and seen how he went about in the poor quarters and
mixed with the enslaved Indians. . . . I lived with
Gandhi in the Indian ' settlement ' in Pretoria and in
various other places where the poor Indians, laundry-
men, vegetable sellers, and labourers, were treated as
pariahs, while all around them the rich were building
their palaces. We all know, too, how the Mahatma
afterwards indefatigably shared the life of the mill-
workers of Ahmedabad, and allied himself to the
oppressed peasants of Kaira. He gained his experience
of the fate of the poor in the only possible way, by
himself living in their midst by the work of his hands. . . .
Mahatma Gandhi is entirely on the side of the poor, and
for this reason they instinctively recognized him as their
true friend and protector. . . ."

Gandhi's loving care for the weal and woe of the great
masses can perhaps be most clearly seen in his particular
interest in the little daily needs and cares of the lower
classes; no circumstance is too trifling for him to devote
himself to it with the greatest conscientiousness. In the
midst of great political undertakings he interested himself in the most trifling needs of his fellow countrymen
with the same seriousness as he had shown in the introduction of the spinning-wheel and the freeing of the
pariahs.

He made a number of speeches on the dirt of Benares,
the miserable lanes which lead to the temple there, and
the uncleanliness of the crowd. He pointed to the

menacing spread of the plague, which is always breaking out in India, and ·violently reproached the English Government on the inadequacy of their measures. But with particular frequency, and this is highly characteristic of his social attitude, he has taken up the question of the scandalous conditions prevailing in the third class of the Indian railways. Far from travelling first class, as would be natural in his position, Gandhi had personal experience through numberless journeys of the intolerable sanitary conditions in the third class. He emphasizes the urgent necessity of altering these conditions, of improving railway arrangements, and of exhorting travellers to more hygienic habits by pamphlets or instructive lectures. He reports that in the compartments, among tightly-packed swearing people, you have to wade in dirt, because the closets are not cleaned, that the refreshments sold in the stations " were dirty looking, handed by dirtier hands, coming out of filthy receptacles, and weighed in equally unattractive scales."

In his *Guide to Health*, too, he emphasizes how important it is to keep privies clean and always to place a pail of ashes in them. He gives the simple people directions how to breathe through the nose instead of the mouth in order to protect themselves against cold, on how uncleanliness leads to epidemics, and how they should use the upper parts of the river for drinking purposes and the lower for bathing and washing clothes, and tells them that there is both hard and soft water, and that hard water is injurious to the digestion.

He almost always illustrates his advice from his own experience: he tells them that he lives on fruits, plantains, and a little olive oil and keeps very well on it; that he has proved that bread made with a handmill is the best, shows how to make a tasty and nourishing dish from coarsely ground wheat with milk and sugar, how necessary it is to chew all food well, and that real good health is only possible with steady work.

He also tries to explain to the ignorant people how to

act in cases of accident; he instructs them in artificial respiration in drowning, the treatment of burns with oil, the ligature of the parts affected, and the opening of wounds in cases of snake bite and scorpion stings. His fundamental idea in all these explanations is always the idea that the human body is the abode of God, and that it is, therefore, man's duty to keep his body pure within and without, in order one day to restore it in its original purity to Him who gave it. He aims less at curing sickness than at preventing it, for this *Guide to Health* is not meant for enlightened, European-trained people, but for the entirely uneducated populace, and is intended to instruct them in the most elementary rules of a healthy life.

Only this intimate connection with all the cares of the poor and suffering, with their slightest and most trifling needs explains Gandhi's enormous influence on the Indian masses. In him, who has descended to them, to where men struggle with the harshest need, whose voice has become a living revelation of all their sufferings, they see their father, their *Bapu*.

"He stopped at the thresholds of the huts," says Rabindranath Tagore, "of the thousands of dispossessed, dressed like one of their own. He spoke to them in their own language; here was living truth at last and not only quotations from books. For this reason the 'Mahatma,' the name given to him by the people of India, is his real name. Who else has felt like him that all Indians are his own flesh and blood? In direct contact with truth, the crushed forces of the soul rise again; when love came to the door of India, that door was opened wide.... At Gandhi's call India blossomed forth to new greatness, just as once before in earlier times, when Buddha proclaimed the truth of fellow feeling and compassion among all living creatures."

VIII

Gandhi is often reproached with having left no place for art in his plans for the renaissance of India; even many of his close adherents deplore the Mahatma's lack of any real understanding of artistic things. When it was pointed out that he had strictly avoided any ornament for the bare walls of his Ashram, and he was asked the reason for this omission, he replied that the walls of a house served purely practical purposes, and therefore needed no adornment: " I am content with my four bare walls," he once said to Ramahandran, a pupil of Tagore, " I hardly need a roof over my head. When I gaze at the star-sown heaven, and the infinite beauty it affords my eyes, that means more to me than all that human art can give me. That does not mean that I ignore the value of those works generally called artistic; but, personally, in comparison with the infinite beauty of nature, I feel their unreality too intensely."

In a conversation with the Indian musician, Dilip Kumar Roy, also, Gandhi said that human art could never attain to the beauty of nature nor compete with the splendour of the starry heaven: " I must confess," he said, " that I cannot conceive of any picture which could arouse in me the same bewildering, enthralling and elevating impression as the vault of heaven with its stars. Are not all human works petty and unreal beside this overwhelming and mysterious artistic achievement of God? "

Gandhi does not, it is true, ignore the importance of art as a medium for representing spiritual and moral strivings, but he thinks that personally he has no need of this means: " As for me, I may say that I do not need external forms to strengthen the powers of my soul."

He feels more love for music: Indian instruments are found on the terraces of his Ashram, and at early morning the day is begun with music, and closed at evening with spiritual songs. Gandhi's friends relate how, during his long fasts in Delhi, the hymns to Krishna and Vishnu meant to him "food for the whole day," and how he never went to bed until the sacred songs had been sung.

Nevertheless, Gandhi's love of music has very little to do with artistic appreciation proper: for him music and song are only a means to meditation, a form of prayer. The sacred *saiten* instruments of India, the *vina*, the *tambura*, and the *sarangi*, accompany the *ragas* which have been handed down orally from generation to generation in the course of the centuries. The methods of expression and principles of Indian musical art are entirely different from those of European music: Indian music has neither harmony nor harmonized accompaniment. It consists rather of very peculiar melodic variations of a definite canonic theme. The old classical music of India had originally about four hundred such *ragas*, but many have been lost in the course of the centuries.

The *ragas* are played and varied in a manner which is only possible within the twenty-two steps of the Indian scale, and which therefore conceals its surprising and alien charms from our ears. If we wish to imagine what this kind of music is like, we must keep in mind that a *raga* consists of a few words, such as "Krishna has conquered me," ceaselessly repeated for half an hour, with no single variation completely harmonized with any other.

The themes of these *ragas* are mostly spiritual love songs celebrating union with the god Krishna; they remind one of the litany-like repetitions in the speeches of Gautama Buddha, and still more of the religious exercises of the Indian *yogis*, who also repeat continually a short sentence or even a single word.

Gandhi's love for music is, therefore, merely a proof of his strong religious feeling. "How could I reject music," he said once to Dilip Kumar Roy, " since I cannot even imagine a religious development of India without it? " As religion in Gandhi's country forms the basis of all social and cultural forms of life, he regards music as a suitable means for influencing the masses, and even desires that it should be as widespread and popular as possible: " I would make compulsory a proper singing, in company, of national songs. And to that end I would have the best musicians in the country place themselves at our disposal and create musical forms suitable for the masses."

Gandhi's object, therefore, is to enlist music in the service of religion and national policy; outside this importance as a factor in organization he cannot recognize anything in music, such as independent abstract enjoyment for example: " I love music and all the other arts, but I do not attach such value to them as is generally done. I cannot, for example, recognize the value of all these activities which require special technical knowledge for their understanding."

Gandhi, therefore, judges art purely by its fitness as a moral and social factor: " Life is greater and must be greater than all art. I would go even further and declare that the man whose life comes nearest to perfection is the greatest artist; for what is art without the sure foundation and framework of a noble life? "

Thus the aesthetic value of art and its beauty lies in its moral content alone; he is convinced that striving for truth is the first and highest task of all artistic activity. To the objection that there are things which in themselves are neither moral nor immoral, but which yet have an effect of beauty, Nature, for example, the Mahatma answered: " Do I not recognize in the beauty of nature the truth and splendour of the Creator? Could the sun or the starry heaven be beautiful if they did not arouse the feeling of the beholder to the truth of God? Whenever I gaze on the marvel of a sunset or the gentle light of the moon, my soul bows in devotion

before the Creator of this world, since in His works I
see Him and His mercy. Without these thoughts of
God, sunrise and sunset would only be a distraction of
man from his daily work, and thus become a stumbling
block in the way of salvation."

" All that is true," he continued, " is in supreme
degree beautiful, not only true ideas, but genuine faces,
genuine pictures, and genuine songs." As an example
of the identity of truth and beauty Gandhi has often
quoted Socrates. Socrates was ugly, but his inner
purity so glorified him that even Pheidias, devoted to
external beauty, recognized the perfection of the apparently so misshapen Socrates.

In Gandhi's view the artist must himself be genuine
if he is to create works of beauty; he also reverses the
dogma and declares that the really pure man is an artist:
" Jesus, who knew and realized truth, was a supreme
artist; so was Mohammed. The Koran is the most
perfect work in the whole of Arabian literature. Because
both of them, Jesus and Mohammed, strove for truth
above all other things, their expression and their form
was also filled with grace and beauty, although neither
was consciously or deliberately aiming at creating works
of art."

Although Gandhi grants art a certain significance, it is
only in so far as it contributes to the moral perfecting of
humanity. Art which produces merely aesthetic works
has in his conception no right to existence, since the
external form has value only as the expression of the
indwelling spirit. As an example of what he thinks a
useless kind of art Gandhi quotes the writings of Oscar
Wilde. He rejects him decisively, nay, he is uneasy
about his influence on the public. He emphasizes that
he is far from wishing to pose as a critic of art; he is
too well aware of the limitations of his understanding;
but he believes that he has the right to judge Oscar
Wilde, because in London he had been a witness of the
disastrous influence exercised by this writer. " For

Wilde," says Gandhi, " the greatest art lies merely in the perfection of form; therefore he did not even shrink from glorifying the immoral."

To the claim that beautiful works are frequently produced by men whose life is anything but perfect, the Mahatma replies: " That merely means that truth and falsehood, good and evil, can often exist side by side. The artist may recognize the truth at one time, and fall into falsehood at another; but perfect beauty only happens if its creator is filled with the most pure knowledge of truth."

This idea that art should be judged solely by its ethical and social value, in many respects recalls Tolstoï's doctrines, especially his work, *What is Art?* But with Gandhi this at first strange way of judging is not the result of any moral speculation; the limitations of Gandhi's understanding of art are conditioned rather by the enormous task which has fallen to his share, by the demands made on him by the misery of the age, which leaves no room for anything else and requires with appalling urgency the application of all his strength and energy.

Like Lenin, Gandhi lacks any understanding of all forms of life and culture which do not serve direct social ends. They are both children of an age in which misery and need appeal more strongly than ever before to the conscience of humanity. Anyone who feels himself so intimately bound up with the fate of the multitude as these two men, can feel but little sympathy for all the things which do not directly serve to help the needy, which seem to be a mere decoration. " I have found it impossible," writes Gandhi, " to soothe suffering patients with a song. The hungry millions ask for one poem—invigorating food! "

Rabindranath Tagore once complained of this gloomy and arid characteristic of Gandhi's policy, and said that he himself had no other alternative during the great political struggle but to devote himself to " inventing

new metres." "They are merest nothings," he said,
"that are content to be borne away by the current of
time, dancing in the sun and laughing as they disappear.
But while I play, the whole creation is amused, for are
not leaves and flowers never-ending experiments in
metre? Is not my God the eternal waster of time?
He flings stars and planets in the whirlwind of changes.
He floats paper boats of ages filled with His fancies on
the rushing stream of appearance. When I tease Him
and beg Him to allow me to remain His little follower
and accept a few trifles of mine as the cargo of His
playboat, He smiles, and I trot behind Him clutching
the hem of His robe. . . . But where am I among the
crowd pushed from behind, pressed from all sides?
And what is this noise about me? If it is a song, then
my own *sitar* can catch the tune and I join the chorus,
for I am a singer. But if it is a shout, then my voice is
wrecked and I am lost in bewilderment. I have been
trying all these days to find in it a melody, straining my
ears, but the idea of non-co-operation, with its mighty
volume of sound, does not sing to me, its congregated
menace of negation shouts. . . .
"The bird awakening in the dawn does not think
only of food. Its wings respond without weariness to
the appeal of the sky, its throat fills with joyous songs
to greet the coming day. Humanity has made its appeal
to us; let the deepest part of us answer in its real voice!"
Gandhi replied to the poet in an essay, *The Great
Sentinel*. He dedicates it simply and gravely to the poor
and destitute of his country, and you feel once again in
his words his deep sympathy with all misery. But his
answer is at the same time also the voice of our whole
age, which is accused of an inartistic, arid, and materialistic spirit: "When all about me are dying for want of
food, the only occupation permissible for me is to feed
the hungry. . . . To a people famishing and idle the
only acceptable form in which God can dare appear is
work and promise of food as wages!" While it is the

privilege of the poet to point to the birds singing their songs of thanksgiving at early morn, there are other men, whose duty it is to care for birds whose strength is exhausted; this is not the moment to hope that humanity will be saved by art, when the starving millions are longing only for bread.

Like everything else in Gandhi's life, his judgment of art and its significance is entirely the expression of his knowledge of the misery of the people. Gandhi, to whom, as once to Buddha, the sorrow of human creatures has shown its uncovered face, could no longer spend his emotions and energies on any activity which did not contribute directly to feeding the hungry, clothing the naked, and comforting those that mourn.

IX

Gandhi's public work and his political system were also the outcome of his passionate desire to help his unhappy, starving brothers as quickly as possible. It was mainly an-economic problem he had to deal with but in order to find the right solution it was necessary to have a clear knowledge of the real causes which had brought about the general impoverishment of India In Gandhi's view, one of the chief reasons for the great economic need was the decline, or rather the enforced abolition, of the once flourishing Indian home industries

Thus India, which produces enough cotton for its own requirements, has been forced since British rule began to send this cotton to England or Japan instead of working it up at home. In this way the Indian people are obliged every year to import cloth from abroad to the value of about six hundred million rupees, while the sum received for exported raw cotton is enormously less. " A country," says Gandhi, " which exports its raw produce and imports it after it has undergone manufacturing processes, a country that in spite of growing its own cotton, has to pay crores of rupees for cloth imported from Europe, cannot be otherwise than impoverished and ruined."

Gandhi, therefore, finds the true cause of the miserable poverty of India in this "robbery of national wealth" caused by the artificial and compulsory export of raw material and import of finished goods, by which the country is deprived of the profits of the manufacturing process, that is, the difference between the value of the raw cotton and that of the re-imported materials.

Gandhi was convinced that in these circumstances the only possibility of saving the country from its desperate economic situation was the return to home industry, to the spinning-wheel, which in earlier times sufficed to supply India's demand for textiles: "Hunger is the argument that is drawing India to the spinning-wheel! . . . We must think of the millions who to-day are less than animals, threatened with the spectre of famine, and almost in a dying state. . . ."

But Gandhi saw in the destruction of home industry another, perhaps worse, danger for India than economic ruin: the Indian people had given up their old occupation, become accustomed to foreign materials, and begun to abandon themselves to a fatal idleness. Before the foreign conqueror appeared, millions of people span and weaved industriously in their homes, and thus earned the surplus necessary to increase their all too modest income from agriculture. For the Indian peasant cannot maintain himself entirely from the yield of the soil; he needs a supplementary trade.

"A hundred and fifty years ago," explained Gandhi in his speech for his defence before the Courts, "our women span fine yarn in their own cottages and supplemented their husbands' earnings. The village weavers wove that yarn and earned their living in this way. It was an indispensable part of national economy . . . and enabled us to utilize our leisure in a most natural manner. To-day our women have lost the cunning of their hands, and the enforced idleness of millions of people has impoverished the land."

On other occasions Gandhi gave an account of the migration of the villagers to the towns, and told how many weavers had had to take jobs as street cleaners and rapidly became physical and moral wrecks through poverty. Many had even to be helpless witnesses of the shame of their daughters, and even their wives. The proud weavers of the Punjab, again, had to enlist as soldiers and fight against innocent Arabs, driven not by conviction, but by need.

Gandhi considers that not even the large sums spent on the army have inflicted such great losses on the national wealth of India as the decay of the home textile industry. " I have travelled through the whole of India and have everywhere heard the heart-breaking, intolerable cries of the people. . . . The whole nation is in want, everywhere people complain that they have not money even for bare necessities of clothing and food. . . ."

Gandhi rightly points out that the real poverty of India can only be seen in the villages. The towns live on the rural districts and do not draw their wealth from foreign nations, but live on the proceeds of the robbery which has for two hundred years been perpetrated on the national wealth of India by foreign industry. " Of the money paid for foreign materials," Gandhi said once in conversation, " only two annas fall to the workers and six or seven to the capitalists. Anyone, however, who buys hand-woven Indian material pays his money direct to the poor weavers and spinners; not a penny of it goes into the pockets of the capitalists."

Gandhi then proceeded to work out his great programme: India must boycott foreign material and re-introduce the spinning-wheel. "I claim that in losing the spinning-wheel we lost our left lung. We are, therefore, suffering from galloping consumption. The restoration of the spinning-wheel arrests the progress of the fell disease." The Mahatma showed how the universal use of hand-woven Indian material, and the complete boycott of imported textile goods, would of itself mean the distribution of six hundred million rupees a year among the Indian people, who would in this way gradually come into possession of their strength and flourish again. Only through the spinning-wheel could India prove to the world that she was determined to make herself completely independent; only by means of the coarse hand-woven khaddar cloth could India be freed from slavery; the spinning-wheel was the only cure for poverty.

Gandhi, therefore, developed an extensive propagandist activity in favour of home-produced cloth and in opposition to imported materials. He exhorted the whole population to supply their requirements in textiles in future entirely from the home market. Even if the khaddar was coarse at first, practice would soon enable the Indian weavers to produce fine makes of cloth, and thus to satisfy the most luxurious demands. He required all his disciples to take a form of vow devised by himself, by which they bound themselves to use only Indian cotton and Indian silk, and to abstain completely from the use of foreign goods, and even to destroy foreign materials which they had already bought. He exhorted the merchants to have their yarns spun from Indian cotton and to use only Indian yarn for weaving. If it rested with him, he said, every Indian would have to learn to spin and weave and devote a certain portion of every day to this occupation: " I would start with schools and colleges, because these with their excellent organization would form the best basis for introducing the spinning-wheel and carrying on propaganda work for this purpose." In this way, he thought, it would be possible to produce millions of yards of khaddar cloth every day.

Proceeding from the assumption that the market for hand-spun yarn and hand-woven cloth in India could be indefinitely extended, if only everybody would abstain from buying foreign textiles, he believed that by the introduction of two million spinning-wheels, *Swadeshi*, the economic freedom of India, could be attained with one blow. But economic independence is an indispensable condition for political *Swadeshi*, that is, for self-government, for *Swaraj*: " The Reform scheme, no matter how liberal it may be, will not help to solve the problem of Indian freedom in the immediate future. But the economic freedom, *Swadeshi*, attained by means of the spinning-wheel can solve it now."

The objection was raised in many quarters against the economic programme of Gandhi that the attempt to revive home industry based on human handwork was a reactionary proceeding in the age of machinery, which could not possibly lead to success. Gandhi replied to these objections with the following argument: " People remind me that in these days of mills, sewing-machines, and typewriters, only a lunatic can hope to succeed in reviving the rusticated spinning-wheel. These friends forget that the needle has not yet given place to the sewing-machine, nor has the hand lost its cunning in spite of the typewriter. There is not the slightest reason why the spinning-wheel may not co-exist with the spinning-mill, even as the domestic kitchen with the hotels. Indeed typewriters and sewing-machines may go, but the needle and the reed pen will survive."

But Gandhi also points out the impossibility of establishing a machine textile industry in India within a reasonable period, because this enormous section of the world, which largely consists of peasant settlements, cannot be industrialized in a day. Therefore it is impracticable to seek a solution of an immediately urgent problem in the erection of Indian textile factories, for the Indian machine industry will not for many generations be in a position to supply the home market.

But Gandhi believes that home industry is to be preferred to large factories for other reasons as well as on account of these considerations of practical feasibility: " If we merely use mill-made cloth, we simply deprive the poor of what they need, or at least increase the price of mill-made cloth. Multiplication of mills cannot solve the problem. They will take too long to overtake the drain and they cannot distribute the sixty crores in our homes. They can only cause concentration of money and labour, and thus make confusion worse confounded. . . . Hand-spinning helps production and cheapens prices."

Gandhi also regarded the factories as a great social danger, because he could not approve of the creation of a proletariat in India: " The workers in the mills of Bombay have become slaves. The condition of the women working in the mills is shocking. . . . It may be considered a heresy, but I am bound to say that it were better for us to send money to Manchester and to use flimsy Manchester cloth than to multiply mills in India. By using Manchester cloth we would only waste our money, but by reproducing Manchester in India, we shall keep our money at the price of our blood because our very moral being will be sapped. We need not, therefore, be pleased at the prospect of the growth of the mill industry on Indian soil."

When he was asked whether he advocated the closing of the factories already in existence in India, Gandhi replied that this was a difficult problem, as it was not easy to do away with a thing that is established: " We cannot condemn mill-owners, we can but pity them. It would be too much to expect them to give up their mills, but we may implore them not to increase them. . . ."

In reply to all the objections of his adversaries Gandhi pointed to existing conditions: " I would ask sceptics to go to the many poor homes where the spinning-wheel is again supplementing their slender resources and ask the inmates whether the spinning-wheel has not brought joy to their homes."

But what influenced Gandhi most strongly in laying such stress on home industry was his hope that in this way the masses stagnating in idleness would be trained in new and useful employment: " Political freedom has no meaning for the millions if they do not know how to employ their enforced idleness. . . . Eighty per cent. of the Indian population are compulsorily unemployed for half the year; they can only be helped by reviving a trade that has fallen into oblivion and making it a source of new income. India must die of hunger so long as the people have no work to provide them with food."

In his wanderings through the country Gandhi inevitably noticed again and again how the compulsory idleness and poverty of the people were gradually producing distaste for work. He tells us that half-starved men apathetically refuse to do any work, in their laziness they would rather be shot than try to do anything. " This indolence," cries Gandhi, " is a greater evil for India even than drunkenness. A drunken sot is prepared to work occasionally, he still retains some judgment, he has still feelings and kindliness. But these moribund creatures who reject all work are almost like animals. Only spinning can free the people from this state of apathy and complete moral degeneration."

X

At the same time Gandhi regarded the spinning-wheel as a symbol of the " dignity of labour," an avowal of the guilt of the rich against the poor. To him weaving and spinning signified a recognition of vital kinship with the masses of the hungry and poor. He inveighed indig-

nantly against the Indian women who themselves
remained idle and resigned to foreigners their pre-
destined work; he issued an appeal to prostitutes, asking
them to weave industriously for eight hours every day
and thus make an honest and worthy existence possible
for themselves. The spinning-wheel signified to him
the key to the true liberation of India, the only means
fitted to restore the economic life of the country to fresh
vigour. Therefore he would endure no interference
from people with other interests and rejected with
indignant contempt the claims urged by foreign manufacturers and Indian importers.

Moreover, Gandhi looked on the resumption of the
old home industry as the best way to unite the population
now split into so many different creeds and castes. In
his opinion nothing could so rapidly unite India and
adjust all religious and social differences as the acceptance of the spinning-wheel and khaddar as the privilege
and duty of every single person. The union of the
whole nation was to be most beautifully and effectively
manifested in the universal practice of hand-spinning
and in the making and wearing of khaddar: "For me
the spinning-wheel and khaddar are the symbols of all-
Indian unity; therefore, I regard them as a national
sacrament."

But weaving and spinning owed their religious importance in Gandhi's eyes not least to the fact that they
allied rich and poor, that everyone who devoted himself
to this occupation of the poor put himself on a level
with the poor, and thereby with all humanity. "I
cannot conceive any higher way of worshipping God
than by doing for the poor, in His name, the work they
themselves do." With religious enthusiasm he proclaims that coarse khaddar is more precious to him than
the finest Japanese silk, for through it he feels himself
linked with his lowly and starving fellow countrymen.
"If we feel for the starving masses of India," he wrote
on one occasion, "we must introduce the spinning-

wheel into their homes and spin daily as a sacrament.
If you have understood the secret of the spinning-wheel,
if you realize that it is a symbol of love for mankind,
you will engage in no other outward activity.   For
khaddar to-day covers all who yesterday were nigh
perishing of starvation, it covers women who used to sit
at home in idleness and demoralization, because no work
called them from their homes."   For this reason khaddar
has become for Gandhi a truly sacred thing, so that he
imagines he can discern a soul in the material.   He once
declared to an English visitor that, if he succeeded in
bringing the spinning-wheel into every cottage in India,
he would be content with the result of his life; his other
plans could, with God's will, be carried out in another
incarnation.

Later, too, the spinning-wheel remained his special
concern.   "I do not want Bombay to mourn over
my arrest," he wrote from prison.   "I would like
Bombay to concentrate on the spinning-wheel. . . .
The women of Bombay, if they really mean to do
their share of the work, should religiously spin for a
certain time every day for the sake of the country. . . ."
Kasturbai, the wife of the Mahatma, also declared in a
message to the Indian people that her husband's last
words before his arrest had been of khaddar; of all the
points of his programme, the Mahatma set the highest
value on the spinning-wheel and khaddar, for the
success of these would not only solve the economic
problem for the Indian masses, but would also set free
the country from its political bonds.   Gandhi wrote to
his friends repeatedly from prison urging them to concentrate all their energies on spinning and weaving:
" We must believe heart and soul in the spinning-wheel."

From his conviction that India could only be restored
to health by means of hand-woven khaddar, Gandhi
finally arrived at the view that the wearing of foreign
materials was a crime against national property, since
it was the taste for foreign textiles that had driven the

Gandhi

spinning-wheel out of India. "It is sinful to eat American wheat and let my neighbour, the grain dealer, starve for want of custom. Similarly, it is sinful for me to wear the latest finery of Regent Street when I know that if I had but worn the things woven by the neighbouring spinners and weavers, that would have clothed me and fed them.... To import even an ell of foreign textiles into India is to snatch the bread from the mouth of a starving man."

Gandhi also drew attention to the fact that the use of factory goods is sinful because these are produced at starvation wages. Among the vows which each of Gandhi's followers has to take is also included one forbidding the use of anything which involves any sort of cheating. In Gandhi's view this command by itself is enough to make the use of foreign cloth impossible, for it is, according to him, the product of exploitation and poverty, manufactured at the expense of the European proletariat, who are cheated of the fruit of their labour.

So Gandhi demanded that materials imported from abroad should not only be rejected, but destroyed, given to the flames. Through this burning of cloth, the sins connected with it were to be symbolically destroyed: "If we are satisfied that we erred in making use of foreign cloth, that we have done an immense injury to India, that we have all but destroyed the race of weavers, cloth stained with such sin is only fit to be burned."

But Gandhi at the same time regarded the destruction of foreign materials as the quickest method of encouraging the production of home-woven khaddar. When he was reproached by many important men, Rabindranath Tagore for example, or his best friend, C. F. Andrews, who frankly declared that they could not understand what advantage it could be to the nation to burn valuable materials, Gandhi in justification developed his "ethics of destruction." This answer, perhaps more than any other utterance of the Mahatma, reveals to us his peculiar and profound realm of thought. First he protested against the assumption that the burning of cloth was an expression of feelings of hostility towards England: "The idea of burning foreign materials springs not from hate, but from repentance of our past sins. . . . In burning foreign cloths we are burning our taste for foreign fineries. . . . The motive was to punish ourselves and not the foreigner. Thus the boycott and burning of foreign textiles has nothing to do with race hatred of England. India cherishes no such hate and does not even feel it."

Gandhi further opposed the assumption that it was a general boycott of all foreign goods: " India does not wish to shut herself out of international commerce. Things other than cloth which can be better made outside India she must gratefully receive. I would exclude only those foreign goods the import of which is injurious to national property, a distinction of great importance. Satan's snares are most subtly laid, and they are the most tempting when the dividing line between right and wrong is so thin as to be imperceptible. But the line is there all the same, rigid and inflexible."

The Swadeshi advocated by Gandhi, the economic independence of India, thus differs to a considerable extent from the weapon of the boycott familiar to the European. Swadeshi is rather an almost religious conception, which does not express revengeful feeling, but aims at advancing the welfare of India. When the pyramids of valuable material and clothes went up in flames amid the jubilation of Gandhi's followers, it was, as he himself solemnly declared, not a symbol of hatred for the foreigner but rather a symbol of India's repentance for her own sins.

When Rabindranath Tagore and many others reproached Gandhi for not having distributed the valuable materials among the poor instead of burning them, he replied to this apparently humane counsel in words which again reveal his deep social and religious feeling: " I must refuse to insult the naked by giving them clothes they do not need instead of giving them the work they sorely need. . . . The ill-clad or the naked millions of India need no charity, but work. Have not the poor any feeling of self-respect and patriotism? Is the gospel of Swadeshi only for the well-to-do? "

" It would have been a crime," he replied on another occasion to remonstrances of the same kind, " to have given such things to the poor. . . . Just imagine the poor people wearing the richest silks. . . . The fact is that the majority of the articles burnt had no relation with the life of the poor. The dress of the middle classes had undergone such a transformation that it was not fit to be given to poor people. It would have been like giving discarded costly toilet brushes to them. I hope, therefore, that the burning process will continue and spread from one end of India to the other, and not stop till every article of foreign clothing has been reduced to ashes or sent out of India."

Gandhi's championing of the spinning-wheel and, in particular, the burning of foreign materials at his instigation, gave rise, as already mentioned, to almost universal opposition. Even men who, like Romain Rolland, held up to admiration the personality and influence of the Mahatma, could not refrain from criticizing him gently on this point. But if one compares Gandhi's procedure with Lenin's attempt to transform in a night an agricultural country, in which industry was but slightly developed, into an industrial state of the most modern kind, Gandhi's ideas suddenly appear in quite a different light. Although he himself never gave concrete form to this idea, it nevertheless appears that Gandhi through his emotions had a more correct understanding of the economic laws of Marxism than Lenin, in refusing to try to industrialize India by artificial means. If, as has already been pointed out, Lenin's " revolutionary jerk," his attempt to try to jump over a

Q

whole epoch in the economic development of his country, must be called an emanation of romantic optimism, Gandhi, on the contrary, by his advocacy of mediaeval home industry, which at first blush sounds romantic, proved himself the more sober practical politician.

It would, therefore, be quite wrong to judge Gandhi's movement by the standard of Western capitalist culture. When Gandhi tried to bring economic relief to his distressed country he could not look for this relief to mechanized industry, which was still almost completely undeveloped, and could not for a long time to come be anything but an insignificant foreign element in India. To be successful he had to direct his efforts rather to the revival of the prematurely crushed, humblest form of industrialism, to the creation of that home industry which, in accordance with the laws of economic evolution, must follow on the purely agricultural system. While thus the violent industrialization of Russia, attempted by Lenin, artificially interfered with the economic position of the country, the khaddar movement of Gandhi in India was much more in harmony with the existing economic situation.

From this point of view Gandhi's action, his bitter fight against the transplantation of industry to India and even against industrialism in general, which at first sight seems utterly absurd to the European, becomes more comprehensible. Even if this hostility to the machine mainly makes use of ethical and religious arguments, nevertheless it contains a core of sober truth from the national and economic point of view. In the economic position of India at the present moment industrialization might in fact be more of a curse than a blessing.

It is most interesting in this connection to note the great difference between the methods of Lenin and Gandhi. The pursuit of one and the same aim led Lenin to an almost religious exaggeration of the value of the machine, whereas it brought Gandhi, almost in the very same years, to the opposite extreme, to a kind

of " machine storming." In both cases, in Russia as
well as in India, it is a question of the reaction of the
East to influences coming from the West; but the
attitude of the two great national leaders to this inruption
of Western civilization was diametrically opposed.

With regard to the particular point of Gandhi's
" machine wrecking," a new light has been thrown by
the extraordinarily pertinent observations of the
well-known Austrian socialist, Julius Braunthal, in his
work, *Mahatma Gandhi und Indiens Revolution*. Braunthal, for the first time I think, has drawn attention to the
very remarkable parallels between Gandhi and the
English factory worker Ned Lud, and indeed the
analogies between the Luddite movement and Gandhi's
are sufficiently striking. But whereas Lud's movement,
which began in Nottingham in the year 1811, led to
bloody outrages and many executions, without having
any permanent success, Gandhi's fight against machine
industry has, by bloodless methods, had important
effects on social conditions in India. In this connection
it may be recalled that the Luddite movement was
publicly supported by no less a personage than Lord
Byron. Lord Byron's first speech in the Upper House
was devoted to opposing the drastic emergency legislation drawn up against the Luddites.

XI

Gandhi's efforts are directed not only against the
industrial manufacture of textiles, but ultimately against
all industry, against machinery as a whole; but here,
too, his views are more in accordance with the specific
position of India than might appear at first. On the
other hand, it is not to be wondered at that his hostility
to machinery frequently met with the most violent

opposition, and that it has called forth the most lively
protests even from many of his own countrymen.
Sankara Nair, for example, declares in a polemical work
that Gandhi obviously does not understand the necessity
of encouraging Indian industry, not only in order to
satisfy the needs of the people, but also to qualify India
for competition with English industry, which is an
absolutely necessary condition for the economic independence of India. " If Gandhi had only applied half
his energies," says Sankara Nair, " to improving the
position of the Indian industrial proletariat, he could
have done away with many of the evils for the sake of
which he wants to destroy all machinery and all industry.
Under the sway of emotional considerations he was led
to advocating the spinning-wheel for India; this may
be quite useful in itself, but it will never be able to be a
substitute for machine production."

But how inconclusive these objections are at bottom
may perhaps be seen most clearly from the views of
Julius Braunthal, to which reference has already been
made. Braunthal, in his study of Gandhi, has grasped
with far-seeing clearness Gandhi's great importance for
the social development of India. Braunthal starts from
the correct assumption, that in order to grasp and judge
Gandhi's movement, it must be treated in its analogy
with the initial stages of European socialism. What the
West may regard as conservative and reactionary in
Gandhi's ideas is, in the conditions prevailing in India,
the only possible preparation for the social revolution.

" The Occidental," says Braunthal, " may call it the
attempt of a *petit bourgeois* reactionary, and it even
appears as such if objectively regarded from a more
advanced historical stage; but if it is looked at from the
angle of the peculiar historical development and the
social and economic conditions of India, this rebellion
against capitalism assumes greater revolutionary significance than, say, the rebellion of the Luddites against
machinery. Luddism was without doubt an aberration

in the class war of the proletariat, but it was an inevitable and to some extent necessary aberration, which was overcome by the modern knowledge of the nature of machinery which increased simultaneously with the rapid development of capitalism and the quick absorption of superfluous labour. . . . It requires time and experience before the worker learns to distinguish between machinery and its capitalist employment and to transfer his attacks from the material means of production to the form of exploitation by society."

For a complete understanding of the Gandhi problem very careful attention should be given to Braunthal's observation that English capitalism, in ruthless pursuit of its own interests, persistently and deliberately ruined the old indigenous Indian home industry without ✓ affording the population, which it robbed of its former means of livelihood, the only possible compensation by means of properly introduced, industrial mass production.

Because it seemed expedient to English capitalism to use India merely as a source of raw materials and a market for finished goods, the Indian home industry was systematically crushed, cotton plantations were introduced in large areas hitherto devoted to rice-growing, and successful efforts were made to accustom the Indian population to the use of English textiles, and thus to drive out home weaving from India. In this way European industry ruined millions of handworkers and reduced to poverty countless millions of small peasants and tenants of tiny plots of land, who had previously lived for six months of the year on their work at the spinning-wheel, without opening up to them any other possibilities of work.

" The hatred of machinery," says Braunthal, " the hatred of capitalism, which burns so strongly in Gandhi, is the reflection of the hate of millions of Indian peasants and handworkers, whose traditional basis of existence was completely destroyed by capitalism and who were excluded from the possibility of existence on a capitalist basis as a factory proletariat. It is the cry of the Luddites which wrings Gandhi's breast, when he condemns capitalism, the capitalist age, and modern civilization as a monstrous depravity, a black age of darkness. . . ."

The correctness of this interpretation may be seen from Gandhi's own views on industrialism and the machine, and also from a research into the impressions which created this hatred of machinery in him. When Gandhi was staying in England in 1908 the great political campaign of the Liberals and the Labour Party against capitalism was being waged. Lloyd George was just about to start his great land campaign, and he was unsparing in his disclosure of all the abuses which existed in large scale industry. Gandhi thus received a terrible impression of the position of the wage worker and of the exploitation of the proletariat practised in English factories. When he returned to India he found similar conditions there, too, in the industrial districts, and saw how Indian labour was shamelessly exploited in the big factories. He was bound, therefore, to recognize that the introduction of machinery had not only not improved the position of the Indian worker, but had actually made it worse, and that the compulsion to work for wages had caught the women and children too. It must not be forgotten that at that time, nearly twenty years ago, the economic position of the English proletariat itself was considerably more unfavourable than it is at the present day, to say nothing of the situation in India, where there were no trade union organizations to protect the workers.

Gandhi, therefore, saw everywhere only the abuse of machinery, and the enslaving of the masses in the interest of a few employers which industrialism had brought about. The " machine wrecking," the " Luddism " of Gandhi, therefore, like all his other doctrines, was the result of personal experience, of a deep social feeling, of sympathy with the exploited. In attacking

machinery Gandhi is protesting against its abuse: this
was the only form in which Western European industrialism presented itself to him,

In a conversation with Ramahandran, Tagore's
disciple, on Ramahandran's asking him whether he
opposed all machinery in principle, Gandhi replied:
" How could that be possible? I know that my own
body is nothing but an extraordinarily delicately constructed machine. The spinning-wheel is also a machine,
and so is every toothpick even. I am not fighting
machinery as such, but the madness of thinking that
machinery saves labour. Men ' save labour ' until
thousands of them are without work and die of hunger on
the streets. I want to secure employment and livelihood
not only to part of the human race, but for all, I will not
have the enrichment of a few at the expense of the
community. At present the machine is helping a small
minority to live on the exploitation of the masses. The
motive force of this minority is not humanity and love
of their kind, but greed and avarice. This state of things
I am attacking with all my might."

For Gandhi the human being remains the only thing
of importance: " Machinery must not strive to cripple
and stunt human limbs. It must one day cease at last
to be a mere tool of acquisitiveness: then the workers
will no longer be overstrained and the machine will be a
blessing instead of a danger. I am aiming at a change
in working conditions of such a kind that the mad race
for money will come to an end, and the worker will not
only be adequately paid but will also find work which is
something more than mere slavery. On those conditions
machinery might be as useful for the men and women
who work it as for the State which possesses it. Once
the mad race has ceased the worker will also be able
to lead a free life under fitting conditions."

It is amazing how closely these words of Gandhi, the
machine stormer, who is decried as a reactionary,
resemble a statement of Karl Marx, also dealing with

capitalistic working methods: " In itself," writes Marx, " machinery shortens working hours, but as used by the capitalist it lengthens the working day; in itself it lightens work, as used by the capitalist it increases the intensity of the work; in itself it is a victory of man over the forces of nature, as used by the capitalist it increases the wealth of the producers; as used by the capitalist it impoverishes those who serve it."

Gandhi, therefore, rejects machinery only because, instead of saving the work of the individual and alleviating conditions of life for the community, it is now useful only to a minority of rich men, and inflicts infinite harm on the working masses. And as in Gandhi's eyes benefit or injury to the masses, to the poor and needy, is the sole criterion for judging every institution, this recognition of the fatal effect of industrialism on the masses leads him to reject machinery.

He expressly excludes from his anathema certain products of European industry, the sewing-machine for example, on the ground that the sewing-machine sprang from an original need to help humanity. But behind this declaration perhaps lurks the unconscious knowledge that the sewing-machine is a tool of home industry and thus a valuable aid to the economic existence for which Gandhi is striving. He would banish from the country all other machines which do not directly serve to help the poor people of India and support them in their struggle for existence; he regards such machines as the works of Satan. Gandhi looks on the great majority of all machine products as entirely unnecessary and even harmful. To the objection that India, if she herself has no factories, must import innumerable commodities, he replies that this idea is entirely wrong. India in earlier times managed to do without these industrial products and can do so again. " As long as we cannot make pins without machinery, so long will we do without them. The tinsel splendour of glassware we will have nothing to do with, and we will make wicks, as of old, with home-grown cotton, and use hand-made earthern saucers for lamps."

For the same reasons Gandhi is opposed to railways, electric tramways, and all modern means of transport; in his opinion these do not satisfy any genuine need: " What is the good of covering great stretches of ground at high speed ? " he asks. " All these things only seem necessary to the European because he is caught in the snares of modern civilization. Machinery is like a snake hole which may contain from one to a hundred snakes. . . . Where there is machinery there are large cities, and where there are large cities there are tramcars and railways, and there only does one see electric light."

All these means of transport seem to Gandhi to be contrary to the original destiny of the human race: " Man is so made by nature as to require him to restrict his movements as far as his hands and feet will take him. If we did not rush about from place to place by means of railways and such other maddening conveniences, much of the confusion that arises would be obviated. Our difficulties are of our own creation. . . . God gifted man with intellect so that he might know his Maker. Man abused it so that he might forget his Maker. Man is so constructed that he can only help his immediate neighbours; but in his conceit he pretends to have discovered that he must with his body serve every individual in the universe. Thus man is utterly confounded. Railways are a most dangerous institution. Man by their means is getting farther and farther away from his Maker."

Gandhi has the happy state of things in India in old days in his mind when he protests against Western innovations. He cries in despair that India was once the abode of the gods, but now it is impossible to conceive gods inhabiting a land which is made hideous by the smoke and din of mill-chimneys, and whose roadways are traversed by " rushing engines."

Both the opponents and the supporters of the Mahatma

have tried again and again to show him the inner inconsistencies of his hostility to machinery. In his pamphlet, *Indian Home Rule*, he deals with all these objections in the form of an imaginary dialogue. When the fictitious " reader " asks how Gandhi squares his attitude with the fact that his own doctrines are printed and circulated by means of machinery, the " editor," that is Gandhi himself, replies: " This is one of those instances which demonstrate that sometimes poison is used to kill poison. The circulation of my ideas by means of machinery thus will not be a good point regarding machinery. As it expires, the machinery, as it were, says to us: ' Beware and avoid me. You will derive no benefit from me.' "

The spiritual and religious side of Gandhi's hostile attitude to the machine is revealed in the conversation of the Mahatma with Ramahandran already referred to. When the visitor asked where the exceptions made by Gandhi were to end, whether the bicycle and the motor-car, as well as the spinning-wheel and the sewing-machine, were to be excluded from his ban, Gandhi replied: " No. For the bicycle and the motor-car do not satisfy the original needs of man. . . . In obedience to the idea, I might indeed exclude all machinery altogether, as I might also reject this body of mine, which is a hindrance to the salvation and liberation of the soul. From this point of view I reject all machinery. Nevertheless, there will always be machines, because these, like the human body, are indispensable. As I have said already, the body is the most perfect machine; but it, too, must be rejected, since it hinders the free flight of the soul."

XII

Gandhi's hostility to machinery is, however, only part of his great fight against the materialistic civilization of the West in general. With the machine Gandhi also rejects the whole world which is bound up with it, as he saw it in all its European manifestations. While so many people in India expected penetration by Western civilization to make the trade and industry of the country flourish and to increase its wealth, Gandhi resisted this economic evolution towards a capitalist system with all his power. What he was striving for in India was not greater riches for the few, but work and bread for the many.

For him the touchstone of a really well ordered society was not the amount of wealth concentrated in a few hands, but the security of livelihood for every individual in the great mass of the people: " The test of orderliness in a country," he wrote once, " is not the number of millionaires it owns, but the absence of starvation among its masses."

At the same time he tried to show the senselessness of all so-called " technical achievements " and the worthlessness of the much extolled European civilization: " The people of Europe to-day live in better built houses than they did a hundred years ago. Formerly they wore skins, and used as their weapons spears. Now they wear long trousers, and for embellishing their bodies they wear a variety of clothing, and instead of spears they carry with them revolvers containing five or more chambers. . . . Formerly in Europe people ploughed their lands mainly by manual labour. Now one man can plough a vast tract by means of steam engines and can thus amass great wealth. Formerly the fewest men wrote books that were most valuable. Now anybody writes and prints anything he likes and poisons other people's minds. . . . Formerly when people wanted to fight with one another they measured between them their bodily strength; now it is possible to take away thousands of lives by one man working behind a gun from a hill. This is civilization. Formerly men worked in the open air only so much as they liked. Now thousands of workmen meet together and, for the sake of maintenance, work in factories. They are obliged to work, at the risk of their lives, at most dangerous occupations for the sake of millionaires. . . . Formerly people had two or three meals consisting of home-made bread and vegetables; now they require something to eat every two hours, so that they have hardly leisure for anything else. . . ."

In Gandhi's view the Western nations are groaning under compulsory labour for the new god, materialism, which stunts their moral growth; Europe no longer worships any god but Mammon and measures its so-called progress in pounds, shillings, and pence. Gandhi tried to show in a wide historical survey how nationalistic cultures had always led to the ruin of great nations; he cites Rome, Egypt, and, lastly, the present age and the world war. "The world war has shown, as nothing else has, the satanic nature that dominates Europe to-day. Every canon of public morality has been broken by the victors in the name of virtue. No lie has been considered too foul to be uttered. But the cause of all these crimes is crass materialism."

India must, according to Gandhi, make every effort to get free as far as she can of the influence of materialistic civilization, and not only not encourage capitalism on the Western model, but even hinder it with all her strength. He rightly says that it would be impossible to amass American riches and at the same time avoid American methods: "It would be foolish to assume that an Indian Rockefeller would be better than the American one."

Independence of Europe, to which Gandhi aspires for India, is, therefore, not a mere political autonomy, but rather a complete severance from the whole world of Western conceptions and ideas. He has declared more than once that he can see no advantage worth mentioning in replacing the present English Government by an Indian Government with English principles and methods. Gandhi desires not only the political independence of India, but its complete detachment from European civilization.

So he directs his attack against all the institutions, vocations, and professions which serve as supports for the gradual Europeanization of the whole of India. But his chief attack is directed against the European system of Government, against parliamentarianism: " Parliament has never yet of its own accord done a single good thing; hence I have compared it to a sterile woman. . . . Parliament is simply a costly toy of the nation." On the strength of this conviction Gandhi asked his followers to boycott the Assembly of the Indian Council, because, unlike many of his countrymen, he was unable to regard this body created by England as a useful institution.

This rejection of the democratic form of Government is also found in Tolstoï: " To ask me for my opinion on parliamentarianism," he said once to his disciple Semeonov, " is like asking the Pope or a monk for advice on the regulation of prostitution. Herzen believed that if men would only devote a hundredth part of the energy wasted on political revolutions to the perfecting of their own nature, they could reach incomparably greater heights. Everything depends on the world's not turning away from the laws of God."

Gandhi has also expressed himself as most decidedly opposed to the law courts; he regards this institution as an instrument of foreign rule forced on the Indians, a contrivance of " satanic civilization." In the same way he opposed lawyers, being convinced that courts and lawyers merely bring confusion into the life of the people, increase disputes, and complicate the relations between man and man.

Gandhi rejects with special vehemence the profession of medicine and the institution of hospitals; he has devoted a special bulky work to this subject, a book which is bound to amaze the European reader. In it he declares that " medical science is the concentrated essence of black magic. Quackery is infinitely preferable to what passes for high medical skill." He regards hospitals as institutions of the devil and the taking of medicine as the greatest sin a man can commit. In his *Guide to Health* he states on this subject:

" We labour under the fatal delusion that no disease can be cured without medicine. This has been responsible for more mischief to mankind than any other evil. It is of course necessary that our diseases should be cured, but they cannot be cured by medicine. Not only are medicines merely useless, but at times even positively harmful. For a diseased man to take drugs and medicines would be as foolish as to try to cover up the filth that has accumulated in the inside of a house. . . . Illness or disease is only Nature's warning that filth has accumulated in some portion or other of the body, and it would surely be the part of wisdom to allow Nature to remove the filth instead of covering it up with the help of medicines. Those who take medicines are really rendering the task of Nature doubly difficult. . . ."

Apart from these doubts of the practical efficiency of the art of medicine, which are to be explained by his utterly inadequate knowledge of the nature and methods of modern medical science, Gandhi has also moral objection to the healing of sickness in general. In his view, the hope of always escaping from all the consequences of dissipation and a wrong way of living by means of medicine, causes men to plunge afresh into vice and sin: " Hospitals are institutions for the propagation of sin; they seduce men into paying less attention to the warnings of their bodies, and giving themselves up more and more to a life of vice."

Gandhi wants to cure all ailments by spiritual means. His most bitter reproach against Western medicine is that it occupies itself exclusively with the body and completely neglects the soul. " I would urge the students and professors," he said once in the course of an address, " to investigate the laws governing the health of the spirit, and they will find that they will yield startling results even with reference to the cure of the body. The man who lives in the proper spirit need never get ill. But because modern medical science entirely ignores this permanent spiritual element, its activities are too restricted to achieve real and permanent success."

Here, too, Gandhi's views are in touch with those of Tolstoï: Tolstoï's hitherto unpublished diaries contain " Thoughts on medicine and doctors," which are strikingly in line with Gandhi's expressed views.[1]

" It is a curious thing," remarks Tolstoï, in these diaries, " that such necessary and beautiful things as bread, fruit, glass, and iron cost so little, while men pay untold sums for the quite unnecessary and often even harmful activities of lawyers and doctors. . . . The art of healing as practised to-day hardly does more good than harm or rather the other way about. . . . The sick man does not know that his life depends on spiritual conditions which are not subject to the laws of matter; instead of seeking for help in the spiritual source of the world and the soul, he prefers to seek it in a living man, a wonder worker, prophet, or doctor. . . . To-day the peculiar but very widespread idea prevails that medicine is useful to life and that its practice is in itself a good work. No such thing exists as good works, there are only good intentions. You can lessen human suffering and be of service to life in a thousand ways, even without medicine. . . ."

[1] Cf. also Der Unbekannte Tolstoi, by René Fülöp-Miller.

Among the resources of European civilization that must be opposed Gandhi also includes schools, at least in the form in which the English have introduced them in India. To understand Gandhi's attitude to the educational problem correctly, we must keep in mind the fact that the English schools in the Indian cities have for long been breeding an educated proletariat of a highly undesirable kind, lacking any real ties with their own people, and detached from their own soil, who scramble in the most unedifying fashion after employment in the few intellectual occupations. Nothing but these serious results of the European educational system can explain Gandhi's desire to make education a privilege of the higher castes and to deprive the lowest classes of any education at all. He considers that education as carried on in India at the present time consists of nothing but the instruction of the children in reading, writing, and arithmetic; and that this is calculated merely to make the simple Indian peasant dissatisfied with his lot. Gandhi's most bitter opponent in India, Sankara Nair, sees a dangerous reactionary element in this attitude: " The educational system advocated by Gandhi," he says in one of his polemical writings, " has for long been practically tested in India; it has created in Hindus and Mohammedans a spirit calculated to produce the sharpest division between the creeds. Not content with this, it has separated the Brahmans from the non-Brahmans, and the caste Hindus from the Hindus without caste. Gandhi wishes to keep all education from the masses, because he wants each class to be resigned to its lot and satisfied with its present position so that the lower castes may continue to be the slaves of the higher."

Gandhi attempted to defend himself against these charges and to prove that the national education given in India to-day is of no value and even harmful: " It is not through the text-books that a lad learns what is right and what is wrong in the home. . . . The higher he goes the farther he is removed from his home. His own civilization is represented to him as imbecile, barbarous, superstitious, and useless for all practical purposes. . . . If I had my way I would certainly destroy the majority of the present text-books, and cause to be written text-books which have a bearing on and correspondence with the home life, so that a boy as he learns may react upon his immediate surroundings. . . . Our children should not be so taught as to despise labour. There is no reason why a peasant's son after having gone to a school should become useless, as he does become, as an agricultural labourer. . . . A word only on the education of the heart. I do not believe that this can be imparted through books. It can only be done through the living touch of the teacher. And who are the teachers in the primary and even secondary schools? Are they men and women of faith and character? Have they themselves received the education of the heart? Are they even expected to take care of the permanent element in the boys and girls placed under their charge? Is not the method of engaging teachers for lower schools an effective bar against character? . . . We know that the teachers in the primary schools are not selected for their patriotism. They only come who cannot find any other employment. . . .

" My uncompromising opposition to English as the medium of education has resulted in an unwarranted charge being levelled against me of being hostile to foreign culture or the learning of the English language. No reader of *Young India* could have missed the statement often made by me in these pages that I regard English as the language of international commerce and diplomacy, and, therefore, consider its knowledge on the part of some of us as essential. As it contains some of the richest treasures of thought and literature I would certainly encourage its careful study among those who have linguistic talents, and expect them to translate those treasures for the nation in its vernaculars.

" Nothing can be farther from my thoughts than that

we should become exclusive and erect barriers. But I
do respectfully contend that an appreciation of other
cultures can fitly follow, never precede, an appreciation
and assimilation of our own. . . ."

Gandhi again and again draws attention enthusiastic-
ally to the superiorities of the old Indian culture. He
thinks that earlier races knew that happiness was not a
material but a spiritual state. He is never tired of
extolling old times and their way of life: " When there
was no rapid locomotion teachers and preachers went on
foot from one end of the country to the other, braving
all dangers not for recruiting their health (though that
followed from their tramps) but for the sake of humanity.
Each one followed his own occupation or trade, and
received a suitable wage for his work. It is not as if we
did not know how to invent technical contrivances!
But our forefathers knew well that if we gave our
attention to such things we were bound to become the
slaves of machinery. Therefore they wisely decided
that we should only perform the work which we can
accomplish with our hands and feet. They recognized
that large towns are a danger and a useless evil, and so
they remained contentedly in their little villages. . . ."

Gandhi shows how India for thousands of years was
the only country to maintain unshaken its wise traditions
and institutions, while everything else in the world was
transient. From quite primitive times India has been
able to cultivate self-control and knowledge of happiness:
" We have nothing to learn from the foreigner. The
traditional old implements, the plough and the spinning-
wheel, have made our wisdom and welfare. We must
gradually return to the old simplicity! Let everyone
proceed to set a good example! "

XIII

But not all his countrymen were prepared to respond to his appeal. Many of them regarded this fight of the Mahatma against Western culture rather as a grave danger for the further development of India. He was reproached with obstinate conservatism, with standing in the way of all reforms, for which the best representatives of India have long been working in peaceful agreement with the English Government. " The success of Gandhi," exclaims Sankara Nair, " would be the success of the forces of reaction in their attempt to attain what they call national independence, which in reality means their sole dominion! "

Rabindranath Tagore, too, India's greatest poet, blamed Gandhi and said that his attempt to divide India from the West was spiritual suicide. " The Occident has a great mission to fulfil for man and humanity; it is wrong to try to cut ourselves off from it by artificial means. No nation can work out its salvation by detaching itself from the others. It is not possible to base the freedom and independence of India on the rejection of everything foreign."

Far from wishing to deny his conservatism, Gandhi insists on maintaining that this strict preservation of traditional Indian custom is the only possible way to make the country free and happy again. He does, it is true, declare in his reply to Tagore that he, too, loves fresh air and does not " want his house to be walled in on all sides and his windows to be stuffed." But no foreign culture can tear him from his native soil: " It is my firm conviction that no culture can show such rich treasures as ours. . . . What we have tried and found to be genuine on the anvil of experience, we refuse to change. In this steadfastness lies India's strength, it is the sheet anchor of her hope."

What gives Indian culture particular value in Gandhi's

eyes is its religious basis; culture and politics are almost
synonymous with religion in India. This reverence of
Gandhi's is connected not so much with the dogmas of
the Hindu creed as with the moral sentiment " which
transcends Hinduism, which changes one's very nature,
which binds one indissolubly to the truth within and
which even purifies. It is the permanent element in
human nature which counts no cost too great in order
to find full expression, and which leaves the soul utterly
restless until it has found itself, known its Maker, and
appreciated the true correspondence between the Maker
and itself."

Gandhi proclaims his pride in being a Hindu and
confesses his faith in the Vedas, the Upanishads, and all
that is united under the name of the Holy Scriptures.
He believes in reincarnation, in Varnashrama Dharma,[1]
" in the strict sense of the word," and in the protection
of the cow " in a much larger sense than the popular."

We must bear in mind in this connection that Gandhi
is by no means ignorant of the other great creeds; on the
contrary, he made himself thoroughly familiar with the
writings and doctrines of Christianity and Islam. We
know what a deep impression was made on him by the
life and work of Christ, especially the Sermon on the
Mount. Nevertheless, he gently but decidedly rejected
his friends' many attempts to convert him, saying that
although he did not believe that Hinduism in itself contained more truth than Christianity, for him personally
the religion of his fathers was the best means for satisfy-
ing his inner needs. " My faith offers me all that is
necessary for my inner development, for it teaches me
to pray. But I also pray that every one else may develop
to the fullness of his being in his own religion, that the
Christian may become a better Christian and the
Mohammedan a better Mohammedan. I am convinced
that God will one day ask us only what we are and what
we do, not the name we give to our being and doing."

---

[1] The caste system.

How little bigotry there is in Gandhi's religious
opinions is best shown by the fact that he always avoids
using the ordinary expression " divine origin " in connection with the Vedas and other Hindu writings. He
explains this by saying that he regards not only the
Vedas, but also the Bible, the Koran, and the Zend
Avesta as divinely inspired. But beyond this his faith
in no way obliges him to regard every line of Holy
Scripture as inspired by God, because in the course of
time much in these books had become confused and
distorted by wrong interpretations.

According to Gandhi, who is in agreement with
Hindu doctrine, a true understanding of religious
writings requires perfection in innocence (*ahimsa*), in
truth (*satya*), and in self control (*brahmacharya*).
" Nevertheless no one must despair of the possibility of
being able to grasp the nature of religion, for the
foundations of Hinduism are unchangeable and easy to
understand."

In very beautiful, most arresting words, Gandhi confesses that he feels most profoundly drawn to the faith
of his fathers, in spite of his clear insight into the many
defects inherent in this creed: " I can no more describe
my feeling for Hinduism than for my own wife. She
moves me as no other woman in the world can. Not
that she has no faults. I dare say she has many more
than I see myself. But the feeling of an indissoluble
bond is there. Even so I feel for and about Hinduism
with all its faults and limitations. Nothing elates me
so much as the music of the Gita or the Ramayana of
Tulsidas, the two books of Hinduism I may be said to
know. When I fancied I was taking my last breath the
Gita was my solace. I know the vice that is going on
to-day in all the Indian shrines, but I love them in spite
of their unspeakable failings. I am a reformer through
and through. But my zeal never takes me to the rejection
of any of the essential things of Hinduism. . . ."

This confidence in the wisdom of the customs

inherited from his forefathers leads Gandhi to support the maintenance of the caste system. It is well known that generally this caste system is regarded as the most dangerous and pernicious legacy which India has inherited from her past; Tagore shares this view and looks on this peculiar social order as the greatest evil existing in India.

The Bengali poet has again and again pointed out that the abolition of caste is the first condition for the real liberation of India, for caste is the root of the weakness and all the social defects of India. Tagore blames the Indian intelligentsia because they have so little understanding of the frightful consequences of this division into castes, and, completely ignorant of true conditions, are still proud of this " stiffness of their social backbone."

But Gandhi recognizes the caste system in all its forms. When it was proposed to him that caste should be abolished and replaced by the European class system, Gandhi answered that he regarded the law of heredity as an eternal law, and that any attempt to alter it must lead to utter confusion. " I can see a very great use in considering a Brahman to be always a Brahman throughout his life. It is easy to imagine the innumerable difficulties if one were to set up a court of punishments and rewards, degradation and promotion. If Hindus believe, as they must believe, in reincarnation and transmigration, they must know that nature will, without any possibility of mistake, adjust the balance by degrading a Brahman, if he misbehaves himself, by reincarnating him in a lower division, and translating one who lives the life of a Brahman in his present incarnation to Brahmanhood in his next. . . ."

Gandhi, also, it is true, confessed the necessity of improvements in existing conditions. He holds only the four main castes to be fundamental, natural, and important, and energetically supports the abolition of the innumerable sub-divisions in these four main castes. But the abuse of the system does not appear to him to

be a sufficient reason for abolishing the system itself:
" I am certainly against any attempt at destroying the
fundamental divisions. The caste system is not based
on inequality, there is no question of inferiority. . . .
Social pressure and public opinion can be trusted to deal
with the problem of the sub-castes. . . ."

In Gandhi's opinion the caste system, along with all
the other traditional religious and cultural rules, has
preserved Hinduism from disintegration. Therefore
all those who are trying to make fundamental changes in
Indian conditions, through the introduction and propagation of modern civilization for example, seem to him
to be enemies and dangers to the nation.

His conviction of the " satanic character " of European civilization, and of the superiority of Indian culture
to all Western institutions, is so strong that he could
even say that he himself preferred the defects in Indian
culture to foreign institutions, because these defects
were merely aberrations of a spirit in itself true and
blessed, whereas the spirit of European civilization was
abhorrent in itself.

No one knows, he declares, the faults of India better
than he does, and no one has opposed them more
strongly; nevertheless, he is convinced that Western
civilization is godless, while Indian civilization is permeated with faith in God. " Whoever really under-
stands and loves India must cling to the culture of his
country as a child clings to its mother's breast."

XIV

All Gandhi's sentiments are closely bound up with the
traditions of his country. This adherence to the old
traditional thought of his race and the ancient doctrines
of his forefathers does not, however, spring from any

narrow-minded rationalism, but, on the contrary, from an all-embracing pity and love. His deep sympathy for all suffering and misery, as shown in his support of the poor and hungry, his fight for the liberation of the pariahs, and for the rescue of women who are the victims of vice, and also his campaign for the spinning-wheel and the freeing of India, are entirely rooted in the Hinduist faith. For the core of that faith is the doctrine of *Ahimsa*, non-killing, the love for all created things.

Ahimsa is the great recognition that all living things find their highest meaning only in love; hate, ill-will, and cruelty are simply transgressions of the fundamental laws of nature, and to abandon oneself to such feelings is to turn away from the divine order of the world. He who truly desires to practise Ahimsa must not anger anyone or wish him ill, not one who has offended him, not an enemy, not even a thief. He must treat every living being with kindness and goodwill, accept all malice quietly, and answer injustice with love.

True Ahimsa is, in fact, an unattainable state of perfection, towards which humanity moves in gradual progress. In our present state we are, according to Hindu doctrine, only partly human; the other part of us is still animal. Only the conquest of our lower instincts by love can slay the animal in us, an idea which is symbolically indicated in the first song of the Bhagavadgita. Ahimsa, love for all creatures, however, embraces not only humanity, but all sub-human life, it includes serpents and wild beasts. If the purposes of the Creator were known to man he would understand that these beasts were not created to be the victims of our lust for destruction.

The Shastras, the ancient holy books of Hinduism, teach that whoever truly practises Ahimsa sees the world at his feet. As soon as we are able to change our inner nature the external world is changed at the same time, dangers cease, foes are transformed into friends, nature itself changes its essence. In its positive form Ahimsa thus signifies the victory over the world by love and compassion, the disarming of evil by good.

The doctrine of Ahimsa is found in Buddhist as well as in Hindu scriptures. Buddhism also contains an unconditional, unlimited, and absolute prohibition of killing and also of the infliction of any kind of pain. Buddhism forbids, as Carl Friedrich Koeppen remarked in his time, plainly and without any exceptions all slaying " not only of man but also of animals," and excepts no case in which this can be done without sin. Therefore it is written in the Buddhist texts also: " There is no conceivable reason for which thou mayst take the life of any creature that breathes, neither because it is useful or harmful to you, neither at the command of a superior, nor from hunger or self-defence, although the guilt may be lessened by such circumstances. The only blood thou mayst shed is thine own, if the giving up of thy life would save or rescue a fellow creature. And not only does he sin who himself lays his hand on a creature, but also he who orders the slaying, who looks on it with approval, who has indirectly caused it, or who benefits by it." Buddha is also supposed to have strictly forbidden his pupils to clothe themselves in silken stuffs or to wear shoes or sandals of leather, " because such clothing is derived from the slaying of living beings." Buddha himself also taught: " Man shall overcome evil by good."

Ahimsa is observed with particular scrupulousness by the adherents of the Jain sect. To this sect Gandhi's parents belonged and he himself was brought up on the strict principles of the Jain religion, so that, as he has declared, from his earliest childhood he was trained in the meaning of " Ahimsa practice."

Later, when he became acquainted with other creeds as well, he sought and always found in them the same commandment to love man and beast, the prohibition of slaying. " I drew many of my convictions," he himself writes, " from Jain religious works, as I have

from the writings of the other great faiths. I found the
same law of pure love in the Hindu scriptures as in the
Bible and in the Koran. Thus, though my views on
Ahimsa are the result of my study of most of the faiths
of the world, they are no longer dependent on the
authority of these works. They are a part of my life,
and if I suddenly discovered that the religious books
read by me bore a different interpretation from the one
I had learned to give them, I should still hold fast to my
views on Ahimsa."

The love for all created beings also led Gandhi to
include in his faith the Hinduist veneration for the cow.
This demand of the Indian creed, which seems so strange
to Europeans, receives a new and deep meaning in
Gandhi: " The central fact of Hinduism is cow protection; cow protection to me is one of the most wonderful phenomena in human evolution. The cow to me
means the entire sub-human world. Man through the
cow is enjoined to realize his identity with all that lives.
Why the cow was selected for apotheosis is obvious to
me. The cow was in India the best companion. She
was the giver of plenty. Not only did she give milk, but
she also made agriculture possible. The cow is a poem
of pity. One reads pity in this gentle animal. Protection
of the cow means the protection of the whole dumb
creation of God. The appeal of the lower order of
creation is all the more forcible because it is speechless.
Cow protection is the gift of Hinduism to the world.
And Hinduism will live as long as there are Hindus to
protect the cow. . . ."

In his writings and speeches Gandhi frequently comes
back to the protection of the cow. He believes that the
moral quality of the Indian race will not be judged either
by its capacity for reciting prayers, nor by the number
of its pilgrimages, nor by its punctilious observance of
the rules of caste, but solely by its ability to protect the
cow.

Gandhi's love for all live nature extends to the lowest

beasts, even to poisonous serpents. Although countless numbers are killed every year in India by snake bites, the Mahatma preaches the practice of Ahimsa even against these dangerous animals: " Let us never forget that the serpents have been created by the same God who created us and all other creatures. God's ways are inscrutable, but we may rest assured that he did not create animals like the lion and the tiger, the serpent and the scorpion, in order to bring about the destruction of the human race. . . .

" The great St. Francis of Assisi, who used to roam about the forests, was not hurt by the serpents or the wild beasts, nay, they even lived on terms of intimacy with him. So, too, thousands of yogis and fakirs live in the forests of Hindustan amidst lions, among tigers and serpents, but we never hear of their meeting death at the hands of these animals. . . . In fact, I have implicit faith in the doctrine that so long as man is not inimical to the other creatures, they will not be inimical to him. Love is the greatest of the attributes of man. Without it the worship of God would be an empty nothing. It is, in short, the root of all religion whatsoever."

Gandhi came more and more to look on the Ahimsa idea as the great message which it was the mission of India to proclaim to the world: " Rightly understood, Ahimsa is the cure for all evils. It does not displace the practice of the other virtues, but renders their practice imperatively necessary. . . ."

During his life in London Gandhi met adherents of the most varied ideas and schools of thought; the bravery of many of these men made a deep impression on him, but he nevertheless always felt that violence and the various forms in which it might be used could be no cure for the maladies of India, and that the civilization of his country required for its protection another and more lofty weapon. This profound conviction of the universal truth of the Ahimsa idea made Gandhi decide to carry on the fight against personal and political enemies in all circumstances by means of love alone.

In his earliest youth strong impressions had established and confirmed in Gandhi faith in the truth and the power of Ahimsa. Once, when J. Doke asked him how the Ahimsa idea took root in him, Gandhi quoted a verse which he learned as a child in school: " If a man gives you a drink of water and you give him a drink in return, that is nothing. Real beauty consists rather in doing good against evil." This verse, according to Gandhi, had a very great influence on him; later the teaching of the Sermon on the Mount had a similar effect on his views: " It was the New Testament which really awakened me to the rightness and value of passive resistance and love towards one's enemies. When I read in the Sermon on the Mount such passages: ' Resist not him that is evil, but whosoever smiteth thee on thy right cheek, turn to him the other also '; or ' Love your enemies, bless them that persecute you, that you may be the sons of your Father which is in Heaven,' I was simply overjoyed."

But of all the utterances of modern ethical doctrine, it was the writings of Tolstoï which most strongly confirmed Gandhi in his ideas of the positive power of non-resistance: " Mahatma Gandhi," writes W. W. Pearson on this subject, " had a profound admiration for Tolstoï and his teaching, and possibly owes more of his present attitude on the value of passive resistance to that great Western teacher than to the teachings of his own religion, although that had from early childhood taught him Ahimsa, the renunciation of all kinds of violence." Romain Rolland has also drawn attention to this similarity between Gandhi and Tolstoï, and in his most excellent monograph on Gandhi, he expressly compares him with Tolstoï: " I have said enough to show Gandhi's great evangelical heart beating under the garb of his Hindu faith. He is a gentler, quieter Tolstoï, a Tolstoï who, if I may use the expression, is a natural

Christian in the universal sense of the word. For
Tolstoï was a Christian less by nature than by force
of will."

Among the posthumous papers of the great Russian
novelist was found a correspondence between Tolstoï
and Gandhi, which made clear the personal relations
which united the two men. It is thanks to the efforts of
the well-known writer Paul Birukov, that this important
correspondence was published.

Gandhi wrote to Tolstoï the first time in 1909, from
London. In his reply to this letter Tolstoï already
showed the liveliest interest in and sympathy for his
Indian disciple: " I have just received your most
interesting letter, which has given me great pleasure.
God help our dear brothers and co-workers in the
Transvaal. The same struggle of the tender against
the harsh, of meekness and love against pride and
violence, is every year making itself more and more felt
among us here also, especially in one of the very sharpest
of the conflicts of the religious law with the worldly laws
in refusals of military service. Such refusals are becoming ever more and more frequent. . . . I greet you
fraternally and am glad to have intercourse with you. . . ."

In April 1910 Gandhi again wrote to Tolstoï, and
sent him his pamphlet, *Indian Home Rule*. In the
accompanying letter Gandhi signed himself Tolstoï's
" humble follower," and asked the novelist to tell him
what he thought of the book.

Tolstoï first replied briefly to this request, and then in
greater detail in a second letter. " The longer I live,
and especially now, when I vividly feel the nearness of
death, I want to tell others what I feel particularly
clearly and what to my mind is of great importance—
namely, that which is called passive resistance, but which
is in reality nothing else than the teaching of love un-
corrupted by false interpretations. That love—*i.e.*,
the striving for the union of human souls and the activity
derived from this striving—is the highest and only law

of human life, and in the depths of his soul every human being (as we must clearly see in children) feels and knows this; he knows this until he is entangled by the false teachings of the world. This law was proclaimed by all —by the Indian as by the Chinese, Hebrew, Greek, and Roman sages of the world. I think this law was most clearly expressed by the Christ, who plainly said that ' in this only is all the law and the prophets.' But besides this, foreseeing the corruption to which this law is and may be subject, He straightway pointed out the danger of its corruption, which is natural to people who live in worldly interests. . . . He knew, as every sensible man must know, that the use of force is incompatible with love as the fundamental law of life, that as soon as violence is permitted, in whichever case it may be, the insufficiency of the law of love is acknowledged, and by this the very law is denied. The whole Christian civilization, so brilliant outwardly, grew up on this self-evident and strange misunderstanding and contradiction, sometimes conscious, but mostly unconscious.

" In reality, as soon as force was admitted into love, there was no more and there could be no love as the law of life, and as there was no law of love, there was no law at all, except violence, *i.e.*, the power of the strongest. . . . This contradiction always grew with the development of the people of the Christian world, and lately it reached the highest stage. The question now evidently stands thus: either to admit that we do not recognize any religio-moral teaching, and we guide ourselves in arranging our lives only by the power of the stronger, or that all our compulsory taxes, courts, and police establishments, but mainly our armies, must be abolished. . . ."

These doctrines of the apostle of Iasnaia Poliana, which had remained purely theoretical, were to be practically realized by Gandhi. In all the political speeches which Gandhi delivered in Ahmedabad, Bombay, or Calcutta, whether he was addressing the

masses, students, women's organizations, or working
men, in the midst of the gravest political confusion,
surrounded by cheers and demonstrations, directly
threatened with arrest, there rang always from his mouth
such words as had never yet been heard from a politician
since the beginning of the history of man.

An enslaved people was rising against their oppressors,
prepared for revolution, and was striving to shake off
the yoke of centuries; but the leader, the organizer of
the movement for liberation, who called on the people
to rise, preached love, understanding, and consideration
for the enemy.

" Through love," says Gandhi, " we seek to conquer
the wrath of the English administrators and their supporters. We must love them and pray to God that they
might have wisdom to see what appears to us to be their
error. It is our duty to let ourselves be slain, but not
ourselves to slay. If we are cast into prison we must
acquiesce in our lot without bad feeling, hate, or any
thought of revenge."

He states emphatically that India can only rise to new
freedom if she meets her oppressors with love, cares
for their lives, and even sacrifices her own rather than
inflict pain on the enemy: " The moment of victory has
come when there is no retort to the mad fury of the
powerful, but a voluntary, dignified, and quiet submission. . . . The secret of success lies, therefore, in
holding every English life and the life of every officer
serving the Government as sacred as those of our own
dear ones. All the wonderful experience I have gained
now during nearly forty years of conscious existence
has convinced me that there is no gift so precious as that
of life. I make bold to say that the moment the Englishmen feel that, although they are in India in a hopeless
minority, their lives are protected against harm, not
because of the matchless weapons of destruction which
are at their disposal, but because Indians refuse to take
the lives even of those whom they may consider to be

utterly in the wrong. . . . We must by our honest conduct demonstrate to them that they are our kinsmen. We must, by our conduct, demonstrate to every English-man that he is as safe in the remotest corner of India as he professes to be behind the machine-gun. That moment will see a transformation in the English nature in its relation to India, and that moment will also be the moment when all the destructive cutlery in India will begin to rust. . . . As soon as a nation no longer fears violence its Government will also see its uselessness and give it up."

Gandhi's revolution is unique in history as a revolution of goodness and non-violence, under the leadership of a man who preaches understanding and sacrifice and whose motto is " Love your enemies." It is true that in earlier times reformers, saints, and founders of religions have preached passive resistance in face of evil, but what distinguishes Gandhi's movement from all those of the past is the fact that the Mahatma regards non-violence not as a religious and ethical precept for individuals or for a small community, but makes it the basis of a political movement, and thus for the first time in history has transformed a moral perception into a practical political system.

Gandhi most energetically stresses the point that his teaching is not only to be followed by a few elect persons, but is rather intended to be universal. " The religion of non-violence is not meant merely for the *Rishis* and saints. It is meant for the common people as well. Non-violence is as much the law of our nature as violence is that of the brute. The spirit lies dormant in the brute and he knows no other law than that of physical might. The dignity of man requires obedience to a higher law, to the strength of the spirit." He appeals to his experiences in South Africa and declares that even his simplest fellow countrymen are able to carry on the war against violence by peaceful means. Non-violence is just as difficult or just as easy to cultivate

as any other virtue, and it is not necessary to know the
complete philosophical basis of the doctrine.

Gandhi demands that children should be instructed
in the principles of Ahimsa at a very early age, for the
child must, even before he learns to read and write,
grasp this fundamental law of all higher spiritual life
and understand also what forces are contained in his
soul. The most important part of education, therefore,
should consist in teaching young people to overcome
hate by love and violence by their own suffering.

His efforts are aimed at " brahmanizing " the whole
Indian nation, that is, at spiritualizing the tactics of war.
The Indian scholar Vidhusekhara, one of the professors
at the Indian University at Santiniketan, presided over
by Rabindranath Tagore, says that hitherto all wars and
struggles for political power have always been carried on
exclusively by the lower castes, the warriors, merchants,
and pariahs, whereas Gandhi is trying to wage his war
with the weapons of the Brahman caste: " The fundamental idea in this struggle is not the principle of ' an
eye for an eye and a tooth for a tooth,' but the more
than two-thousand-year-old commandment of Buddha:
' Man shall conquer anger by love, evil by good, avarice
by generosity, and the liar by truth.' "

The Mahatma, by exhorting the nation to wage their
war for political freedom with the spiritual weapons of
Brahmanism, is raising the whole nation to the rank of
the highest caste, and attributing to every Indian the
capacity to think, feel, and act like a Brahman. India's
great settlement with England was to be brought about
exclusively by the weapons of love and sacrifice; the
deep political conflict between two races was to be
waged in a war without violence or bloodshed.

In the decrees of this peculiar statesman the appeal
to love recurs again and again: " We may not attempt
to chasten the enemy with violence, still less may we
force him to share our views. . . . The attainment of
freedom will not be possible until we make it our strict

rule never to exercise any undue pressure on anyone. The one permissible way of convincing our enemy is by friendliness and kindness. . . . Many of us believe, and it is my opinion also, that we have a message to give to the whole world. I would gladly use the British race to spread our ideas over the whole earth; but this can only happen if we conquer our so-called conquerors by love."

Gandhi made the attempt to prove the superiority of moral and spiritual weapons to a world in the toils of faith in violence. For he is convinced that Ahimsa, the practice of love and understanding, is not the weapon of weakness, but the concentrated form of spiritual and moral force, a mysterious power stronger than all the violence of brutal oppression: " I believe," he says, " that Ahimsa is infinitely superior to violence, forgiveness is more manly than punishment. Forgiveness adorns a soldier. But abstinence is forgiveness only when there is the power to punish. It is meaningless when it pretends to proceed from a helpless creature. Therefore it is only the stronger who can forgive the weaker. . . . Strength does not come from physical capacity. It comes from an indomitable will. An average Zulu is any way more than a match for an average Englishman in bodily capacity. But he flees from an English boy, because he fears the boy's revolver or those who will use it for him. He fears death and is nerveless, in spite of his burly figure. We in India may in a moment realize that one hundred thousand Englishmen need not frighten three hundred million human beings. A definite forgiveness would, therefore, mean a definite recognition of our strength. With this enlightened forgiveness must come a mighty wave of strength in us, which would make it impossible for a Dyer or a Frank Johnson to heap affront upon India's devoted head. It matters little to me that for the moment I do not drive my point home. We feel too downtrodden not to be angry and revengeful. But I must not refrain from saying that India can gain more by waiving the

right of punishment. . . . It may be that in other
countries Governments must be overthrown by brute
force; but India will never gain her freedom by the
naked fist. For the destiny of this country is different
from that of the other great empires. India is thus pre-
destined to exercise religious domination over the whole ✓
world. She needs no weapons of steel, she formerly
fought with divine weapons. She will do so in the future,
and win wholly and solely by soul-force. . . ." Gandhi,
therefore, does not ask India to practise Ahimsa because
she is weak; he rather desires that his country should
cultivate love from a consciousness of inner strength.
" I want India to recognize that she has a soul that cannot
perish, and that can rise triumphant above every
physical weakness and defy the physical combination
of a whole world. . . ."

He even goes so far as to declare that he would sever
his connection with India the moment she adopted the
creed of violence: " If India takes up the doctrine of
the sword she may gain a momentary victory; then
India will cease to be the pride of my heart. I am wedded
to India, because I owe my all to her. I believe absolutely that she has a mission for the world; however,
India's acceptance of the doctrine of the sword will be
the hour of my trial. My religion has no geographical
limits. If I have a living faith in it, it will transcend my
love for India herself. My life is dedicated to the service
of India through the religion of non-violence, which I
believe to be the root of Hinduism. . . ."

XV

One of the essential features of Gandhi's teaching is
thus the positive character of Ahimsa. He again and
again emphasizes the fact that the non-violence which
he preaches is not a passive state, but rather the setting

of a higher violence against oppression. In order to describe this spiritual power, Gandhi has borrowed the Sanskrit word *Satyagraha*, which means the " power of truth," and is intended to designate the active force of love in opposition to the merely passive form of passive resistance.

For this reason Gandhi draws a sharp distinction between Satyagraha and passive resistance; passive resistance, it is true, avoids violence, but only so long as violence is not in the power of the weaker; it does not in principle exclude its use. It is accordingly the weapon of the weak, which is used only while these are not capable of meeting force with force. The Satyagraha recommended by Gandhi is intended for the strong and in no conceivable case sanctions the use of force. For Gandhi no idea exists, not even the loftiest, for the realization of which the use of brute force is permissible.

He himself is the protector of the poor and has devoted his whole life to a ceaseless fight for the interests of the needy and suffering, but he has never made use of force even in the struggle for a lofty and ideal aim. An utterance of the Mahatma in a conversation with the German writer, Arthur Holitscher, quoted by him in his most interesting book, *Das Unruhige Asien*, is very characteristic. Holitscher had drawn attention to the injuries inflicted by capitalism and remarked that this evil could only be attacked by force. Gandhi, however, replied in one of his metaphors that his faith forbade him to kill a serpent. " That is not to say," he went on, " that I am forbidden to shudder when I catch sight of a serpent. I will not play with it or caress it, I will inspire it with confidence and make it clear that I do not wish to hurt it; then it will also spare me. I would not destroy capitalism, I would only change its temporary form—its essence I cannot destroy, because I offer it no resistance."

It is, therefore, not surprising that Gandhi vigorously

rejects the methods of Bolshevism. In spite of all the claims put forward to the effect that the liberation of the poor and oppressed can only be accomplished by a violent upheaval, Gandhi has never let himself be led astray in his views on this subject. " I believe in the conversion of humanity not in its destruction," he replied to the Indian Bolshevik, M. N. Roy. " I do not believe in the success of violent action; however much I sympathize with and admire deserving arguments, I nevertheless remain an inflexible opponent of all violent methods in however good a cause they may be employed. The doctrine of force can never be brought into harmony with our own outlook. The faith of Bolshevism is ruthless self-indulgence, whereas Satyagraha means self-restraint."

Truth cannot be upheld by inflicting pain on the enemy, but only by voluntary endurance of suffering. All progress is to be measured by the amount of suffering undergone by the sufferer; thus the sacrifice of Christ sufficed to free a sorrowing world. Gandhi is convinced that the liberation of India cannot be attained by bloody reprisals on her oppressors, by physical force and destruction, but only by the voluntary assumption of suffering. The active side of the Satyagraha idea preached by Gandhi consists in this, that everyone must be prepared, of his own free will and for the sake of truth, to undergo pain, privation, and even death, for voluntary suffering produces an overwhelming spiritual strength and leads to the liberation of the oppressed and the abolition of all wrongs and injustices.

Gandhi points out that no country has ever risen without having been " purified through the fire of suffering." " Will India rise from her slavery without having fulfilled the eternal law of purification by pain? " Gandhi, with a proud gesture, declares that he has undertaken to re-establish in India the old law of sacrifice, for Satyagraha is " a new name for suffering," without which freedom can never be attained.

Just as he tried to show that Satyagraha can only be the weapon of the really strong, so he also endeavours to prove that force is in truth not only not a proof of courage, but, on the contrary, a proof of cowardice. It is from cowardly fear that man takes refuge in brute force. Therefore, the resolution to practise Satyagraha and voluntarily take suffering on oneself is the conquest of cowardice. No one can, in Gandhi's words, practise Satyagraha and at the same time be a coward; Satyagraha calls forth the greatest courage. It is the most soldierly of soldiers' virtues. For while Satyagraha means the rejection of all physical force, it does not imply helpless submission to the power of the evildoer. Gandhi's followers are not to submit to evil, but rather oppose their full soul-force to the will of the oppressor, in order to overcome him by the weapons of the soul. Anyone may defy brute force and effectively defend the right by the exercise of his spiritual strength, whereas armed resistance only brings fresh injustice into being without causing any change of heart in the enemy.

Gandhi has again and again set a good example of readiness joyfully to accept all injustice for his righteous ideal. When he was threatened with arrest he welcomed the news with joy, and instructed all his followers to submit unresistingly if they were taken prisoner. " Anyone summoned to appear before a Court should do so. No defence should be offered and no pleaders engaged in the matter. If a fine is imposed with the alternative of imprisonment, imprisonment should be accepted. If only a fine is imposed, it ought not to be paid. . . . There should be no demonstration of grief or otherwise made by the remaining Satyagrahis by reason of the arrest or imprisonment of their comrade. It cannot be too often repeated that we court imprisonment and may not complain of it when we actually receive it. When once imprisoned it is our duty to conform to all prison regulations. . . . A Satyagrahi may not resort to surreptitious practices. All that the

Satyagrahis do can only and must be done openly.
To evade no punishment, to accept all suffering joyfully,
and to regard it as a possibility for further strengthening
his soul-force, is the duty of every single one of my
followers."

When Gandhi actually was put in prison he regarded
this as a trial of his spiritual strength. " I calmly
acquiesced in all the troubles bodily given to me by the
warder," he wrote of his time in prison, " with the result
that not only was I able to remain calm and quiet, but
that he himself had to remove my fetters in the end.
If I had opposed him my strength of mind would have
become weakened and I could not have done those more
important things that I had to do. By my submissive-
ness I overcame most difficulties in prison. But the
greatest good I derived from these sufferings was that
by undergoing bodily hardships I could see my mental
strength clearly increasing, and it is even now maintained.
I feel that divine help is always with those who suffer
for the sake of a righteous cause. Jesus Christ, Daniel,
and Socrates represented the purest form of passive
resistance, of soul-force. All these teachers counted
their bodies as nothing in comparison with their soul.
In India the doctrine was understood and commonly
practised long before it came into vogue in Europe."

As a model for the conduct of a true Satyagrahi,
Gandhi also quotes the example of Thoreau, who wrote
with regard to his life during his imprisonment, that
the thick walls surrounding him were unable to confine
him: " The walls seemed to me a great waste of stone
and mortar. I could not but smile to see how industriously they locked doors on my body, while my medita-
tions followed them out again without let or hindrance.
My gaoler wanted to punish my body, as boys, if they
cannot come to some person against whom they have
a spite, will abuse his dog."

But for Gandhi the voluntary acceptance of suffering
is not confined to letting oneself be imprisoned without

resistance; it includes also the overcoming of the fear of death. Only those who have mastered the fear of death can tread the path of Satyagraha. For this reason Gandhi sometimes calls the great aim of his Swaraj movement, the liberation of India, an " abandonment of the fear of death," for true freedom cannot consist of political freedom alone, it involves rather the complete freedom of every individual from every kind of fear: " So long as we let ourselves be influenced by the fear of death, we can never attain to freedom. . . . We are not yet completely free, because we are not prepared to look death quietly in the face."

This teaching of Gandhi's is particularly important for India, for the Indian races are generally, apart from exceptional cases, rather inclined to abandon themselves helplessly to all pain and are in particular dominated by a great fear of death. Gandhi has therefore, again and again, to point out most emphatically that the freedom of the country can only be won if the population is able to overcome its " fear and helplessness in the face of death."

For the followers of the Satyagraha doctrine the body is only a means to a higher end, and must therefore be given up as soon as it becomes an obstacle to the free development of the soul. The disciple of Satyagraha is, therefore, ready to die if he believes that his death would convert his enemies to truth. In the knowledge that the soul survives the body, the sacrifice of the body becomes a triumph of truth as it was with the early Christian martyrs.

XVI

Satyagraha, the power of truth and sacrifice, had not only to be practised in the life of the individual, it must also regulate the relations between the citizen and the State, and even the relations between nations: " The people," says Gandhi, " must do away with the error and injustice of a State which are expressed in the form of bad laws, by enforcing the repeal of these enactments through voluntary acceptance of suffering. It is, therefore, necessary not only to transgress an unjust law, but also voluntarily to accept the penalty which this transgression brings."

The resistance to the injustice of the State recommended by Gandhi, " civil disobedience," was in future to be the only means to be used in the fight against political oppression. The expression " civil disobedience " was coined by Thoreau, but whereas the American wanted to limit this weapon to the fight against a few specific laws, especially against unjust taxation, Gandhi extends its application to all immoral laws, and enjoins on his followers the strictest abstinence from all violence. This public disobedience is intended to form a protest against an act for which the population cannot recognize any moral and ethical justification. If the State issues unjust orders it oversteps the limits ✓ of its powers and thereby renounces its authority. The citizen who refuses to submit to these orders transgresses them quite openly and voluntarily accepts the prescribed penalty. This protest of the Satyagrahi against unjust laws can, however, only be effective if he at the same time submits willingly to and obeys all laws which he recognizes as just. Only the man who can obey the laws is competent to refuse to obey them. For, according to Gandhi, submission to State laws is the price which the citizen pays for his personal freedom. Subjection to a State which is wholly or largely unjust is, however, an " immoral barter for liberty."

The " civil disobedience " preached by Gandhi is thus a " rebellion without any signs of violence," an insurrection of the people in an unarmed and silent protest against the authority of the State.

Gandhi employed this weapon for the first time in South Africa in his fight against injustice and oppression,

and won remarkable success by its means. When all
the attempts of the Indians living in South Africa to
convince the Government peacefully of the injustice of
their exceptional laws had failed, Gandhi finally decided
to secure the rights of his oppressed fellow countrymen
by means of Satyagraha and civil disobedience.

In the year 1906 the South African Government had
passed an Act which placed the immigrant Indians in
some respects on the level of criminals: they had to
report to the police and allow their thumb prints to be
taken and registered. The Indians felt this measure to
be an offensive and provocative insult; great meetings
were held and finally they adopted Gandhi's proposal
to adopt civil disobedience in face of the new order.
It was then that Gandhi's Satyagraha idea first began to
prove its practical effectiveness.

Although non-observance of the new registration
order involved heavy penalties, almost all the Indians
in South Africa categorically refused to enter their names
in the police lists or to allow their thumb prints to be
taken. Imprisonment after imprisonment followed with
unrelenting severity; soon the prisons in the Transvaal
were full of disobedient Indians; Gandhi also was
sentenced to two months in prison.

A conciliatory movement led to the institution of
negotiations between Gandhi and the South African
authorities, but these were only temporarily successful,
and as a protest against fresh humiliations the passive
resistance of the Indians began again. Again thousands
allowed themselves to be imprisoned voluntarily, and
Gandhi himself was again put in gaol.

The whole dispute, which lasted for many years,
reached its climax in 1912, when by an award of the
South African Union Court all marriages celebrated
according to Indian rites were declared to be null and
void. Almost simultaneously a new Act obliged the
Indians in South Africa to pay a poll tax of three pounds
a year. Gandhi proceeded to proclaim passive resist-

ance in the form of complete stoppage of work. The
Indian women, who had risen in protest against the
nullification of their marriages, toured the mining
districts and called on the Indian workers to strike
until the Government had repealed this unjust legislation. Under pressure of this great strike movement a
conference was called, at which Gandhi was present,
and finally the Government announced that they were
prepared to repeal the poll tax.

In order to make the authorities keep their promises,
Gandhi decided to organize a great procession of all the
Indian immigrants through the Transvaal. The London
Times called this great march one of the most remarkable
historical manifestations of passive warfare.

The programme was to carry on the march until all
those taking part in the demonstration had either been
put in prison or reached the town of Johannesburg.
The Government called out large military forces to act
as police, and began by arresting Gandhi in the hope of
thus bringing about the collapse of the whole movement. But when it became clear that this " non-violent
army " were not to be stopped in their march by the
imprisonment of their leader, Gandhi was released. He
at once hastened back to his people and led the procession
onwards until the police declared all the demonstrators
arrested and took them back to their homes by rail.

This peculiar form of protest and the tenacious
stubbornness of Gandhi's followers were not without
effect on public opinion. Although Gandhi himself
was again sentenced to fifteen months' imprisonment,
the South African authorities were at last forced to yield.
In 1913 the poll tax was repealed and the validity of
Indian marriages recognized. The Government by a
special law granted the immigrants complete freedom
and equality of rights. But Gandhi had won even more
than the realization of his aims. By the peaceful and
dignified nature of his warfare he succeeded in the end
in completely converting his most bitter enemy, the

Boer General and Prime Minister, Smuts. Smuts, in
1906, declared that he would never erase from the
statutes the exceptional measures against the Indians,
but in 1913 he confessed that he was very glad to do
away with them.

XVII

Gandhi's second attempt to defend the rights of the
oppressed against unjust Government measures by the
help of Satyagraha was undertaken in his own country,
in the province of Gujerat. After the successful conclusion of his struggle for the liberation of the South
African Indians, Gandhi had returned to India with all
the honours of a conquering hero. When, in 1918,
an agrarian movement started in Kaira in opposition
to the unjust taxation of the peasantry, Gandhi inter-
vened, although up till then, right through the war, he
had remained loyally on the side of the British
authorities.

After he had for long tried in vain to convince the
authorities of the injustice of their actions, he advised
the peasants to refuse to pay taxes and to accept voluntarily the penalties prescribed. Events showed that the
peasants of Kaira could display the same endurance as
their brothers in South Africa. More than two thousand
simple country people, in spite of all the threats of the
authorities, refused to pay the unjust taxes and suffered
all the penalties inflicted on them. Finally they succeeded in carrying their point, made the Government
give in, and enforced the repeal of the taxes. Soon
afterwards Gandhi also undertook the leadership of disaffected workers in Virangan and Ahmedabad and there,
too, achieved surprising success with his passive resistance methods.

But the system of non-resistance and soul-force did
not find its true political expression until the great

political struggle to free India from English rule. Gandhi, by "non-co-operation," by the complete refusal to work with the British authorities, tried to assemble all the long existing efforts to free the Indian people from English overlordship into a common non-violent struggle, and to oppose to the military predominance of the foreign conquerors the purely spiritual power of the Indian people.

The political weapon of non-co-operation had occasionally been used in India in earlier times; but it was only through Gandhi that it received its true ethical and revolutionary importance, and was at the same time formed into a lofty philosophical and political system. The abstinence of the people from all participation in Government business in India was more than a mere protest against the measures of unjust governments; the idea was deeply rooted in the feeling, thought, and action of the Indian, for since the time of Buddha a distaste for all forms of armed rising had been general among orthodox Indians. It was only the Mohammedan Indians who had from time to time had recourse to the sword in their fight against oppression.

Passive resistance to British rule was tried for the first time in Benares · in 1812, as a protest against a certain measure of the British administration which seemed to the people to be unjust. All the shops in the city remained shut for a long time and the populace did no work; the masses obeyed absolutely the instructions of their leaders and maintained the strictest discipline. This movement was successful; the Government had to yield and repeal the taxes which had led to this outburst of protest.

Another attempt of the kind was made in 1830 in the principality of Mysore, the native ruler of which cruelly oppressed his subjects. The report of the British representative on these events says: " The population left the villages, ceased all work in the fields, drove out the officials and refused to pay taxes in any form whatever. But no excesses occurred anywhere and no one had recourse to arms. The people assembled in the jungles and maintained themselves there with all sorts of provisions brought from the villages at night-time. The various measures by the help of which the natives defend themselves against the abuses of the Government are familiar to the population. The most frequent and most effective means is to refrain completely from any participation in administrative business."

At the beginning of the twentieth century the people of Bengal, under the leadership of the great Indian thinker and politician, Aurobindo Ghose, carried out a movement which has many claims to be called the fore-runner of Gandhi's "non-co-operation." The English bureaucracy intended to introduce a new administrative division of districts which was a menace to interests important to the people of Bengal. In answer to this measure the Bengalis decided, on the advice of Auro-bindo Ghose, to proclaim a boycott of all British goods and to cease all co-operation with the English authorities. To this period belong Rabindranath Tagore's first songs of freedom, in which he exhorts his fellow citizens to devote their whole strength, lives, and property to the freeing of their native land. The Bengalis replied enthusiastically to the appeal of their poet and their political leader. In all parts of the province men and women cast off their clothes of English manufacture and burnt them on great bonfires; at the same time almost all the native officials retired from their posts and boy-cotted the British administrative authorities.

Aurobindo Ghose, like Gandhi after him, was con-vinced that India should educate her children in the spirit of her own culture and make a clean sweep of the half-education which had previously been in force. But so long as the people were unfed and unclothed, they could not be expected to take sufficient interest in spiritual training. For this reason Aurobindo Ghose demanded financial self-administration for India, so that

the Indian people could relieve the universal need from
their own resources. When England proved disinclined
to grant this financial autonomy Aurobindo turned
against the British Government altogether, but wished
to avoid all use of violence in the struggle. Therefore,
he asked the people to develop their own moral fitness
for independence by mutual support and help, and at the
same time by passive resistance to the English. India
must encourage her industry and agriculture from her
own resources instead of expecting help from her foreign
overlords. Because England refused India economic
protection by means of customs duties, the people,
according to Aurobindo Ghose, must provide protection
for themselves by the boycott of English goods. The
nation should make every effort to crush the devastating
epidemics by clearing the jungles, laying out new roads,
and abolishing the unhygienic conditions in the villages
and towns, to build as large a number as possible of new
Indian schools in order to increase the spiritual and
moral strength of the young, and to prepare the people
systematically for political and economic independence.

This movement in Bengal did not long preserve its
peaceful character. The leadership of the excited
masses soon slipped from the hands of Aurobindo
Ghose into those of other politicians, who preached
armed rebellion. Soon a bloody revolt occurred, which
was quickly crushed by the English.

XVIII

Before the appearance of Gandhi the political leadership of the movement for Indian independence had been
in the hands of Bal Gangadhar Tilak. Tilak, who bore
the honorary title of " Lokamaya " (leader of the people),
had raised the cry of " Swaraj," self-government for
India, for the first time at the All-Indian National

Congress in 1905, and after a series of hard struggles had enforced many reforms in the English administration of India. After the appearance of Tilak the nationalists had gained leadership in the Congress and had finally wrung a number of concessions from the Government: first the " Morley-Minto reforms," and then, after the war, the " Montagu-Chelmsford reforms," which first really created a sort of autonomous Indian administration.

Tilak is one of the political leaders of whom Gandhi always speaks with respect and reverence. The Mahatma relates that Tilak honoured him with his confidence and approved his methods on his death-bed. Gandhi also includes among his chief political teachers the Parsee, Dadabhai, the " uncrowned king of Bombay," who first taught him how to apply Ahimsa in public life, and finally the great Indian politician and national leader, Gokhale. " Gokhale seemed to me," says Gandhi, " all I wanted in a political leader. He was pure as crystal, gentle as a lamb, brave as a lion, and chivalrous to a fault."

Under the influence of these teachers, and in obedience to his own views, Gandhi, in India as in South Africa, first attempted a peaceful and friendly settlement of all differences with the British administration. In an open letter to all Englishmen in India he later, in the days of the most violent struggle, pointed out how he had worked hand in hand with the British Government for twenty-nine years, under the most difficult conditions. " I ask you to believe me when I tell you that my co-operation was not based on the fear of the punishment provided by your laws or on any selfish motive. It was free and voluntary co-operation based on the belief that the sum total of the activity of the English Government was for the benefit of India."

It was events during and after the war that changed Gandhi's views on loyalty to England. Great Britain, soon after the beginning of the war, made far-reaching promises in order to secure the support of India, includ-

ing an undertaking to grant India complete autonomy
and equality with the other British dominions. Relying
on this promise India not only gave England financial
help during the war, but even raised a large army in the
recruiting of which Gandhi himself took part.

But when England, after the defeat of Germany, no
longer depended on the help of India, she took her own
time over the fulfilment of her promises and paid no
particular attention to the disappointment of the Indians.
Gandhi still believed that London intended only a
postponement, and would sooner or later fulfil its
pledges. This faith was not finally shattered until the
time when, in 1919, the " Rowlatt Bill " was introduced,
which was nothing but an indefinite prolongation of the
exceptional state of affairs established during the war.

The rushing of this Bill through the Imperial Legislative Assembly at Delhi was the real cause of Gandhi's
finally abandoning his confidence in the loyalty of
England and deciding on open war for the independence
of his race. " I felt that the Rowlatt Bills," he wrote,
" were so restrictive of human liberty that they must be
resisted to the utmost. . . . I submit that no State,
however despotic, has the right to enact laws which are
repugnant to the whole body of the people, much less
a Government guided by constitutional usage and
precedent such as the Indian Government."

The whole of India, under Gandhi's influence,
suddenly awoke to the liveliest political activity, and
joined in a mighty demonstration of protest on 6th April
1919. " I felt," Gandhi wrote later, " that the on-
coming agitation needed a definite direction if it was
neither to collapse nor to run into violent channels. So
I ventured to present Satyagraha to the country. . . ."
Throughout the whole of India a " hartal," or general
stoppage of work, was held, accompanied by religious
celebrations. But even this hartal was hardly more than
a demonstration, it was directed merely against a definite
law and kept entirely within the limits of law and order.

T

With the exception of some trouble in Delhi, the demonstration passed off without any violence.

However, when Gandhi, having heard of the outbreak in Delhi, set off for the town to quiet the people, the Government in an excess of zeal had him arrested on the way and brought back to Bombay. The news of this arrest had disastrous results. It led to trouble in the Punjab, to proclamation of martial law, and a little later to he notorious massacre at Amritsar, when the English General Dyer ordered machine-guns to fire on the unarmed crowd and butchered hundreds. It is true that, on pressure from the Indian nationalists, a committee of enquiry was set up soon after this frightful occurrence, whose findings confirmed the atrocities, but the English Government took no steps to punish the guilty officials.

At the same time as the Hindu population was thrown into a state of violent excitement by these events in the Punjab, the " Khalifat movement " began among the Indian Mohammedans, and added to the general unrest. The Indian Moslems consented to support England during the war only on condition that Turkey should not be too severely treated after the victory. So when peace negotiations began at Sèvres, and it became known that severe conditions had been imposed on Turkey, the Mohammedan population of India was full of indignation. They appealed to the promises made by Lord Chelmsford and Lloyd George, and forcefully demanded the reinstatement in his former sovereign state of the Sultan, who as Khalif represented the spiritual head of all Islam. When the English Government disregarded this demand the two Ali brothers organized the Indian Mohammedans in an energetic movement of protest.

Gandhi's keen eye recognized this as an opportunity for bridging over the gulf of hostility which had for centuries separated Hindus and Mohammedans in India and for uniting the adherents of the two creeds in

common movement against England. He himself took
the chair at the great Mohammedan Khalifat Conference
which met on 24th November 1919, zealously supported
their demands, and declared that the Hindus would
make the Mohammedan cause their own.

XIX

Although Gandhi's " non-co-operation " was at first
a negative movement with the object of restraining the
Indian people from any participation in the English
administration and any contact with official institutions,
his political thought became an active force the moment
he reminded his countrymen that non-co-operation
with England presupposed the co-operation of all Indians.
Gandhi's success in establishing this unity in India,
even although it was but temporary and incomplete,
and in bridging over the profound differences which
had existed for centuries, especially between Hindus
and Mohammedans, is perhaps his greatest achieve- ✓
ment as a statesman. He was the first to be able to
create something like an Indian nation, to weld together
the population of this gigantic empire, so riven with
religious and ethical differences, in a uniform national
sentiment.

Just as Lenin recognized the union between peasants
and workers, between the urban proletariat and the
enormous mass of the rural population, to be the chief
condition for the success of the revolution and the
maintenance of his new political system, so Gandhi
regarded the union between Hindus and Mohammedans
as a fundamental condition for a new and free India.

More than once in earlier times attempts had been
made to put an end to the century-old deep hostility
between the Mohammedan conquerors and the Hindus

whom they subdued. As early as the seventeenth
century the Emperor Akbar the Great prepared the way
for reconciliation by an extraordinary tolerance towards
all religious creeds. Nanak, the founder of the Sikh
sect, tried to bring about an adjustment of differences
from the religious side. But the doctrines of Nanak,
whose cry was " There are no Hindus and no Mohammedans," later led to the exact opposite of a religious
reconciliation, for the Sikh sect developed into an
extremely intolerant and entirely warlike religious
community.

At the present time many efforts, especially in intellectual circles, might be mentioned which all aim at
bringing about a union between Hindus and Mohammedans by the propagation of Western ideas of tolerance;
particular mention should be made of the reform movements of Rannohun Roy, Debendranath Tagore, and
Kesub Zunder Sen, with whom Rabindranath Tagore is
closely allied.

As the number of Mohammedans in India has never
amounted to more than a fifth of the total population,
they for long formed an alliance with the English and
adopted a friendly attitude to them in order to preserve
their superior position. It is well known that Great
Britain would never have been able to put down the
dangerous Sepoy rising in 1859 without Mohammedan
support. This friendly alliance between England and
Islam naturally contributed greatly to making the
contrast with the Hindus more acute, oppressed as they
were by both sides. As long as the Mohammedans made
common cause with the English, any union between
them and the Hindus was practically inconceivable.

In the year 1919 the political situation of centuries
was changed at one blow. By the Mohammedan
Khalifat movement the Mussulman population of India
became alienated from the English regime and approached
correspondingly nearer to the Hindu Swaraj movement.
Gandhi, by knowing how to take advantage of the new

situation, and persuading his followers to make the claims
of the Mohammedans their own, succeeded for the first
time in uniting Hindus and Mohammedans in a common
movement against the English Government.

Although here and there there was a revival of the
hostility between the two faiths, which sometimes even
led to grave excesses, as at the time of the bloody
Moplah rising, nevertheless unity was realized in practice
to a greater extent than ever before through Gandhi's
initiative. The Mohammedan leaders worked hand in
hand with Gandhi, both parties put forward the same
programme at the All-Indian Imperial Congress, and
in the years that followed Hindus and Mohammedans
supported each other in the movement against England
in an honourable alliance.

In all his speeches and writings on Hindu-Mohammedan unity, Gandhi championed absolutely equal
rights for both religions. In his opinion unity was
independent of all differences of creed and culture:
" I never realize any distinction between a Hindu and
a Mohammedan. To my mind both are sons of Mother
India. I know that the Hindus are a numerical majority,
and that they are believed to be more advanced in
knowledge and education. Accordingly, they should be
glad to communicate some of their knowledge to their
Mohammedan brethren. When Hindus and Mohammedans act towards each other like blood brothers, then alone
can there be true unity, then only can the dawn of
freedom break for India."

Gandhi hoped that the ultimate result of this union
would mean not only the political liberation of India,
but also the awakening of a homogeneous national
culture. In order to advance this aim, he founded an
Indian University at Ahmedabad, at which the students
were to be made familiar with all Asiatic cultures and
languages, Arabic and Persian as well as Sanskrit.
" My university," he wrote in his paper, *Young India*,
" is not intended merely to feed on or repeat the ancient

cultures, but to build a new culture based on the traditions of the past and enriched by the experiences of later times. The ideal is a synthesis of all the different cultures that have come to stay in India, that have influenced Indian life, and that, in their turn, have themselves been influenced by the spirit of the soil. This synthesis will naturally be of the Swadeshi type, where each culture is assured its legitimate place, and not of the American pattern, where one dominant culture absorbs the rest and where the aim is not towards harmony, but towards an artificial and forced unity. . . . One thing only is barred by the university, that spirit of exclusion which permanently claims for its sole use any field of human interest whatever. . . ."

It is not surprising that this bold idea of breaking with all the deeply rooted prejudices of India's past and uniting Hindus and Mohammedans in a common movement was not accepted with unanimity in India, and even led to strong opposition in many circles. One of Gandhi's most bitter enemies, the politician and writer, Sankara Nair, expressed the view that the Mohammedans understand by unity merely their own hegemony over the Hindus and that Gandhi had gone far to meet them on this point. " Gandhi," Sankara Nair maintains, " has had to make very great concessions to the Mohammedans, and has thereby delivered the Hindu cause into the hands of Islam."

In reply to the objection that the Mohammedans, even by religion, are in principle supporters of war, and can, therefore, find no place in a system of passive resistance, Gandhi stated: " My association with the noblest Mussulmans has taught me to see that Islam has spread not by the power of the sword but by the prayerful love of an unbroken line of its saints and fakirs. Warrant there is in Islam for drawing the sword; but the conditions laid down are so strict that they are not capable of being fulfilled by everybody. Where is the unerring general to order a Jehad? Where is the

suffering, the love, and purification that must precede
the very idea of drawing the sword? "

Other Indian publicists again, like Chatterjee and
Chandarvarkar, have expressed the view that it would
be wrong to expect a religious agreement from the fact
that the Hindus have adopted the Mohammedan
demands in the Khalifat dispute, for the victory of the
followers of the Khalifat could only help to make Indian
Islam even stronger than before and gravitate to some
centre outside India.

However justified some of these objections may in
themselves appear to be, the greatness of Gandhi's
undertaking remains beyond dispute. The fact that he
succeeded, even if only partially and perhaps not permanently, in reaching a national agreement in the century-
old hostility between the two creeds, remains an historic
fact, which is bound to be numbered among the most
important in the history of India.

XX

The influence of this united movement of all Indian
parties under Gandhi's leadership caused the English
Government to make certain concessions. On 24th
December 1919 an amnesty for political prisoners was
proclaimed, and a Reform Act was approved which
granted the Indian people a number of important rights
both in the central government and in district administration. On the assumption that England intended to
relent, and in his desire to preserve peace as long as
possible, Gandhi accepted the British proposals and
also carried them in the National Congress.

But in 1920 Gandhi found himself compelled to make
a final break with the British Government. After the
death of Tilak he became the universally recognized

leader of the Indian nationalists at the very moment when the disastrous peace terms for Turkey became known, and almost at the same time as the provocative resolutions of the Committee of Investigation on the atrocities in the Punjab were published. The Mohammedans felt that their religious sentiments had been wounded by the unjust treatment of the Osman Empire, while the Hindus regarded the immunity of the officers guilty of the massacre at Amritsar as a grave insult and a maddening injustice. The two great parties therefore, on Gandhi's advice, resolved on the joint execution of " non-co-operation." Gandhi informed the Viceroy of this decision in a letter, in which he also explained the motives for the adoption of passive resistance against the English authorities; but he also, on this occasion too, emphasized his willingness for a peaceful settlement.

Gandhi's *Open Letter to All Englishmen in India* perhaps affords a better insight than any other document into the reasons which led him to start his non-co-operation campaign. Moreover, the whole spirit of his programme is clearly shown in this pamphlet. " Up to the present I fully believed that Mr. Lloyd George would redeem his promise to the Mohammedans, and that the revelations of the official atrocities in the Punjab would secure full reparation for the Punjabis. But the treachery of Mr. Lloyd George and the condonation of the Amritsar atrocities have completely shattered my faith in the good intentions of the Government and the nation which is supporting it. You have shown total disregard of our feelings by glorifying the Punjab administration and flouting the Mussulman sentiment.

" I know that you would not mind if we could fight and wrest the sceptre from your hands. You know that we are powerless to do that, for you have ensured our incapacity to fight in open and honourable battle. Bravery on the battlefield is thus impossible for us. Bravery of the soul still remains open to us. I know that you will respond to that also. I am engaged in evoking that bravery. Non-co-operation means nothing less than training in self-sacrifice. . . ."

Gandhi published innumerable appeals to the population and made speeches and gave addresses in the attempt to familiarize the masses with his ideas and his programme. He declared that from time immemorial it had been the right of the people to refuse to work with an unworthy authority. But if this movement were to be successful, it must be conducted with the strictest discipline, and discipline was possible only if no violence were used. For this reason abstinence from any form of armed warfare was the first condition of success: " If violence is employed against the representatives of the Government or against persons who refuse to join our movement, it means retrogression in our case and a useless waste of innocent lives. Therefore, all who earnestly desire that non-co-operation be successful in the shortest possible time must regard complete order as his first duty. . . ."

Gandhi explained in detail how every citizen unconsciously and tacitly supported the ruling Government and thus made himself responsible for its actions. There was nothing against this while the Government acted justly; but it became the duty of everyone to refrain from co-operation with unjust rulers: " If a father does any injustice it is the duty of his children to leave the parental roof. If the head master of a school conducts his institution on an immoral basis the pupils must leave the school. If the chairman of a corporation is corrupt the members thereof must wash their hands clean of his corruption by withdrawing from it. Even so, if a Government does a grave injustice the subject must withdraw co-operation wholly or partially, sufficiently to wean the ruler from his wickedness. In each of the cases conceived by me there is an element of suffering, whether mental or physical. Without such suffering it is not possible to attain freedom."

The Indian people, therefore, in order not to be

responsible for the deeds of the English Government, were to refrain from giving their active and passive support; they were as it were to terminate the *contrat social* and withdraw from the political community. Until reparation was made for the unjust acts of the Government, Gandhi's followers were to take no notice whatever of any official institution, much less make use of it. Gandhi, however, in this case tried to show that this non-co-operation was quite distinct from the boycott; the boycott was the expression of revengeful sentiments and therefore in conflict with the Ahimsa idea. " To proceed from non-co-operation to the boycott would be a descent from the sublime to the ridiculous. . . . Non-co-operation, in the sense used by me, must be non-violent, and therefore neither punitive nor vindictive, nor based on malice, a desire to punish, or ill-will or hatred. . . . What makes our movement a moral and peaceful struggle is the law of love which we have made its basis. Our non-violence must be something more than merely refraining from injuring the enemy physically; otherwise every siege or blockade would be a form of peaceful warfare, whereas in reality they are as much an expression of brute force as a regular battle."

Gandhi was convinced that the Government could overthrow any armed rising with their military resources, but that they were unable to stop peaceful non-co-operation. It was certainly an important condition for success that the whole movement was not animated by the idea of embarrassing the Government at any price, but that the whole Indian people, even in the midst of the strictest non-co-operation, was full of goodwill and kindliness towards the oppressors, for it was only in this atmosphere that the all-prevailing power of Satyagraha could develop. The greatness of the success depended, as Gandhi often emphasized, not on the amount of embarrassment that non-co-operation caused the authorities, but solely on the amount of goodwill prevailing in the people of India.

" Non-co-operation," wrote Gandhi, " is a movement intended to invite the English to co-operate with us on honourable terms or retire from our land. It is a movement to place our relations on a pure basis, to define them in a manner consistent with our self-respect and dignity."

There is no charge which Gandhi rebuts so decisively as the idea that his fight for Indian freedom has anything in common with nationalism in the ordinary sense: " It is true that I work for the freedom of India; I was born in India, I inherited its culture, and was created to serve my country. But my love for my fatherland has not only no desire to injure any other nation, it rather aims at serving as best it can all other nations in the truest sense of the word. The freedom of India, as I conceive it, can never be a danger to the world."

Gandhi's nationalism contains none of those elements which make the nationalist movements of the Western countries seem a menace to peace. Gandhi's national ideal is not the principle of narrow concentration on his own nation and a hostile attitude to all other nations; it is rather a consciousness of having a specific task to fulfil for India. Whenever nationalism ceases to use violence, and consciously and unconditionally rejects violence, it will become a principle fundamentally different from the nationalist imperialism of Europe. Gandhi has awakened the Indian people to a national ethical system which can never be a danger to other countries.

This is best seen in Gandhi's definition of his own patriotism: " For me," writes the Mahatma, " patriotism is the same as humanity. I am patriotic because I am human and humane. My patriotism is not exclusive. I will not hurt England or Germany to serve India. Imperialism has no place in my scheme of life."

Gandhi drew up a most precise and carefully thought-out plan of campaign for his non-violent warfare, in which he fixed four stages of non-co-operation, which were to be applied consecutively as need required. The first stage consisted in the resignation by Indians of all titles and honorary offices; the second stage provided for the recall of all Indian officials from their posts, at the third stage the Indian police and military forces were to resign from the service of the English, while the fourth stage prescribed a general refusal to pay taxes.

To start with, Gandhi announced the first part of his programme and asked the population to resign all honorary titles and offices conferred by the English Government, not to participate for the time being in any State loans, not to invoke the aid of the courts, to remove their children from the State schools, and not to send deputies to the Legislative Councils provided for in the Constitution. He himself announced in his letter to the Viceroy that he resigned all the English titles and orders conferred on him.

His example was almost generally imitated in India. Numerous officials sent in their resignations, the schools emptied, the law courts were no longer used. The All-Indian National Congress not only sanctioned all the measures proposed by Gandhi, but also made known that, if necessary, they were ready to proceed to the fourth stage of the struggle, refusal to pay taxes. About a year later, when violent measures were expected from the English authorities, the National Congress handed over all its functions to Gandhi, that is, conferred the right of dictatorship on him, and at the same time authorized him, in case he were arrested, to appoint his successor and transmit his authority to him.

The aim of Gandhi's efforts was *Swaraj*, complete self-government for India. The Indian people must in future be able to decide their destiny, independent of all foreign influences. In this connection Gandhi believes that this freedom cannot be a gift to India, for Swaraj is a treasure to be purchased with a nation's best blood, which can only come to the country as the fruit of " incessant labour and suffering beyond measure."

So long as they had no legal pretext for intervention the English authorities looked on more or less quietly at the non-co-operation movement. Gandhi had also reckoned on this, at least in the first stages of his programme, when he maintained that the Government would be powerless in face of a non-violent movement.

But if the English did nothing to compel the Indian population to co-operate, neither did they show any signs of submitting to Gandhi's demands and granting self-government to the country. And just as the Mahatma, according to programme, was on the verge of going on to the next stage of non-co-operation, and proclaiming civil disobedience, the excited crowd was guilty of serious excesses in Chauri Chaura, which caused the death of several police officers. Under the shattering impression of this serious breach of the principle of non-violence, Gandhi recognized that the people were not ripe for carrying out civil disobedience in a dignified and peaceful manner, and desisted from proclaiming it. He imposed a five days' fast on himself as an atonement for the crime committed by the infuriated mob.

In the spring of 1922 the English Government, after a long period of uncertainty and vacillation, at last decided to make an example of Gandhi and to bring him to trial. The ostensible pretext for this action was afforded by four articles published by the Mahatma in his periodical, *Young India*, in which the Advocate-General discovered the crime of " exciting disaffection towards His Majesty's Government as established by law in British India." On 10th March 1922 Gandhi was arrested and detained in the prison of Sabarmati. On his first appearance before the examining magistrate Gandhi pleaded guilty; his friend Shankarlal Banker, the publisher of *Young India*, who had been arrested and charged with the same offence, also from the very beginning accepted full responsibility before the law.

On 18th March the case was heard before C. N.

Broomfield, the district judge of Ahmedabad; the accused declined to be defended. A great part of the case was taken up with a controversy between the Advocate-General and the judge; the judge wished to give his verdict immediately after Gandhi had pleaded guilty, but the Advocate-General insisted that the procedure should be carried out in full; his aim was to make Gandhi responsible for the riots and bloodshed at Chauri Chaura, Madras, and Bombay, and to influence the sentence by proving aggravating circumstances.

Then Gandhi rose and made his great speech. He began by acknowledging that he was really responsible for the popular excesses with which the Advocate-General had charged him: " I wanted to avoid violence. But I had to make my choice; I had either to submit to a system which I considered had done an irreparable harm to my country or incur the risk of the mad fury of my people bursting forth when they understood the truth from my lips. I know that my people have sometimes gone mad. I am deeply sorry for it, and I am, therefore, here to submit not to a light penalty, but to the highest penalty. I do not ask for mercy nor plead any extenuating act. I am here, therefore, to invite and cheerfully submit to the highest penalty that can be inflicted upon me for what in law is a deliberate crime, and what appears to me the highest duty of a citizen."

Gandhi explained that he had for thirty years been loyal to England, until finally all his hopes were destroyed and he felt compelled to take up the fight against the British Government.

" I have no personal ill-will," he declared, " against any single administrator, much less can I have any disaffection towards the King's person. But I hold it a virtue to be disaffected towards a Government which in its totality has done more harm to India than any previous system. India is less manly under British rule than she ever was before. Holding such a belief, I consider it to be a sin to have affection for the system. And it has been a precious privilege for me to be able to write what I have in the various articles tendered in evidence against me. . . . I am endeavouring to show to my countrymen that violent non-co-operation only multiplies evil, and that as evil can only be sustained by violence, withdrawal of support of evil requires complete abstention from violence. Non-violence implies voluntary submission to the penalty for non-co-operation with evil. I am here, therefore, to invite and submit cheerfully to the highest penalty that can be inflicted upon me. . . . The only course open to you, the Judge, is either to resign your post and thus dissociate yourself from evil, if you feel that the law you are called upon to administer is an evil and that in reality I am innocent; or to inflict on me the severest penalty if you believe that the system and the law you are assisting to administer are good for the people of this country, and that my activity is, therefore, injurious to the public weal."

After Gandhi had finished the judge began his address. He prefaced it by saying what a heavy task had fallen to him, as he was personally perfectly convinced of Gandhi's lofty mindedness and ideal motives. " There are probably few people in India," he went on, " who do not sincerely regret that you should have made it impossible for any Government to leave you at liberty. . . . I feel it my duty to sentence you to six years imprisonment, and I would like to say in doing so that, if the course of events in India should make it possible for the Government to reduce the period and release you, no one will be better pleased than I."

Soon after Gandhi went to prison an important change began in the Indian Independence Party. Under the leadership of C. R. Das, a group of Swarajists was formed who, in distinction from Gandhi's followers, do not boycott the Legislative Councils introduced by the English Government, but try to oppose them by internal obstruction. The Montagu-Chelmsford Reforms granted

by England provided for a sort of gradual transformation of India into a British Dominion, and adopted a
transitional period of ten years, during which the Indian
people were to be politically trained and prepared for
self-government by participation in the Legislative
Councils. Gandhi had ordained strict non-co-operation
tion with regard to these Legislative Councils, and
had forbidden his followers to appear in them or
to take part in elections to them. C. R. Das, however, now believed that it would be better if he
Indian nationalists secured as many seats as possible in
this parliamentary body, and tried to " boycott the
Councils from within." C. R. Das was able to bring the
majority of the All-Indian Congress over to his side,
alter Gandhi's programme, and replace it by his own.
Apart from this change in tactics towards the Legislative
Councils, Das upheld Gandhi's general principles,
especially strict non-violence. With regard to Western
civilization, too, C. R. Das shared Gandhi's attitude:
" The wheels of the machine," he said once, " will
draw us into a vortex until we ourselves become unreal
and dead parts of the machine. The machine is a work
of the devil; it sows the germ of corruption among
the people."

Meanwhile, after a considerable period of imprisonment in Yeroda gaol, Gandhi became seriously ill, and
after having undergone an operation he was released on
account of his weak health. On his return to political
life he found the situation completely changed by the
rise of the Swarajists. To the surprise of his own
followers he contrived to adapt himself cleverly to the
existing situation. He compromised with the Swarajists,
gave up non-co-operation with regard to the Legislative
Councils, and in return secured from the Swarajists
the recognition of the other points of his programme,
Hindu-Mohammedan unity, equal rights for the pariahs,
and his propaganda for the spinning-wheel. Like
Lenin, Gandhi had also to face the bitterest opposition

from many of his own followers on account of his unexpected compromise with the political necessities of
the moment; this went so far that one group, who called
themselves "non-changers," separated from Gandhi
and persisted in non-co-operation with the Legislative
Councils.

Henceforward, Gandhi withdrew almost entirely from
active political life for a considerable time, and applied
his undivided energies to propaganda for the spinning-
wheel. In the autumn of 1925 he founded the All-
Indian Spinners' Association, and with the help of this
organization tried to promote the economic independence of his country more effectively than hitherto. The
actual day to day political work he left to the Swarajists
who, after the death of C. R. Das, were led by the Pandit
Moti Lal Nehru.

Meanwhile a new party had been formed, the Justice
Party, consisting mainly of politicians, lawyers, and
journalists, which aimed at the Europeanization of India
and the overthrow of the caste system. Naturally this
party, of professions so ardently fought by Gandhi, was
from the very outset strongly opposed to the Mahatma.
Most of the attacks on the ideas and political methods
of non-co-operation came from its ranks.

In November 1926 the new Indian provincial elections
took place and, especially in Madras, resulted in the
annihilating defeat of the Justice Party and the complete
victory of the Swarajists. This result was received with
almost universal jubilation in India; processions were
organized which carried the pictures of C. R. Das and
Gandhi.

The Congress of the Oppressed Colonial Nations
which met at Brussels in February 1927, proved that
Gandhi's doctrines had spread far beyond India. The
representative of the South African negroes, the Zulu,
Gumedi, brought vehement charges of oppression of the
black workers and peasants, and declared that the
negroes also wished to follow the example of India and

U

start a non-violent war against their oppressors. Perhaps this programme of the South African negroes is not unconnected with the fact that Gandhi himself made practical application of his passive resistance methods for the first time in South Africa.

XXI

As may be seen from the political developments in India in recent years, Gandhi's programme has not been unopposed. We must not fail to note that many objections, some not easily disposed of, have been raised against Gandhi's ideas in general and against his system of non-co-operation in India in particular. The chief argument against the Swaraj for which Gandhi is striving is the doubt whether India, as a completely independent State deprived of the military assistance of England, would be able to protect its frontiers against foreign invasion.

The publicist, B. C. Chatterjee, editor of the *Modern Review*, declares that an independent India would never be able to maintain the hegemony over the Indian Ocean at present exercised by Delhi. Without the help of the English army it would prove to be impossible even to preserve political unity on the Deccan Peninsula itself. As soon as the English troops left India the country would again sink into the disastrous system of petty states and the demoralizing struggle between conflicting religious antagonisms which existed before the beginning of British rule in India. Chatterjee believes that the North-West passes on the boundary between India and Afghanistan even now can only be defended against their warlike Mohammedan neighbours by a perpetual guerilla warfare; after the withdrawal of the English the Indians, unarmed and entirely without military skill or practice, would be helpless against the incursions of these frontier tribes. Moreover, the independence of India is also threatened from another side. The warlike Japanese, seeking for an outlet, would at once seize the opportunity for capturing an enormous colony which would no longer be defended. In Chatter-jee's view Gandhi's Swaraj would only be a brief transitional state, and would ultimately mean only that India exchanged one master for another.

Many of Gandhi's opponents also draw attention to the danger of a Russian invasion of India, which would become a menace the moment the power of Great Britain no longer protected the Indian frontiers. In fact, Soviet Russia has already contrived to establish itself in Afghanistan, and is thus near enough to the Khyber Pass, the chief point for invading India, to cause anxiety. The founding of the new Soviet Republics, Turkmanistan, Uzbekia, Taikistan, and Kara Khirgis, is also something of a menace to India; for it is well known that Tsarist Russia was always striving to expand towards the south and that the Soviet state has made no change in this policy.

In reply to such objections Gandhi declares that India has no need to be afraid of Bolshevism; the people are too peace-loving to make common cause with anarchy. The Mahatma believes that all the psychological con-ditions for the success of Bolshevism are lacking in India, and thus it will be impossible for Russian agitators to prepare the ground for an invasion: " If anything can possibly prevent this calamity descending on our country, it is Satyagraha. Bolshevism is the necessary result of modern materialistic civilization. Its insensate worship of matter has given rise to a school which has been brought up to look upon materialistic advancement as the goal, and which has lost all touch with the final things of life. . . . If I can but induce the nation to accept Satyagraha, we need have no fear of Bolshevik propa-ganda."

At the Brussels Congress Jawahar Nehru, the general secretary of the Indian National Congress, also declared that, while India sympathized with Russia, because the Soviet State was also fighting English imperialism, Bolshevik doctrines as such were practically unknown in India and would never gain any following worth mentioning among its population.

Chandarvarkar attacks Gandhi from another side and states that it was England and English education that first awakened the spirit of patriotism in India. " The English teachers called the attention of the young people of India to the treasures of Sanskrit literature; service in offices under the direction of Englishmen trained the Indian officials in responsibility and social ideas. To cut ourselves off from all English influence, as Gandhi preaches, would be a serious injury to the growth of Indian national and civic sentiment."

A further objection in principle to Gandhi's non-co-operation movement is the reproach frequently levelled at it that this doctrine is purely negative and is, therefore, entirely inconsistent with the ancient Indian principle that only saying yea to life can be of any value. Chatterjee made a comparison between Gandhi and the Bengali national leader, Aurobindo Ghose, in which he called Gandhi the high priest of renunciation and Aurobindo the prophet of life. For Chatterjee, Gandhi, on account of his tendency to renunciation, is the suitable guardian of religious feelings, but not the right political leader. Gandhi belongs to the type of the Sanyasi, who repress the flesh, consciously reject all the colour and warmth of life, denounce everything which is not necessary for bare livelihood, and hasten the dissolution of the body, so that the spirit imprisoned in it may the more quickly be united with the divine. It has been the mission of India from its earliest days to produce men of this type and to keep its face always turned to God. Chatterjee tries to show, however, that the Indian people have to thank this asceticism and estrangement from life for their loss of freedom and their abasement.

" If we look back, we discover that foreign dominion over India is a terrible revenge on the country, a revenge which life has taken on a nation which tried to deny life. By the assimilation of the doctrine of complete abstinence from violence, India has lost its real self; in exposing its soul utterly to the absolutely good God, it at the same time committed the error of also stripping itself before humanity, which, however, is a mixture of good and evil. . . ."

Aurobindo Ghose, on the other hand, according to Chatterjee, appeared as the apostle of life and proclaimed that modern India must take the way of true Brahmanism, freedom through life. " The great philosophy of divine knowledge must no longer remain locked in the breast of the Brahmans; all India must take the way of Brahmanism and win its freedom through joy in life."

Rabindranath Tagore also states that Gandhi is content to " recite the chapter of negation and dwell eternally on the faults of others." In Tagore's opinion the non-co-operation movement, with its negative idea, corresponds to the teaching of Buddhism, which demanded the extirpation of all joy in life. Buddhism lays the chief stress on avoidance of evil, whereas Brahmanism expressly calls attention to the necessity for positive joy in life.

Gandhi, in his answer to this reproach, said that rejection is as much an ideal as acceptance, and that it is as necessary to reject untruth as it is to accept truth: " All religions teach us that two opposite forces act upon us, and that human endeavour consists in a series of eternal rejections and acceptances. Non-co-operation with evil is as much a duty as co-operation with good. . . . This deliberate refusal to co-operate is like the necessary weeding process that a cultivator has to resort to before he sows. . . . Non-co-operation is the nation's notice that it is no longer satisfied to be in tutelage. The nation has taken to the harmless (for it), natural, and religious doctrine of non-co-operation in the place of the unnatural and irreligious doctrine of violence. And if India is ever to attain the Swaraj of the Poet's [1] dream, she will do so only by non-violent non-co-operation...."

Gandhi, however, regarded these methods of political warfare by non-violent means as more than a weapon for winning independence for India. He looked on the Ahimsa doctrine as a message of salvation for the whole world: " The programme which I have drawn up and carried out for India will not only have a favourable influence on the political position of India and England, but also on that of all the world."

By his message of " truth-force," and of non-violence, Gandhi wished to prove to the world that it was possible " to free the soul from the body even during life, and to deliver up the body to the enemy without endangering the freedom of the soul." India was to give all the other nations the great example of how the moral freedom of every individual and of whole nations could be effectively defended against all oppression by new means: " Non-violence has come to men and will remain. It is the annunciation of peace on earth."

Gandhi was reproached because, though he was trying to proclaim a new doctrine of salvation for the whole world, he nevertheless busied himself with petty national problems. The Mahatma replied to this objection by saying that the great work of universal liberation required an apparently " petty local beginning." He appealed to Tolstoï, who once said that we need forgive only our nearest neighbours to restore peace to the whole world, for in this way the circle of harmony would grow wider and wider, until at last it was conterminous with the circle of the world. Gandhi also quoted the saying of an Indian wise man: " What happens on a handful of earth happens on the whole globe."

Therefore Gandhi regarded the Indian non-co-operation movement as a very great achievement in the

[1] Tagore.

interest of the whole of humanity: " However rich may
be the harmonies with which the rest of the nations can
enrich the human symphony, they would be of subordinate importance if the powers of Asia did not
become the bearers of a new justification of life, death,
and action, if they could not show a new way of salvation
to exhausted Europe."

Thus Gandhi's peaceful fight for the freedom of India
was bound to find a lively response in Europe as well
and to call forth a mass of differing opinions. While
many important men, chief among whom is Romain
Rolland, who declared to the author that he regarded
Gandhi as a " Christ who only lacked the Cross," see
in Gandhi's doctrines and methods the dawn of a new
morality, many others doubt whether it is possible to
attain political success with peaceful weapons.

Upton Sinclair, in a letter to the author, said that he
followed Gandhi's life work with the greatest interest,
that he himself had never used violence and would be
very glad if it could be proved that humanity could
solve all its problems by Gandhi's method. But after
the experiences of the world war, he was not convinced
that the West would be able to take Gandhi's way:
" My own forefathers got their political freedom by
violence; that is to say, they overthrew the British
Crown and made themselves a free Republic. Also by
violence they put an end to the enslavement of the black
race on this continent. . . . If there is any chance of
oppressed peoples getting free by violence I should
justify the use of it. At the same time I recognize that
a man like Gandhi may quite possibly put me to shame
as an adviser to oppressed races."

Bernard Shaw also gave the author his opinion on
Gandhi: " For myself," writes this English writer,
" I can only say that I do not believe in the efficacy of
any purely negative policy except for stupidly conservative purposes.

" The objection to military coercion is not that it is

ineffective: it is, on the contrary, terribly effective, but
that its effects are incalculable. They are as often as
not precisely the reverse of those contemplated; and in
all cases they go far beyond the intentions of those who
resort to it. The late Tsar of Russia began the war of
1914 with the object of preventing Austria from sub-
jugating Serbia. The British Empire went into it with
the object of keeping Belgium in its condition of a
power greatly inferior in military strength on the shores
of the North Sea, and of preventing any of the major
powers from establishing a military hegemony in
Europe. The Tsar achieved his object most effectively;
but the forces he set in motion, instead of stopping
there, went on to exterminate himself and his family
and set up a Communist Republic in Russia. The
British Empire did not even achieve its object. It gave
France a military hegemony, and consolidated Belgium
and France into a single military unit. If this was the
reward of the victors, that of the vanquished can be
imagined.

"India has been subjugated by violence and held
down by violence. India can be freed by violence just
as Ireland has been freed by violence. It is idle in the
face of history to deny these facts: it might as well be
said that tigers have never been able to live by violence
and that non-resistance will convert tigers to a diet of
rice. But the logical end of it will be that England will
never be safe whilst there is an Indian left alive on
earth, nor India ever safe whilst an Englishman breathes.
The moment violence begins men demand security at
all costs; and as security can never be obtained and the
endless path of it lies through blood, violence means
finally the extermination of the human race. That is
why the conscience of mankind feels it to be wicked and
finally destructive of everything it professes to conserve.
Christ and Buddha and Shelley, Tolstoï and Gandhi,
were the mouthpieces of this conscience; but though
they did not revenge evil it can hardly be said that they

did not resist it, the confusion between revenge and
resistance, between the attempt to balance one evil by
creating another, and the determination to eradicate
evil and disarm or even destroy its agents, must be
cleared up before men will enter on the path of peace,
or on any path which they are asked to pursue without
weapons and without responsibility."

XXII

Like Lenin, Gandhi is also accustomed to carry out
any idea once recognized to be right with unshakable
resolution and without regard for the opinions of his
opponents or his followers. Gandhi also has that courage
to be lonely which is the mark of the truly great; he,
too, despises the homage of the crowd for whose welfare
all his strength is expended. He once declared that
every leader must make up his mind " to oppose " if
necessary " even the will of the people " in the interest
of his ideas; on another occasion he wrote bluntly:
" I have become literally sick of the adoration of the
unthinking multitude; I would feel more certain of my
ground if I were spat upon by them." He vigorously
refuses " to have anything to do with truckling to the
multitude."

Thus it is not surprising that Gandhi, like Lenin, has
been accused of being obstinate and autocratic even by
his direct followers; more than once he has been
reproached with being a tyrant and striving after dicta-
torial power. He also alienated many of his supporters
by his stubborn inflexibility, so that he, as he himself
has told us, sometimes had scarcely a dozen followers,
and in India at the beginning was often almost completely isolated. Obsessed by his faith in his idea,
Gandhi regarded this isolation as only a stronger stimulus

to fresh efforts: " The best and most solid work," he once said, " is done in the wilderness of minority."

In spite of this complete refusal to make any concessions to the will of the majority at the expense of truth, the Mahatma has, nevertheless, always been ready to acknowledge the limitations of his own knowledge and to confess his mistakes publicly. This clear insight into his own imperfection also led him immediately to repeal any measures which he recognized to be wrong without any feeling of false shame. " How could I," he once asked, " go on proclaiming a thing to be right which I had discovered to be wrong? "

Thus he undauntedly called a halt in the revolutionary movement he himself had begun, as soon as he became convinced that India was not yet ripe for the civil disobedience he had proclaimed. He broke off his own movement three times, but this retirement did not mean for him the abandonment of his faith in the ultimate victory of his idea, just as unexpected tactical *volte-face* meant for Lenin anything but doubt of the communist idea. Gandhi has always held that the truth he preaches is " independent of temporary successes or failures."

When the Mahatma, under pressure of the bloody excesses at Amritsar, Bombay, and Chauri Chaura, ordered the cessation of the movement which had already begun, he was trying to come nearer to the knowledge of truth: " I am but a seeker after Truth. I claim to have found the way to it. I claim to be making a ceaseless effort to find it. But I admi I have not yet found it. To find truth completely is to realize oneself and one's destiny, in other words, to become perfect. I am painfully conscious of my imperfections and therein lies all the strength I possess. . . ."

But confession of error does not imply in Gandhi any attempt to escape from responsibility for what has happened. On the contrary, he feels himself personally liable for all the consequences of his policy. When twenty-one police officers were cruelly massacred by the infuriated mob in Chauri Chaura Gandhi treated this event as a warning from God: he had been shown that India was not yet sufficiently permeated by the spirit of non-violence, but at the same time he took complete responsibility for this crime of the mob which he loathed, because it had been committed in his name, and he was therefore stained with blood.

Although he had sent the English Government an ultimatum a few days previously, and although this retirement exposed him to the derision of his enemies, he nevertheless submitted to this " most bitter humiliation " and immediately cut short the civil disobedience movement already started. " Let the opponent," he wrote on this occasion, " glory in our humiliation and so-called defeat. It is better to be charged with cowardice than to be guilty of denial of our oath and sin against God. It is a million times better that I should be the laughing stock of the world than that I should act insincerely towards myself. . . . I know that the drastic reversal of practically the whole of the aggressive programme may be politically unsound and unwise, but there is no doubt that it is religiously sound. The country will have gained by my humiliation and confession of error. . . . I lay no claim to superhuman powers. I wear the same corruptible flesh as the weakest of my fellow beings wear, and am therefore as liable to err as any. . . ."

In court, too, Gandhi agreed with the Advocate-General, when the latter tried to make him responsible for the excesses committed by the people: " I wish to endorse all the blame that the learned Advocate-General has thrown on my shoulders in connection with the incidents in Bombay, Madras, and Chauri Chaura. Thinking over these deeply and sleeping over them night after night, it is impossible for me to dissociate myself from these diabolical crimes. . . ."

The peculiar character of Gandhi's whole policy,

however, is most clearly shown in the curious and unique way in which the Mahatma tried to manifest his responsibility to the country. When he ascribed his mistaken estimate of national psychology to his inadequately developed understanding of the national atmosphere, he undertook a personal purification by prayer and a strict fast of several days. According to his own account, he tried in his way to make his perceptions more delicate and to " become a fitter instrument able to register the slightest variation in the moral atmosphere about me."

He kept before him, as an example and a model, the conduct of the prophet Mohammed, who prayed and fasted before every important decision until a revelation was vouchsafed to him. The Mahatma is convinced that the power of perception increases in proportion as the flesh is overcome by strict fasting. He also imposed several days of fasting and prayer on himself before the proclamation of non-co-operation, for he hesitated for a long time as to whether he should place this " dangerous weapon " in the hands of the people.

Later, when new dissensions arose between Hindus and Mohammedans, and all his attempts to allay this revival of hostility by speeches and negotiations had failed, he again had recourse to the original method of fasting. " I blame no one," he wrote on that occasion, " I blame myself alone. I have lost the power to make myself audible to the people; beaten and helpless, I turn to God, who alone can hear me."

Gandhi betook himself to Delhi to the house of the Mohammedan leader, Ali, at the foot of the old citadel, and there began the " great fast " which he hoped would give their old effect back to his words and his personality. For two thousand five hundred years ago Gautama Siddharta, the lofty one, had extolled spiritual concentration through fasting, which, hand in hand with Ahimsa, " never intent on violence, leads to the goal of strict discipline " (*Lakkhanasuttam*). And, in fact, this curious attempt to evoke political decisions by the aid of fasting and self-mortification was crowned with success. On the twenty-first day of the fast the leaders of all the religious congregations and political parties gathered in fear and anxiety about the Mahatma, and made peace with each other, so that his precious life might no longer be endangered.

Below among the ruins and hills muscular young Englishmen were swinging their golf clubs, while above, on the terrace of the house at the foot of the citadel, a protocol was being drafted which certainly deserves to be numbered among the most curious documents in history: " The leaders here present are impressed by the decision of Mahatma Gandhi to fast for twenty-one days, and are profoundly moved by it. . . . All those participating pledge themselves to do their utmost to, ensure that his resolutions are carried out and that all violations are strictly condemned. We empower the President personally to communicate to Mahatma Gandhi the solemn resolution of all those taking part to preserve peace, and to announce to him our unanimous desire that he should break his fast immediately so that he may be present at the meeting and favour it with his co-operation, his advice, and his leadership. He himself shall select the means to be used to check the spread of the existing evil as rapidly and effectively as possible."

It is not to be wondered at that, in spite of this success, an objection was raised in many quarters against Gandhi's whole activity on the ground that religion and politics cannot be reconciled. People were ready to recognize Gandhi as a saint, but disputed his title to be a politician, and appealed to him to remember the maxim of the great Indian leader, Tilak, that politics is no field for saints. Rabindranath Tagore, in particular, implored Gandhi not to risk such a precious treasure of power in the frail barque of politics, allowing it to sail across endless waves of angry party warfare, and not to let himself be used for cunning moves on the political chessboard.

But no one protested more vehemently than Gandhi himself against any separation between religion and politics. He felt all too clearly that the whole of life at the present time is so interspersed with social, political, and religious considerations that it would be impossible to try to set up strictly separate categories: " I do not believe that religion has nothing to do with politics. Politics divorced from religion is like a corpse, only fit to be burned."

The Mahatma regarded this separation between statesmanship and morality as one of the causes of the political degeneration of the nations. He points out that in earlier times all the great founders of religions were also statesmen, and appeals in particular to Christ and Mohammed.

" Jesus," says the Mahatma, " was in my humble opinion a prince among politicians. The politics of his time consisted in securing the welfare of the people by teaching them not to be seduced by the trinkets of the priests and pharisees. The latter then controlled and moulded the life of the people. To-day the system of government is so devised as to affect every department of our life. It threatens our very existence. If, therefore, we want to conserve the welfare of the nation, we must religiously interest ourselves in the doings of the governors, and exert a moral influence on them by insisting on their obeying the laws of morality."

The Mahatma is thus firmly convinced that it is only through the penetration of politics by religious elements that politics can be ennobled. He has an unshakable belief in the possibility and necessity " of introducing uncompromising truth and honesty into political life."

Thus, for the first time for centuries, through Gandhi, politics and diplomacy have been imbued with the principles of candour, sincerity, and morality. Never once in his whole life has Gandhi made use of secret

egotiations, misleading explanations, tactical subter-
uges, or surprise strokes. He has rather ostracized from
olitical life and stigmatized as disgraceful all this
landestine trafficking hitherto looked on as indis-
ensable.

Convinced that only questionable schemes need fear
he light of full publicity, he has always given his
pponents notice beforehand of every step he is going
o take, published full and truthful accounts of all
eliberations, and never concealed or even tried to make
xcuses for a failure. And by this very unconditional
traightforwardness he has succeeded in disarming his
nemies, so that the Delhi Government finally had to
bandon as useless all supervision of his actions by
ecret police.

XXIII

Gandhi, who, like Lenin, makes it his chief concern
o " transform ideas into facts," has called himself a
' practical idealist," thus decisively repudiating the idea
hat his teaching is nothing but an unrealizable dream, a
Jtopia.

It is true that Gandhi's revolution, like that of Lenin,
as not yet succeeded in reaching its real goal. English
ule in India continues as firmly established as before,
nd it even seems that Gandhi's movement has for the
noment receded into the background. But the practical
nd positive side of the great political experiment he
nitiated must nevertheless not be ignored.   He was the
irst to succeed in making the idea of abstinence from
iolence one of the highest ideals of humanity, the
ractical policy of a nation of hundreds of millions.

It is precisely by the fact that he has never over-
stimated actual possibilities, always kept his demands
vithin the practical limits of the actual situation at the

moment, had the courage at once to repeal orders that had miscarried, it is just by the restrictions he imposed on himself, that Gandhi proves himself an able practical politician. He does, it is true, proclaim the law of perfect love, but he declares at the same time that it would be unreasonable to expect the masses to submit completely to this law at present. He knows quite well that the moral demands he puts forward cannot be realized in a day, and has declared that his ideal is " like Euclid's line, which exists only in imagination, never capable of being physically drawn. It is nevertheless an important definition in geometry yielding great results."

Gandhi looks on the non-co-operation movement as merely the first step towards a future ideal world. He reminds the representatives of the old political methods, who call his plans impracticable and fantastic, that " the steam engineer was laughed at by the horse dealer till he saw that even horses could be transported by the steam engine. The electrical engineer was no doubt called a faddist and a madman in steam-engine circles till work was actually done over the wires. It may be long before the law of love will be recognized in international affairs. Yet if only we watched the latest international developments in Europe and Eastern Asia with an eye to essentials, we could see how the world is moving steadily to realize that between nation and nation, as between man and man, force has failed to solve problems. . . ."

But even in Gandhi's strange-seeming attempt to permeate politics with religious elements, in this curious mixture of prayer, fasting, and statesmanship, the Mahatma proves himself a practical politician. For India the " holy man " is the only possible form of national politician; for throughout the whole history of this race the great statesmen have almost always been the product of the spirit of religion.

The many thousand year old Indian Empire is now undergoing a mighty historical process. The European civilization takes hold of India by means of modern methods of government and administration, with schools, factories, railways, and motor-cars. Enormous factory buildings, hotels, and warehouses are forcing their way among the fantastic palaces and temples, motor-cars and motor-bicycles are mingling with the heavy tread of the sacred cows and elephants, the pattering of the herds of asses, and the creaking of the teams of oxen.

The old India is once again girding herself for a mighty effort, is uniting to withstand the invasion of an alien Europe, and is ready to sacrifice deeply rooted traditions, if only the hated " satanic civilization " can in this way be checked. Thus one of the greatest liberation movements in all history is beginning: the calling of the pariahs to free humanity so that they, too, may take part in the fight against the foreigner. So terrible does the danger threatening from the West seem to the Indian people that the whole country has united, and all the profound conflicts between races and creeds give way before the anxiety to save their menaced Asiatic culture. All religious castes and races, Hindus and Mohammedans, Parsees and Sikhs, Brahmans and pariahs, rich and poor, are taking their stand as a unified Indian nation against Europe. In religious defiance the whole country is gathering round a symbol of the most primitive hand work, of a long superseded archaic machine, round the banner of the spinning-wheel.

Three hundred million men are obeying the command of the man who first created a nation out of these countless creeds and tribes, a man who is entirely their own, who speaks their language and prays their prayers, who appeared before the Viceroy clad in a loin-cloth like the humblest of his countrymen, to treat of the future of India on equal terms with the all-powerful representative of the British World Empire.

Gandhi's followers are in line with truth when they believe that the real India wants no other leader than the Mahatma and no other policy than the preaching of the ancient ideal of Ahimsa, and that India was well advised when she decided to follow the prophet of sympathy and truth.

The figure of the modern cosmopolitan professional politician imported from Europe is alien to the nature of India, and would never arrive at any real inner understanding with the people. What India needs is just that blending of the religious and the political which is incorporated in Gandhi, the type of the " political guru."

GANDHI'S LETTERS FROM PRISON

To C. F. Andrews.

Sabarmati Prison,
17th March 1922.

MY DEAR CHARLIE,

I have just got your letter.... I should certainly like your going to Ashram and staying there a while, when you are free. But I would not expect you to see me in gaol; I am as happy as a bird! My idea of a gaol life—especially that of a civil resister—is to be cut off entirely from all connection with the outside world. To be allowed a visitor is a privilege—a civil resister may neither seek nor receive a privilege. The religious value of gaol discipline is enhanced by renouncing privileges. The forthcoming imprisonment will be to me more a religious than a political advantage. If it is a sacrifice, I want it to be the purest.

With love,

Yours

MOHAN.

To Hakimji.

Yeroda Prison, 14th April 1922.

DEAR HAKIMJI,

Prisoners are allowed to have a visit once a quarter and to write and receive one letter. I have had my visit in the persons of Devandas and Rajagopalachari, but the one letter allowed I want to write to you.

As you will of course remember Banker and I were brought to the prison on the 18th of March, a Saturday. On the following Monday at 10 p.m. we were informed that we were to be moved to an unknown destination. At 11.30 the police superintendent escorted us to a special train which was waiting for us at Sabarmati.

We received a basket of fruit and were well treated during
the whole journey. For reasons of religion and also for
considerations of health the doctor of the Sabarmati
prison permitted me to have the food to which I am
accustomed, but Banker was ordered bread, milk, and
fruit on medical grounds. The deputy police superintendent, who accompanied us, was instructed to see that
I had goat's milk and Banker cow's milk on the journey.

We left the train at Khirki, where a police van was
standing ready which brought us to the prison from
which I am writing this letter.

As I had heard from former prisoners that life in this
prison was not exactly pleasant, I was prepared for all
kinds of difficulties. I had previously said to Banker
that I would have to refuse food if they tried to forbid
me to spin—for I had taken a vow on the Hindu New
Year's Day to spin for at least half an hour a day, unless
I were ill or travelling. I told him he was not to get
excited if I had to adopt a hunger strike, and that he
was not to follow my example out of a mistaken feeling
of solidarity. He was thus aware of how I looked at the
affair.

Thus we were not surprised when the director
announced as we entered the prison that we must leave
our spinning-wheel and the basket of fruit. I told him
emphatically that we had both been allowed to spin
every day in Sabarmati prison, and that I must insist on
spinning in accordance with my vow. That brought the
reply that Yeroda was not Sabarmati.

I also said to the director of the prison that, for
reasons of health, we had been allowed to sleep in the
open air at the Sabarmati prison. But here we could not
hope for this favour either.

Our first impression was thus rather unfavourable.
I did not let this trouble me, and, moreover, the fact that
I had practically fasted for the last two days prevented
me from being affected. Banker felt everything much
more hardly. He is afflicted with nightmares and so

does not like to be alone at night. Besides, this was the first painful experience of his life, whereas I was accustomed to the cage.

Next morning the director appeared to ask how we were. I saw that my judgment of him, formed on a first impression, had been mistaken. In any case he had been in a flurry the night before. We did not arrive till after the prescribed time, and besides he was quite unprepared for what must have seemed to him an extraordinary request. Now he understood that I did not want to keep my spinning-wheel out of crankiness, but—rightly or wrongly—from a religious need. When he also perceived from conversation with us that there was no question of a hunger strike, he gave the order that we should both be allowed to have our spinning-wheels again. Also, he no longer held out against the view that the food we asked for was a necessity for us. So far as I have had the opportunity for observation, physical needs are well looked after in this prison. I found both the superintendent and the head warder tactful and friendly. The first days are of no account. My relations with these two officials are as cordial as is possible between a prisoner and his warders.

I see quite clearly, however, that our prison system is almost, if not quite, devoid of humanity. The superintendent tells me that the other prisoners are not treated differently from myself. If that is the case, then the physical needs of the prisoners are completely satisfied, but there is no consideration for human needs. The prison rules are not adapted to this.

This may be seen for example from the attitude of the prison committee, which consists of the administrator, a clergyman, and some other persons. It happened to meet on the morning after our arrival and came to ask us our wishes. I pointed out to them that Banker suffered from nervousness and should for that reason sleep in my cell with the door open. I cannot describe the contempt and unfeeling indifference with which this request was treated. As the gentlemen went away I heard one of them say disdainfully: " Nonsense! " What do they know of Banker, his position in life, and the education he has enjoyed? It was not even their task to go and see him to discover what had moved me to make this request, which seemed so natural to me. Undisturbed sleep was certainly more important for Banker than good food.

An hour after this conversation a warder informed Banker that he was to be transferred to another section. I felt like a mother who has been robbed of her only child. It had seemed to me a happy dispensation that Banker was arrested and sentenced along with me. While we were still at Sabarmati I informed the authorities that I would esteem it a particular favour if they would leave Banker with me, and pointed out that we could be mutually helpful to each other. I read to him from the Gita and he looked after my feeble body. Banker had lost his mother only a few months before. When I was speaking to her a few days before her death she said to me that death would not be hard for her now that she knew her son was under my protection. The noble woman could not know how completely powerless I was to prove when it was a question of protecting her son. When Banker left me I recommended him to the care of God, and awakened confidence in him that God would preserve His own.

Since then he has received permission to come to me for half an hour every day to teach me carding, in which he is proficient. This takes place in the presence of a warder, who has to see that we speak only of matters necessary to our occupation. At present I am trying to induce the general inspector and the prison superintendent to allow us to read the Gita for the few moments we are together. This request of mine is being considered.

I had to use all my ingenuity to get leave to keep seven books, five of a purely religious character, an old dictionary which I value greatly, and an Urdu manual, which Maulana Abdul Kamal Azad gave me. My wish was against the strict order that prisoners may only read books taken from the prison library. So I was urged to present the seven books to the library and then borrow them back again. I remarked in a friendly way to the superintendent that I would gladly do this with all my other books, but that he might as well demand my right arm as these books, which were dear to me partly because of their contents and partly because of their importance as souvenirs. I do not know what means the superintendent had to use in order finally to persuade the higher authorities to let me keep the books. . . .

The use of a pocket knife presents another problem. If I want to prepare my toasted bread (I cannot bear it otherwise) I must cut it into slices. And I must also cut up my lemons if I want to squeeze them. But a pocket knife is regarded as a " lethal weapon " which would be a great danger in the hands of a prisoner. I gave the superintendent the choice of either depriving me of bread and lemons or allowing me a knife. After a great deal of fuss my own penknife was again placed at my disposal. But it remains in the keeping of the warder and is only handed to me when I actually need it. Every evening it has to be given up to the head warder, who gives it back again to the convict warder in the morning.

This species will be new to you. " Convict warders " are generally prisoners on a long sentence who are given warder's uniform for good conduct and entrusted with tasks which do not involve any great responsibility. They are allowed to wear warder's uniform, but remain under continual supervision. One of these warders, who was sentenced for murder, has to watch me during the day. At night he is given an assistant, whose appearance reminds me of Shaukat Ali. This last, it is true, has only been the case since the general inspector gave orders that my cell door might remain open. Both warders are very harmless fellows. They do not molest me in any way, and I never permit myself to talk to them. I have to exchange a few words now and then with the warder who watches me in the day time about my desires and needs, but otherwise I have no communication with him.

My cell is situated in a triangular block whose longest side—it faces West—contains eleven cells. One of my fellow prisoners quartered in the same section is, I surmise, an Arabic State prisoner. As he does not speak Hindustani and I unfortunately have no mastery of Arabic, our intercourse is limited to a mutual good-morning. The base of the triangle is formed by a stout wall, and the shortest side by a barbed-wire fence with a door which opens on to a spacious square. The triangular space within the central block was formerly divided in two by a chalk line I was forbidden to cross. Thus I had a space of about seventy feet long at my disposal on which I could move freely. When Mr. Khambata, an inspection official, was here recently on a visit of inspection, I drew his attention to this white line as a proof of the lack of human feeling in the orders of the prison administration. He himself was not in favour of this restriction and reported in this sense, with the result that the whole triangle was made free to me. It is about a hundred and forty feet long. Now my desires are set on the open square on the other side of the door. But that is perhaps too human to be allowed. But since the white line has been removed I may perhaps hope that the barbed-wire fence will also fall and I may have still more freedom of movement. It is certainly a ticklish matter for the director, and he will need time for deep reflection.

I am in solitary confinement and may not speak to anyone. Some of the Dharvad prisoners are in the same gaol with me, the great Gangadhar Rao of Belgaum, for example, Verumal Begraj, the reformer of Sukkem, and Lalit, a Bombay publisher. I do not see any of

them, though I really do not see how my society could
do them any harm. They again could not harm me.
Nor would we make arrangements for our escape nor
conspire for this purpose. Besides, by acting in this
way we would do the Government the greatest favour.
But if it is a question of protecting them from the
infection of my dangerous ideas, the isolation has come
too late. They are already thoroughly infected. And
there is only one thing I could do here, make them still
more enthusiastic about the spinning-wheel.

What I said about my isolation is not intended as a
complaint. I feel happy. My nature likes loneliness.
I love quietness. And now I have an opportunity of
engaging in studies that I had to neglect in the outside
world.

But not all prisoners feel like me and enjoy solitary
confinement. It is as inhuman as it is unnecessary.
It could be avoided by a proper distribution of the
prisoners. But now the prisoners are arbitrarily shut up
together, and no director, however human his feelings,
could be just to all the men and women of different sorts
who are entrusted to his care, while he has not a free
hand. So he merely does his best to be just to their
bodies and neglects their souls.

Hence it comes that prisons are abused for political
ends, and, therefore, the political prisoner is not safe
from persecution even within their walls.

I shall end the description of my life in prison with a
description of the course of my day. My cell is in itself
decent, clean, and airy. The permission to sleep in the
open air is a great blessing to me who am accustomed to
sleeping in the open. I rise at four o'clock to pray.
The inhabitants of Satyagraha-Ashram will, I am sure,
be glad to know that I have not ceased to say the morning
prayers and sing some of the hymns which I know by
heart. At six-thirty I begin my studies. I am not
allowed a light. But as soon as it is light enough for reading I start work. At seven in the evening, when it is too

dark to read, I finish my day's work. At eight o'clock I
betake myself to rest after the usual Ashram prayer.
My studies include the Koran, the Ramayana of Tulsidas,
books about Christianity I got from Standing, exercises
in Urdu, and much else. I spend six hours on these
literary efforts. Four hours I devote to hand-spinning
and carding. To begin with, when I had only a little
cotton at my disposal, I could only spin for thirty
minutes. But now the administration has placed sufficient cotton at my disposal, very dirty, to be sure—
perhaps very good practice for a beginner in carding.
I spend an hour at carding and three at spinning.
Anasuyabai and Maganlal Gandhi have sent me bobbins.
I want to ask them not to send me any more for the
moment. On the other hand, some fine well cleaned
cotton would be a great service, but they should not
send me more than two pounds at a time. I am very
much set on making my own bobbins. To my way of
thinking every spinner should learn to card. I learnt
in an hour. It is more difficult to manage than spinning,
but it is easier to learn.

Spinning becomes more and more an inner need with
me. Every day I come nearer to the poorest of the poor,
and in them to God. The four hours I devote to this
work are more important to me than all the others.
The fruits of my labour lie before my eyes. Not one
impure thought haunts me in these four hours. While
I read the Gita, the Koran, or the Ramayana, my
thoughts fly far away. But when I turn to the spinning-
wheel or work at the hackle my attention is directed on
a single point. The spinning-wheel, I know, cannot
mean so much to everyone. But to me the spinning-
wheel and the economic salvation of impoverished India
are so much one that spinning has for me a charm all its
own. My heart is drawn backwards and forwards between the spinning-wheel and books. And it is not impossible that in my next letter I will have to tell you that
I am spending even more time on spinning and carding.

Please say to Maulana Abdul Bari Sahib, who recently informed me that he had begun to spin, that I count on his keeping pace with me in progress. His good example will cause many to make a duty of this important work. You may tell the people at Ashram that I have written the promised primer and will send it to them if I am allowed. I hope it will also be possible for me to write the contemplated religious primer, and also the history of our fight in South Africa.

In order to divide the day better I take only two meals instead of three. I feel quite well on it. With regard to food the prison superintendent is most accommodating. For the last three days he has let me have goat's milk and butter, and I hope in a few days to be able to make my own chapatis.

Besides two new warm blankets, a cocoa mat and two sheets have been placed at my disposal. And a pillow has also arrived since. I could really do without it. Up till now I have used my books or my spare clothes as a pillow. But Rajagopalachar used all his influence to have a pillow given to me. There is also a bathroom with a lock available which I am allowed to use every day. A special cell has been put at my disposal for work, at least while it is not required for other purposes. The sanitary arrangements have been improved.

So my friends need not be at all anxious about me. I am as happy as a bird. And I do not feel that I am accomplishing less here than outside the prison. My stay here is a good school for me, and my separation from my fellow workers should prove whether our movement is an independently evolving organism or merely the work of one individual and, therefore, something very transient. I myself have no fears. Thus I am not eager to know what is happening outside. If my prayers are sincere and come from a faithful heart they are more useful—of this I am certain—than any fussy activity.

I am very anxious, on the other hand, about the health of our friend Das, and have good reason to reproach his wife for not informing me how he was. I hope that Motilalalji's asthma is better.

Please try to convince my wife that it is better for her not to visit me. Devandas made a scene when he was here. He could not bear to see me standing in the superintendent's presence when he was admitted. The proud and sensitive boy burst into tears, and I had difficulty in calming him. He should have realized before that I am now a prisoner, and as such have no right to sit in the prison superintendent's presence. Of course, Rajagopalchar and Devandas should have been offered seats. That this was omitted was certainly not due to want of courtesy. I do not think the superintendent is accustomed to be present at meetings of this kind. But in my case he declined to take the risk. But I should not like the scene to be repeated on a visit from my wife, and even less that an exception should be made for me and chairs offered. I can keep my dignity even standing. And we must have patience for a little until the English people have advanced enough to extend on every occasion and universally their lovable politeness with unforced cordiality to us Indians. Besides, I do not long for visitors and would like to ask my friends and relations to restrain themselves in this matter. People may always come to me on business affairs, since for this it doesn't matter whether external circumstances are favourable or not.

I hope that Chotani Nian has distributed the spinning-wheels he has given among the poor Mohammedan women of Panchmahals, Ostkandesh, and Agra. Unfortunately I have forgotten the name of the woman missionary who wrote me from Agra. Possibly Kristodas will remember it.

I have almost finished with the Urdu manual and would be very grateful for an Urdu dictionary, and also any other book you or Dr. Ansari may select for me.

I hope that you are well. To ask you not to overwork would be to demand the impossible. I can only pray that God will keep you well and strong in all your work. With loving greetings to all fellow workers,

Yours,

M. K. GANDHI.

To the Governor of Yeroda Central Prison.

Yeroda Central Prison,
1st May 1923.

You were good enough to show me the order to the effect that certain prisoners sentenced to simple imprisonment will be assigned to a special section and to inform me that I was of the number. In my view some of the prisoners condemned to hard labour, like Messrs. Kaujalgi, Jeramdas, and Bhansali, are not worse criminals than I am. Besides, they had probably had a much higher position than I, and in any case they were accustomed to a more comfortable life than I have led for years. So long as such prisoners are not also assigned to the special group, it is impossible for me, however much I might like it, to avail myself of the advantage of special prison orders. I would therefore be very grateful if you would strike my name off the list of the special section.

Yours obediently,

M. K. GANDHI.

To the Governor of Yeroda Central Prison.

Yeroda Central Prison,
12th November 1923.

At the time that you informed my comrade, Mr. Abdul Gani, that the prison rules did not allow you to grant him food which cost more than the official ration, I drew your attention to the fact that your predecessor permitted all my comrades as well as myself to arrange our own diet. I further informed you that it was very unpleasant for me to enjoy a favour denied to Mr. Abdul Gani, and that for this reason my diet must also be restricted to what is in accordance with the rules and what is allowed to Mr. Abdul Gani. You were good enough to ask me to accept the old rations for the time being, and to say that the whole question would be discussed with the general inspector, who was shortly to visit the prison. I have now waited ten days. If I am to keep a good conscience I cannot wait any longer, for I have nothing at all to discuss with the general inspector. I have no reason to complain to him of the decision you took in the case of Abdul Gani. I willingly recognize that you are powerless, even if you were inclined to help my comrade. Nor is it my aim to work for a change in the food regulations of the prison. I desire one thing only, to protect myself against any preferential treatment. . . .

I therefore ask you from next Wednesday to give me no more oranges and grapes. In spite of this my food will still be more expensive than the official ration. J do not know if I need four pounds of goat's milk, but so long as you refuse to reduce my food so that its cost is in accordance with the rules I must, although reluctantly, accept the four pounds of milk.

I do not need to assure you that there is no question of dissension. . . . It is only for the sake of my own inner peace that I propose that you should restrict my diet, and I beg for your understanding and approval.

Yours obediently,

M. K. GANDHI, No. 827.

BIBLIOGRAPHY

A. LENIN

ADORATSKIĬ. *Marxistskaia dialektika v proizvedeniiakh Lenina. Pechat' i Revolutsiia.* No. 2, 1922.

Authors and Politicians on Lenin. 1924.

AXELROD. *The Development of the Social Revolutionary Movement in Russia.* 1881.

BAKUNIN. *Dieu et l'Etat.* 1892.

BAUER, O. *Bolschewismus oder Sozialdemokratie?* 1920.

BONCH-BRUEVICH. *Nekotoryia svedeniia o iunosheskikh godakh V . I. Lenina pro offitsial'nym Dokumentam.* (*Proletarskaia Revolutsiia.* No. 2, 1921.)

BRÜCKNER, A. *Peter der Grosse.* 1879.

BUKHARIN, N. *The Programme of the Communists.* 1919.

BUKHARIN, N. *The Way to Socialism.* 1923.

BUKHARIN, N. *The Peasant Question.* 1923.

BUKHARIN, N. *From the Overthrow of Tsarism to the Overthrow of the Bourgeoisie.* 1923.

BUKHARIN, N. and PREOBRAZHENSKI. *A.B.C. of Communism.* 1921.

CHEREVANIN. *The Proletariat and the Russian Revolution.* 1908.

DEBORIN, A. *Lenin the Fighting Materialist.* 1924.

DRAHN, E. *Bibliography for the Life of Lenin.* 1925.

ELIZAROVA. *Stranichkie vospominanii.* (*Proletarskaia Revolutsiia.* No. 2 (14), 1923.)

EMELIANOV. *Tainstvennyĭ Shalash.* 1922.

EPSTEIN, I. *Lukacs' Lenin.* (*The Word.* 1924.)

FĒDORCHENKO, L. *Ot Ul'ianova k Leninu.* 1923.

FÜLÖP-MILLER, R. *Geist und Gesicht des Bolschewismus.* 1926.

GOREV. *Ot Tomasa Mora do Lenina " glava o Lenine."* (*Izd. Krasnaia Nov' M.* 1923.)

Y

322 Lenin and Gandhi

GOREV, B. *Lenin v épokhu vtoroi emigratsii.* (*Katorga i ssylka.* No. 3, 1924.)

GUILBEAUX, H. *Vladimir Il'ich Lenin.* 1923.

KAGANOVICH, H. *The Organizational Structure of the Russian Bolshevik Party.* 1923.

KAMENEV, L. B. *Istoriia partii Komunistov i V. I. Lenin.* (*Izd. VTSIK. M.* 1919.)

KAMENEV, L. B. *Lenin's Literary Remains.* 1925.

KAUTSKY, K. *Terrorism and Communism.*

KRAINII and BEZPALOV. *Lenin.* 1923.

KRAMAŘ, K. *The Russian Crisis.* 1925.

KRUPSKAIA, N. K. *Lenin and Questions of National Education.* 1924.

KUN, BELA. *The Propaganda of Leninism.* 1924.

LANDAU-ALDANOV, M. A. *Lenin and Bolshevism.* 1920.

LENIN, V. *The International Communist Movement.*

LENIN, V. *The New Economic Policy.*

LENIN, V. *On Climbing Higher Mountains.*

LENIN, V. *The Caricature of Marxism and the Imperialist Machinery.* (*O karikature Marxisma i ob imperialisticheskom Ekonomisme. Zvezda.* No. 1, 1924.)

LENIN, V. *What Shall We Learn and How Shall We Learn It?* (*Chem uchit'sia i kak uchit'sia?*) 1923.

LENIN, V. *The Characteristics of Economic Romanticism. Sismondi and Our Sismondists.* 1923.

LENIN, V. Collected Works:

Vol. i. *The First Steps of the Social Democratic Labour Movement.* (1894-1899.)

Vol. ii. *Economic Studies and Articles.* (1897-1899.)

Vol. iii. *The Development of Capitalism in Russia.*

Vol. iv. *The Spark.* (1900-1903.)

Vol. v. *The Fight for the Party.* (1901-1904.)

Vol. vi. *The Year* 1905.

Vol. vii. *The Year* 1906.

Vol. viii. *The Year* 1907.

Vol. ix. *The Agrarian Question.* (1899-1919.)

Vol. x. *Marxism and Empirio-Criticism.*

LENIN, V. Collected Works (*continued*):
Vol. xi. *In the Years of the Counter-Revolution.* (1908-1911.)
Vol. xii. *New Uprising.* (1912-1914.)
Vol. xiii. *The World War.* (1914-1916.)
Vol. xiv. *The Bourgeois Revolution.* (1917.)
Vols. xv-xviii. *The Proletariat in Power.* (1917-1921.)
Vol. xix. *The National Question.* (1920-1921.)
Lenin. A volume in memory of Lenin, containing contributions from Bukharin, Chicherin, Iaroslavskiĭ, Kamenev, Karpinskiĭ, Krshishanovskiĭ, Krupskaia, Larin, Lepeshinskiĭ, Lomov, Miliutin, Podvoĭskiĭ, Preobrazhenskiĭ, Radek, Rotstein, Rykov, Ryskulov, Sorin, Stalin, Trotskiĭ, Ul'ianova, Zinov'ev, and Zosnovskiĭ. 1924.
Lenin as Seen by his Contemporaries. Views of Leading Personalities. 1924.
Lenin's Letters. Edited by L. Kamenev. 1924.
Lenin's Letters to Gor'kiĭ, 1908-1913. With an Introduction by L. Kamenev. 1924.
LEPESHINSKIĬ. *Na povorote.* (*Izd. GITS. M.* 1923.)
LUKACS, G. *Lenin.* 1924.
LUNACHARSKIĬ, A. *Revolutsionnye Siluetti.* 1923.
MARTINOV. *From Menshevism to Communism.* 1924.
MARX, KARL. *Capital.* 1885.
MARX, KARL. *The Communist Manifesto.* 1903.
NEVSKIĬ. *V. I. Ul'ianov-Lenin.* (*Izd. VTSIK. M.* 1919.)
OL'MINSKIĬ. *Lenin.* (*Vestnik zhizni.* No. 2, 1918.)
Osinskago, Radeka, Preobrazhenskago, Zemashka, Mitskevicha, " Dvadtsat' piat' R.K.P." *Sbornik. Izd. Oktiabr' Tver'* 1923, *Stat'i o Lenine.*
PAVLOVICH. *Lenin kak razrushitel' narodnichestva.* (*Pod znamenem marxisma,* Nr. 4-5 za 1923 g.)
PLEKHANOV, G. *Fundamental Problems of Marxism.* 1908.
POPOV, N., and IAKOVLEV, I. *Zhizn' Lenina i Leninism.* 1924.

Pososkhov, I. *Ideas and Conditions in the Time of Peter the Great.* 1878.

Preobrazhenskiĭ, E. *Morality and Class Standards.* 1922.

Present Day Russia, 1917-1922. (Official Publication.) 1923.

Radek, Karl. *The Ways of the Russian Revolution.*

Rykov and Trotskiĭ. *Trade and Industry in Soviet Russia and Western Europe.* 1920.

Seĭfulina, L. *A peasant Legend of Lenin. Labour Literature.* March-April 1924.

Semashko, N. *Ob izuchenii Lenina.*

Shidlovskiĭ. *Lenin—Mificheskoe litso.* (*Proletarskaia Revolutsiia.* No. 3, 1921.)

Sovremennik. *Russkiĭ.* No. 1, 1924.

Stalin, I. *Lenin and Leninism.* 1924.

Steklov, Georg. *Mikhail Bakunin.* 1913.

Sverchkov, D. *In the Dawn of Revolution.* 1925.

Trotskiĭ, L. *Questions of Daily Life.* 1923.

Trotskii, L. *The Birth of the Red Army. Speeches, Orders, Appeals, and Theses belonging to the Year the Red Army was founded.*

Trotskiĭ, L. *The New Economic Policy of Soviet Russia.*

Trotskiĭ, L. *The Russian Revolution of 1905.* 1922.

Trotskiĭ, L. *From the October Revolution to the Brest Treaty.* 1922

Universities and Labour Faculties of the U.S.S.R. (*Vyshiia shkoly i rabochie fakultety.*) 1923.

Vilenskiĭ, Vl. *Lenin.* (*Katorga i ssylka.* No. 2, 1924.)

Voronskiĭ, A. *Lenin i chelovechestvo.* 1923.

Wiedenfeld, K. *Lenin und sein Werk.* 1923.

Witte, A. *Reminiscences.* 1923.

Zelikson, Bobrovskaia. *Zapiski iadovogo podpol'shika : chast' pervaia.* (*GITS. M.* 1922.)

Zetkin, C. *Memories of Lenin. Labour Literature.* March-April 1924.

Zetkin, C. *Lenin's Work. Labour Literature.* March-April 1924.

ZINOV'EV, G. *Five Years of the Communist International.* 1923.

ZINOV'EV, G. *Tov. Lenin i natsional'nyĭ vopros.* 1923.

ZINOV'EV, G. *History of the KPR.* (Bolsheviki.) 1923.

ZINOV'EV, G. *The War and the Crisis of Socialism.* 1924.

ZINOV'EV, G. *Lenin geniĭ, uchitel', vozhd' i chelovek. Zvezda.* 1924.

ZINOV'EV, G. *Lenin-V. I. Ul'ianov. Ocherk zhizni i deiatel'nost'.* (*Izd. VTSIK'a M.* 1919.)

B. GANDHI

ALI, MOHAMMED. *Speeches.* Ganesh and Co., Madras, 1921.

ANDREWS, C. F. *Indian Independence.* Ganesh and Co., Madras, 1921.

ANDREWS, C. F. *How India can be Free.* Ganesh and Co., Madras, 1921.

ANDREWS, C. F. *Speeches and Writings of M. K. Gandhi.* Natesan and Co., Madras, 1922.

ANDREWS, C. F. *The Indian Problem.* Natesan and Co., Madras, 1922.

BASU, SRI UPENDRANATH. *Gandhi-Mahatma.* Bharat Grantha Bhandar, Calcutta, 1922.

BAUER, OTTO. *Das Weltbild des Kapitalismus.* Thüringer Verlagsanstalt, 1924.

BEER, M. *Geschichte des Sozialismus in England.* Stuttgart, 1913.

BIRUKOV, PAUL. *Tolstoi und der Orient.* Rotapfel-Verlag, 1925.

BRAUNTHAL, JULIUS. *Mahatma Gandhi und Indiens Revolution. Der Kampf*, October 1924.

BROCKWAY, F. A. *India and its Government.* Tagore and Co., Madras, 1922.

CHANDAVARKAR, NARAGAN. *Pamphlets.* N. M. Joshi, Bombay, 1921.

CHATTERJEE, B. C. *Gandhi or Aurobindo?* The Saraswaty Library, Calcutta, 1921.

Current Thought. (Periodical.) S. Ganesan, Madras, 1922-1926.

DAS, BHAGAVAN. *The Philosophy of Non-Co-operation.* Tagore and Co., Madras, 1922.

DAYAL, LALATTAR. *Our Educational Problem.* Tagore and Co., Madras, 1922.

DEUSSEN, PAUL. *Die Geheimlehre des Veda.* Brockhaus, 1911.

DOKE, JOSEPH J. *M. K. Gandhi.* Natesan and Co., Madras, 1921.

Freunde indischer Weisheit. Vivekananda. Adolf Saal, 1921.

Friends and Foes. M. K. Gandhi. Saraswaty Library, Calcutta, 1921.

FÜLÖP-MILLER, RENÉ. *Der Unbekannte Tolstoj.* Amalthea-Verlag, 1927.

GANDHI, MOHANDAS KARAMCHAND. *Indian Home Rule.* Ganesh and Co., Madras, 1920.

GANDHI, MOHANDAS KARAMCHAND. *Swaraj in One Year.* Ganesh and Co., Madras, 1921.

GANDHI, MOHANDAS KARAMCHAND. *Young India.* 1920-1924.

GANDHI, MOHANDAS KARAMCHAND. *Freedom's Battle.* Ganesh and Co., Madras, 1922.

GANDHI, MOHANDAS KARAMCHAND. *Gaol Experiences.* Tagore and Co., Madras, 1922.

GANDHI, MOHANDAS KARAMCHAND. *Guide to Health.*

GHOSE, AUROBINDO. *A System of National Education.* Tagore and Co., Madras, 1922.

GHOSE, BARINDA KUMAR. *The Truth of Life.* S. Ganesan, Madras, 1922.

GLASENAPP, HELMUTH VON. *Der Hinduismus.* Kurt Wolff, 1922.

GLASENAPP, HELMUTH VON. *Lloyd George über den Indian Civil Service und die Indianisierung der indischen Verwaltung. Der Neue Orient*, November 1922.

GLASENAPP, HELMUTH VON. *Indien*. 1927.

GOKHALE, G. K. *Speeches and Writings*. Natesan and Co., Madras, 1921.

HAUSHOFER, KARL. *Das erwachende Asien*. Süddeutsche Monatshefte, November 1926.

HAUSHOFER, KARL. *Geopolitik des Pazifischen Ozeans*. Vohwinkel-Verlag, 1925.

HILLEBRANDT, ALFRED. *Aus Alt- und Neuindien*. M. and H. Marcus, 1922.

HOLITSCHER, ARTHUR. *Das unruhige Asien*. S. Fischer, 1926.

HOLMES, JOHN H. *The Christ of To-day*. Tagore and Co., Madras, 1922.

HOUGHTON, BERNARD. *Advance India*. Tagore and Co., Madras, 1922.

HOWSIN, HILDA M. *India's Challenge to Civilization*. Tagore and Co., Madras, 1922.

HYNDMAN, H. M. *The Awakening of Asia*.

KALE, V. G. *Indian Industrial and Economic Problems*. Natesan and Co., Madras, 1922.

KASSNER, RUDOLF. *Der indische Idealismus*. Hellerauer-Verlag, 1915.

KERN, MAXIMILIAN. *Das Licht des Ostens*. Union, Deutsche Verlagsgesellschaft.

KOEPPEN, KARL FRIEDRICH. *Die Religion des Buddha*. F. Schneider, 1859.

KOLWEY, KARL. *Studien über Britisch-Indien*. *Archiv für Sozialwissenschaften und Sozialpolitik*, vols. 50 and 51.

MARX, KARL. *Das Kapital*. Hamburg, 1885.

MARX, KARL. *Uber China und Indien*. *Unter dem Banner des Marxismus*. July 1925.

MIRA. *Die politische Bewegung in Indien und ihre Tragweite*. *Österreichische Rundschau*. July 1922.

NAIDU, SAROJINI. *Mahatma Gandhi, Life, Writings, and Speeches*. Ganesh and Co., Madras, 1921.

NAIR, SANKARA. *Gandhi and Anarchy*. Tagore and Co., Madras, 1922.

328 Lenin and Gandhi

NATORP, PAUL. *Stunden mit Rabindranath Thakkur*. Diederichs, 1921.
NEUMANN, KARL EUGEN. *Dhammapadam*. R. Piper and Co., 1922.
NEUMANN, KARL EUGEN. *Die Reden Gotamo Buddhas. Längere Sammlung*. R. Piper and Co., 1922.
NEUMANN, KARL EUGEN. *Die Reden Gotamo Buddhas. Mittlere Sammlung*. R. Piper and Co., 1922.
PRAGER, HANS. *Das indische Apostolat*. Rotapfel-Verlag, 1924.
RAJOGOPALACHARIAR, T. *The Vaishnavaite Reformers of India*. Natesan and Co., Madras, 1920.
REUTHER, OSKAR. *Indische Paläste und Wohnhäuser*. Leonhard Preiss, 1925.
ROHDE, HANS. *Der Kampf um Asien*. Vol. II. Deutsche Verlagsanstalt, 1926.
ROLLAND, ROMAIN. *Mahatma Gandhi*.
RONIGER, EMIL. *Eurasische Berichte*. Rotapfel-Verlag, 1925.
RONIGER, EMIL. *Mahatma Gandhis Leidenzeit*. Rotapfel-Verlag, 1925.
ROY, MANABENDRA NATH. *Indien*. Verlag der Kommunistischen Internationale, 1922.
ROY, MANABENDRA NATH. *Perspektiven der Nationalen Bewegung in Indien. Die Kommunistische Internationale*, January 1927.
RUTHNASWAMI, M. *The Political Philosophy of Mr. Gandhi*. Tagore and Co., Madras, 1922.
SAUTER, J. A. *Unter Brahminen und Paria*. K. F. Koehler, 1923.
SCHLAGINTWEIT, EMIL. *Indien in Wort und Bild*. Schmidt and Günther, 1880.
SCHROEDER, LEOPOLD VON. *Indiens Literatur und Kultur*. H. Haessel, 1887.
TAGORE, RABINDRANATH. *Nationalism*.
TRUMPP, ERNST. *Die Religion der Sikhs*. Otto Schulze, 1881

VASWANI, T. L. *Creative Revolution.* Ganesh and Co., Madras, 1922.

VASWANI, T. L. *India's Adventure.* Ganesh and Co., Madras, 1923.

VASWANI, T. L. *The Gospel of Freedom.* Ganesh and Co., Madras, 1921.

VIDHUSEKARA, S. *The Next War of the World. Modern Review*, Bombay, February 1921.

WEBER, MAX. *Die Wirtschaftsethik der Weltreligionen. Archiv für Sozialwissenschaften und Sozialpolitik*, vols. 41 and 42.

INDEX

A. LENIN

Index

B. GANDHI

340 Lenin and Gandhi

Index   341

"Non‑co‑operation" with, 284, 288, 289.
LENIN, 168, 171, 172, 212, 225, 226, 275, 288, 297, 298.
LLOYD, MR., 161, 168, 170.
London, 211, 251, 253, 267, 273.
Gandhi in, 189-190.
Lucknow, 171.
LUD, NED, 227.
Luddite Movement, 227, 228-229, 230.

Madras, 286, 289, 299.
Bishop of, 192.
"Mahabharata," 185.
Maharajahs, 164.
Manchester, 219.
MARX, KARL, 231-232.
Modern Review, 290.
MOHAMMED, 300, 302.
Mohammedan Khalifat Conference, 1919, 295.
Movement, 276.
League, Calcutta, 171.
Mohammedans, 163, 164, 269, 274-275, 280, 300, 305.
Union with Hindus, 275-279, 288.
Montagu-Chelmsford Reforms, 272, 287-288.
Moplah Rising, 277.
Morley-Minto Reforms, 272.
Moslems (Indian), 274.
MOTILALALJI, 318.
MURRAY, GILBERT, 172.
Mussulmans, 278.
Mysore, passive resistance in, 1830, 269-270.

NAIDU, SAROJINI, 166, 193.
NAIR, SANKARA, 228, 240, 243, 278.
NANAK, 276.

NEHRU, JAWAHAR, 291-292.
MOTI LAL, 289.
NEUMANN, KARL EUGEN, x.
New York, 194.
World Magazine, 167.
NIAN, CHOTANI, 318.
"Non-Changers," 289.
"Non-co-operation" Movement, 165, 199, 204, 269-271, 273-274, 275, 280-288, 300, 301.
Benares, 1812, 269.
Bengal, 270-271.
Distinct from boycott, 282.
Justice Party, hostility, 289.
Mysore, 1830, 269-270.
Objections to, 290-297.
"Non-violence," 281-287, 288, 290, 294, 299.
North Sea, 296.
Nottingham, Luddite movement, 1811, 227, 228-229, 230.

Orange Free State, 204.
Osman Empire, 280.
Ostkandesh, 318.

Panchmahals, 318.
Pariahs, India, 194, 195-199, 248, 288, 305.
Parsees, 163, 164, 305.
PEARSON, W. W., 252.
PHEIDIAS, 211.
POLAK, J., 167-168.
Poona, 165.
Porbander, 186, 187.
PRAGER, HANS, x.
Pretoria, 203, 205.
Punjab, 216.
Disturbances, 274, 280.
Puri, 201-202.

Raikot, 187.
RAJACHANDRA, Influence on Gandhi, 190, 191.